NATIONAL SECURITY IN THE DIGITAL AGE

BITCOIN AS A TOOL FOR MODERN STATECRAFT

This Book is the Second Installment
in the Bitcoin Today Coalition's American Dream Series

Proudly Presented by the BTC VETS Council

A Special Thank You To Our:

Volunteer Authors:

Julia Nesheiwat PhD, Matthew Pines, Ben Kincaid,
Robert Malka, James McGinniss, Lee Bratcher, Pierre Rochard,
Lindsey Daley, Gabriel Royal PhD, Thomas Wood DBA,
Ian Gaines, and Kyle Schneps

Strategic Advisory Team:

Lyn Alden, Alexandra DaCosta, and Julia Nesheiwat PhD

Core Editorial Team:

Alexander Brammer PhD, Jayson Browder MPA, Victoria Corriere,
Ben Kincaid, Robert Malka, and Kyle Schneps

© 2024 by: The Bitcoin Today Coalition

All rights reserved

The Bitcoin Today Coalition is a 501(c)(4) non-profit, non-governmental, non-partisan civic organization advocating on behalf of the business ecosystem enabling over 67 million Americans to own and secure bitcoin. The Coalition helps to educate leaders at the Federal, State, and Local levels about bitcoin's positive impacts to innovation in energy and grid stability, national security, future-oriented job growth, and financial inclusiveness. BTC's members represent a broad constituency, including bitcoin entrepreneurs, veterans, national security practitioners, energy industry stakeholders, and human rights activists.

The Bitcoin Today Coalition's Veterans for Energy and Technology Security community leverages veterans, ex-intel, and national security experts to articulate the national security and foreign policy benefits of the bitcoin network. The BTC VETS aims to engage with and advise stakeholders in the DoD, intelligence, and foreign service communities to maintain American dominance in the bitcoin space.

No part of this book may be reproduced, or stored in a retrieval system, or transmitted in any form or by any means, electronic, mechanical, photocopying, recording, or otherwise, without the express written permission of The Bitcoin Today Coalition.

ISBN — Hardcover: 979-8-9906253-1-0
ISBN — Paperback: 979-8-9906253-0-3
ISBN — E-book: 979-8-9906253-2-7

Cover Design by: Crox Road | Bitcoin Newsletter

Printed in the United States of America

Table of Contents

Foreword — *Julia Nesheiwat, PhD*

Chapter 1 — Great Power Network Competition and Bitcoin: An Assessment for Policymakers — *Matthew Pines*

Chapter 2 — Bitcoin, Africa, and U.S. National Security Interests — *Ben Kincaid*

Chapter 3 — Bitcoin and the Middle East: An Epoch Beyond the Petrodollar — *Robert Malka*

Chapter 4 — Securing America's Future in the Age of the Electron — *James McGinniss*

Chapter 5 — Bitcoin and Energy Security: How Bitcoin Stabilizes and Reinforces the Grid and Why It's a Matter of National Security — *Lee Bratcher and Pierre Rochard*

Chapter 6 — Nuclear Power Plants and Bitcoin Mining: Synergies for a Clean Energy Transition — *Lindsey Daley*

Chapter 7 — China's Crypto Ban: How Decentralized Networks React to Hostile Policy Interventions — *Major Gabriel Royal, PhD*

Chapter 8 — The Implications of Bitcoin on Global Illicit Finance — *Thomas Wood, DBA*

Chapter 9 — Bitcoin and Economic Empowerment — *Ian Gaines*

Chapter 10 — Defection 2.0: Winning Hearts and Minds with Bitcoin — *Kyle Schneps*

Conclusion

Strategic Advisory Team Biographies

Core Editorial Team Biographies

FOREWORD

By Julia Nesheiwat, PhD

Dr. Julia Nesheiwat is a distinguished fellow and Board Member with the Atlantic Council's Global Energy Center, as well as a recognized expert for energy, environment, climate change, and national security issues as a public servant, academic, former military officer, and US diplomat. In government, she most recently served in the White House as Homeland Security Advisor to the President and as Florida's first Chief Resilience Officer. Julia has served as the Corporate Advisor to TeraWulf, Inc., as a Board Member for Bridger Solutions, and on the Advisory Council of Sustainable Bitcoin Protocol, PowerEdison, and others.
She has also published numerous articles in the Stanford Review and Energy Source. In prior administrations, Julia served as Deputy Assistant Secretary of State for the Energy Resources Bureau at the US Department of State. Prior to holding those positions, she served as Chief of Staff to the US Special Envoy for Eurasian Energy as well as the Under Secretary for Energy, Environment, and Business. Her Ph.D. dissertation is from Tokyo Tech titled "Post-Disaster Reconstruction in Energy Policy & Resilience" and she's been a visiting professor at the Naval Post Graduate School on Energy Security. Julia served multiple combat tours in Afghanistan and Iraq and has been awarded the Bronze Star Medal.

If you've ever found yourself wondering what bitcoin is, or what it does, you're in good company. I hear these questions all the time, both in my professional political circles as well as in my personal life. And given the recent launch of several exchange traded funds backed by bitcoin, these conversations have become much more common. Far from the clickbait headlines, celebrity endorsements, and gaudy "crypto" Superbowl commercials, bitcoin stands apart in its ability to affect improvements both in policy and in practice, here in the US and also for people seeking out economic freedom and self-sovereign principles across the globe.

In the essays that follow, you will dive deep into the first successful, digitally native, peer-to-peer currency, bitcoin. Springboarding off the first book in this series, Bitcoin and the American Dream: The New Monetary Technology Transcending Our Political Divide, which looked at the ways bitcoin could provide potential consensus on domestic issues that typically divide political partisans, this second installment, National Security In The Digital Age: Bitcoin As A Tool For Modern Statecraft, applies a more rigorous, scholarly thinking to the role of bitcoin in foreign policy and national security.

Because bitcoin is a revolutionary technology — commonly compared to the novelty and growth of the internet — it disrupts some of our longest held beliefs about statecraft, geopolitics, and national security. And it's why bitcoin is subject to much of the same skepticism that the internet experienced as it became publicly adopted, such as pointed attacks regarding criminality, terrorist financing, and energy usage. These concerns are compounded by the fact that our often-inflexible regulatory apparatuses are not built to adapt to new technologies as quickly as needed. The chapters in this book address these concerns, not by dismissing them, but by offering context, nuance, and education on the larger picture for US policymakers and the public to consider.

Each chapter brings fresh insight and contextual analysis to the various aspects of bitcoin as a tool for modern statecraft. Many of the authors are U.S. Military Veterans, and all are experts in their subject matter, guided by their own real-world experiences into the effects of this new technology on our national and global security.

As the old saying goes, politics ends at the water's edge. The chapters in this book give us new ways to think about that old saying, effectively applying the adage to a technology that does not obey, and is in fact intended to overcome, international borders.

In **Chapter 1**, Matt Pines evaluates bitcoin in the context of grand strategy, ultimately arguing that US policymakers must master its implications before their foreign counterparts do.

In **Chapter 2**, Ben Kincaid offers a vision of how bitcoin may provide stability in Africa, overcoming sources of instability on the continent and offering alternatives to outside influencers, like China and Russia.

In **Chapter 3**, Robert Malka takes the reader to the Middle East, and especially the United Arab Emirates, offering a glimpse of how the UAE's pro-bitcoin policies are making it a major FinTech hub that could unseat US leadership if not matched.

In **Chapter 4**, James McGinniss looks at the forces at play as the US shifts from oil-based to electron-based energy, and money.

In **Chapter 5**, Lee Bratcher and Pierre Rochard discuss the implications and the benefits of bitcoin mining on energy consumption and the power grid.

In **Chapter 6**, Lindsey Daley evaluates the possibility that clean energy — particularly nuclear energy — may have a reciprocal relationship with bitcoin mining.

In **Chapter 7**, Gabe Royal describes policy decisions of the People's Bank of China to outlaw cryptocurrency transactions and mining, then outlines the effect of those decisions on the global bitcoin network.

In **Chapter 8**, Tom Wood looks at bitcoin in the hands of non-state actors, like international terrorist organizations and extremists, and underscores the importance of strengthening networks in order to clamp down on illicit finance.

In **Chapter 9**, Ian Gaines describes bitcoin as a "financial awakening" that can bring fairness and financial access across markets, domestically and abroad.

And in **Chapter 10**, Kyle Schneps details how bitcoin offers those living under authoritarian or corrupt regimes a way to "defect" away from those tyrannical systems and join one that is undergirded by the democratic principles of the US Constitution.

While every writer looks at different aspects of bitcoin, they all deepen the understanding of its role in our national security. In the pages ahead, you will find new facts, or a new twist on something that you thought you already knew.

Benjamin Franklin wrote that "an investment in knowledge pays the best interest." We are all richer for the insights of the thinkers in this book.

CHAPTER 1

GREAT POWER NETWORK COMPETITION AND BITCOIN: AN ASSESSMENT FOR POLICYMAKERS

By Matthew Pines

Matthew Pines *is the Director, Security Advisory at SentinelOne where he leads geopolitical intelligence and cybersecurity risk advisory engagements with private sector clients. He is also a National Security Fellow at the Bitcoin Policy Institute, where he contributes research and analysis on the intersection of bitcoin, national security, and geoeconomics. Prior to joining KSG, Matt spent over ten years leading U.S. Government assessments of national preparedness, strategic resilience, and emerging technology. Matt holds an M.Sc. in Philosophy and Public Policy (with Distinction) from the London School of Economics and a B.A. in Physics and Philosophy from Johns Hopkins University (University Honors).*

Introduction

Geopolitical competition in the 21st century is a competition, to the first order, over and through global technology networks. As the status quo power leading an era of technology-driven globalization, the U.S. has enjoyed decades of dominance over tightly coupled networks of trade, finance, critical technology supply chains, and digital/telecommunications infrastructure. Rising from a position of exceptional relative weakness,

China is implementing a long-term strategy to displace, co-opt, and undermine the U.S.'s power over, and derived from, these networks. The fight for the future is on.

This great power competition will define how the geopolitical order evolves this decade. Its spillovers and escalations are the principal source of risk facing the U.S.'s global position, and humanity at large. As a result, U.S. policymakers must analyze every aspect of this dynamic network power competition, hedge every downside scenario, and explore every possible advantage, even those that at first blush might seem counterintuitive, or even radical, like bitcoin.

Network power consists in the ability of a state to exercise surveillance and chokepoint controls over a global network.[1] For example, signals intelligence collection on global communications,[2] suspicious activity reports on banking transactions,[3] and end-user inspections on semiconductor technology[4] are all forms of surveillance power from which the U.S. derives immense geopolitical advantage.

(Figure 1: Many geopolitically relevant digital and monetary networks show features of a Barabási–Albert structure, where a small number of nodes have outsized influence.)

More overtly, the U.S.'s ability to conduct global cyber operations,[5] apply blocking financial sanctions,[6] and restrict technology exports to adversary nations[7] is a chokepoint power of increasing strategic importance. Monitoring and controlling global networks is modern power.

These strategically critical global networks have a scale-free topology[8] that greatly facilitates hegemonic power — new nodes "preferentially attach" to existing well-connected nodes, resulting in a structure where most of the network runs through a small number of nodes.

Think of that friend you know who "knows everyone" or that parent who leads the school chat group and directs all social planning, capturing most of the gossip along the way. Being such a key node in a social graph gives asymmetric information about, and influence over, one's peers. At the nation-state level, digital communications and transaction networks are the source of most national intelligence collection[9] and strategic influence and are increasingly the focus of adversary efforts to co-opt, displace, and degrade the United States' hegemonic geopolitical position.

We see this strategic game — between the G7 and China, and also Europe to an extent — over network influence playing out most visibility in the trade, critical technology, and telecommunications domains. For example, US and China trade competition,[10] semiconductor export controls,[11] sanctions on Chinese tech firms,[12] and subsea cable rivalry[13] have drawn much attention. The watchword among G7 policymakers and multinational corporation boardrooms is "de-risking,"[14] as a diplomatic cover for what amounts to a slow, messy, and halting "de-coupling" of the strategic technology, trade, and telecommunications infrastructure interdependencies still binding East and West in this fraught moment of global disorder. Our connected world threatens to pull itself apart.

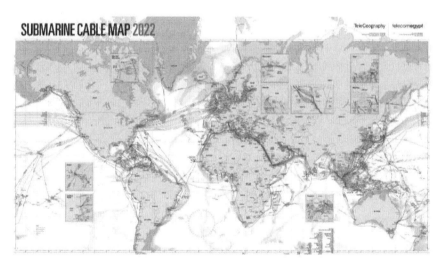

(Figure 2: The physical contours of global network competition can be seen in the laydown of undersea fiber optic cables, which undergird the Digital Foundations of Human civilization and through which great powers seek to spy, influence, coerce, and even attack one another.)

Another key locus of strategic network competition is the dollar-based global monetary system and its interrelated network of correspondent banking, shadow banking, cross-border payments systems, and sovereign balance sheets. While economists and policymakers are familiar with the macroeconomic implications of this system,[15] the fragilities of this network — and its exploitation by the U.S.'s principal adversary — are an underappreciated source of strategic vulnerability.

For digital networks are dynamic, self-healing systems, and they respond to interruption by forging alternative paths. For example, the U.S. might be concerned that broad-scale financial sanctions (e.g., on Russia's FX reserves[16]) and payment system exclusions (e.g., on Russian banks' SWIFT access[17]) could trigger changes to sovereign reserve manager behavior and stimulate alternative financial arrangements that result in a global structure where its incumbent network power is attenuated.[18]

The short run effect may be to impose higher costs and frictions on bad actors, but with the long-term consequence that other network participants forge alternate arrangements that bypass the legacy — tightly surveilled and controllable — corresponding banking system. This effect may be amplified by key network participants (namely China and its key Eurasian and Middle Eastern "friends"[19]) accelerating digital, cross-border clearing and settlement systems[20] while shifting the marginal unit of bilateral trade to non-dollar currencies[21] and changing reserve strategies.[22]

These changes are occurring in the context of a geopolitical dynamic that is generating increasing stress across the three key pillars of the global system, namely the "frenemy" relationship that previously existed between financial capital (dominated by the G7), energy/commodities (dominated by OPEC+), and goods production (dominated by China). Each leg of this tripartite order is undergoing significant stress, from G7 sanctions on Russia (and an attempted oil price cap) to tech controls and fraught "decoupling" of western supply chains in China, all while China and OPEC+ build increasingly tight digital, economic, trade, military, and diplomatic relations. This is a recipe for global instability and presents an unprecedented challenge to the U.S.-led world order.

One shouldn't expect any major shift to happen quickly, but the structural forces and geopolitical incentives are in place to push it forward in the coming years. The inertia and strength of status quo network effects can absorb some degree of volatility, but the tight feedback loops between key nodes in the global system mean change, if it does come, could unfold rapidly. U.S. policymakers must grapple with the strategic implications before these nascent developments reach a critical point.[23] Intelligence analysis that ignores these developments are vulnerable to strategic surprise.

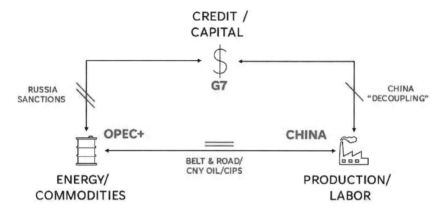

(Figure 3: A simplified view of the geoeconomic relationships between key power centers shows how sanctions, Economic Warfare, strategic capital flows, and Technological "decoupling" interact to place strain on the current global system.)

This brief presents an assessment of the strategic vulnerabilities posed by the current monetary system, the strategic challenges presented by adversary monetary arrangements, and explores potential advantages, and risks, of emerging non-state cryptocurrency monetary networks.

1. Strategic U.S. Vulnerabilities from its Current Monetary Network Dominance

This section argues that the dollar system has turned from "exorbitant privilege" to "exorbitant burden" and is a source of increasing strategic vulnerability to the U.S. This brief argues that these strategic vulnerabilities emerge across critical financial, political, and geopolitical dimensions of national power.

The current dollar system is complex and opaque, but its key features can be boiled down to two core elements: the status of the **dollar** (USD) as the dominant **Global Reserve Currency** (GRC) and the status of **U.S. Treasury Securities** (USTs) as the dominant **Global Reserve Asset** (GRA).

The former takes its value from the network effects of the "dollar" as a popular unit of account for denominating economic and financial transactions and as a medium of exchange for global payments and clearing systems. The latter takes its value from the credibility of the U.S. government as an exceptionally reliable servicer of its debts, which sustains strong and enduring demand for USTs as safe and liquid stores of value.

(Note that "safety" derives the guarantee of redeemability (and low likelihood of sovereign seizure), while "liquidity" refers to the ability to buy/sell or collateralize/repo large notional transactions quickly and without large spreads. One could argue that the former took a hit after Russia's FX reserves were seized, and the latter after the March 2020 market panic that saw the "off-the-run" UST market completely froze.)

The USD as the GRC has sustained the surveillance and chokepoint power of the U.S. over global financial networks. The Financial Crimes Enforcement Network (FinCEN), a bureau of the U.S. Department of the Treasury, implements this surveillance power via analysis of global financial transactions, which it collects via global compliance with its anti-money laundering (AML) and counter-terrorism financing (CTF) reporting requirements.

The Office of Foreign Assets Control (OFAC) implements this chokepoint power via enforcement of sanctions designations that can block any entity's ability to engage in the global dollar system. Note that each of these powers is exercised extraterritoriality and is strong to the extent that evasion (from either FinCEN monitoring and/or OFAC enforcement) is limited.

This has been a very important — and often morally and politically justified — use of national authorities to disrupt terrorist financing and rogue states' weapons of mass destruction programs. But like a sword over-wielded, its blade has grown dull. As the go-to, bloodless instrument of international coercive force, it has given U.S. security officials a misplaced confidence in the ability to achieve "action-at-a-distance" without blowback. That is no longer the case.[24] New tools and strategic approaches are needed to adapt to a world that is rapidly vaccinating itself to the threat of U.S. sanctions via alternative national settlement systems that bypass U.S. clearing infrastructure.

The old playbook of economic coercion and network exclusion may work for minor powers, but it certainly isn't going to suffice, and may even backfire, in an era of great power competition. Note that China's geoeconomic allies across OPEC and Russia (and the expanded BRICS) dominate the oil market, most commodities trade, and are increasingly at the center of global value chains.[25]

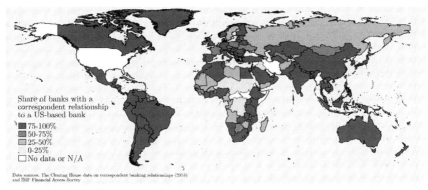

(Figure 4: On average, around 80 percent of banks in a given country have a correspondent relationship with a U.S.-based bank, giving US authorities visibility and potential blocking power over a large majority of global transactions.)[26]

While the USD gets its network effect from more organic, mostly offshore private decisions to choose the most salable medium of exchange, the UST security has been strategically embedded — as a function of geoeconomic policy[27] — as the essential monetary asset at the foundation where the entire global financial system rests.

As long as that system is perceived as stable and enduring, the baseline perception of USTs as the bedrock, safe reserve asset for global institutions, central banks, and householder savers remains unchallenged. If this changes, look out below…

For, as the Global Reserve Asset, the UST has sustained the fiscal power of the U.S. to outspend its geopolitical rivals and run large and persistent structural deficits that readily absorb the surpluses of the rest of the world. Given its status as the global safe haven asset, the UST has historically — at least up until recently — been the beneficiary of capital flight during periods of economic or financial stress.

The function of the UST as "safe and liquid" capital given favorable accounting treatment by international banking regulations has implanted a structural demand, and its "cash-equivalent" status makes it the go-to form of collateral greasing the gears of global money and repo markets.

However, U.S. geoeconomic dominance is not inevitable or invulnerable, even if policymakers have grown, perhaps hubristically, accustomed to unchallenged unipolarity. The global dollar system has evolved in such a way as to generate potential strategic vulnerabilities that policymakers need to honestly reckon with, especially as we enter an era of acute Great Power Competition.

1.1 Financial Vulnerabilities

1.1.1 The Federal Reserve Becomes the Marginal Source of Financing to the USG

The U.S. continues to run persistent deficits even as the economy has rebounded from the pandemic. The Congressional Budget Office now projects the deficit will be 5.8% of gross domestic product (GDP) in 2023, declining to 5.0 percent by 2027, and then "grows in every year, reaching 10.0 percent of GDP in 2053".[28] Note these projections assume no additional future exogenous economic, geopolitical, public health, or unanticipated shocks. (That is quite optimistic…)

These projections come in the aftermath of an unprecedented (if necessary) fiscal expansion to public debt from COVID-19: in only six fiscal quarters (from Q4 2019 to Q2 2021), total public debt as a percentage of GDP increased by 18.5% to over 125%.[29] This measure peaked at 130%, a level historically associated as a "point of no return", exceeding levels attained because of WWII. Since 1800, 51 of 52 times a country's debt reached this level, it led to restructuring, devaluation, inflation, and/or outright default.[30] The last time a reserve currency issuer's debt was this high was the United Kingdom in the 1920's. It didn't end well.

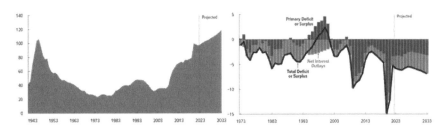

(Figure 5: U.S. public debt is projected to reach 119 percent of GDP at the end of 2033 — about 22 percentage points higher than it was at the end of 2022 and about two and one-half times its average over the past 50 years.)[31]

The last 15 years has followed a well-studied pattern[32] whereby: 1) private debts surge prior to a banking crisis, 2) private debts become public debts after the crisis, and 3) public debts after such banking crises precipitate sovereign debt crises.[33] We may now find ourselves at the end of this ominous series. Even if we avoid an outright crisis, it is likely that official balance sheets — namely that of the Fed and its proxy Global Systemically Important Banks (G-SIBs) — will be enlisted to provide the marginal source of financing to the U.S. Government,[34] a form of financial repression that may soon combine with (explicit or implicit) yield curve control to ensure official solvency.

If not well-managed, the current moment may be seen, in retrospect, as a structural inflection point for the U.S.'s monetary, fiscal, social, and geopolitical stability. Social Security started drawing down trust fund reserves (USTs) for the first time in 2021, with a projected depletion by 2034.[35]

Financial market participants know that increasing debt leads to increasing fragility, and that increasing fragility increases systemic risk.[36] Now, increasing systemic risk increases the need for volatility suppression. But suppressing volatility doesn't make risk go away — it merely pushes it to the tails, where it lies in wait for a "high sigma" event that triggers a systemic crisis.[37]

1.1.2 Instability Requires Ever Larger Interventions and the Federal Reserve Becomes Market Maker of Last Resort to the U.S. Treasury Market

As the G30 Working Group on Treasury Market Liquidity has noted, the smooth functioning of the U.S. debt market is imperative for the stability of the global financial system.[38] As a result, the Federal Reserve has had to develop extensive facilities that increase the "moneyness" of U.S. Treasury Securities (USTs) by increasing their fungibility as a "cash equivalent" and shore up this $23+ trillion market.[39] These efforts have come in halting response to periodic disruptions to the UST market after the global financial crisis.

The first signs of disturbance appeared with the flash rally in 2014, then the repo spike in 2019, and the particularly concerning sell-off in March 2020, when the secondary market for USTs essentially froze. In addition, while written off as an "operational error," the technical failure of the Fedwire system on February 25, 2021, left a lasting imprint in the debt market.[40]

The Fed also invoked its emergency authorities under Section 13(3) of the Federal Reserve Act to deploy an unprecedented series of lending and credit facilities in coordination with the Treasury Department, marking the beginning of what some are calling an era of "fiscal dominance".[41]

In the wake of the failures of Silicon Valley Bank and Signature Bank in March 2023, the Federal Reserve created a new Bank Term Funding Program (BTFP) backstopped by up to $25 billion from the Treasury Department's Exchange Stabilization Fund.[42] The function of this program was to allow the conversion of illiquid (out-of-the-money) collateral into liquid (money good) dollar reserves (at par).

These emergency Fed measures were necessary to prevent the balance sheet destruction (caused by the drop in banks' UST assets value from the Fed's own rate hikes) from metastasizing into a system-wide bank run as depositors lost confidence. Regulators were concerned that this could spiral out of control as the banks further liquidate assets to meet withdrawals and trigger a broader financial panic as selling begets selling across the system.

It worked, but at the cost of increasing the explicit and implicit scope of official guarantees (moral hazard), bailing out unsecured depositors (including Chinese account holders), and temporarily reinflating the Federal Reserve's balance sheet (contrary to its stated monetary policy objectives). It also revealed the strategic vulnerabilities associated with the fragilities of the UST market and the emergency interventions needed to prevent a regional banking collapse and further financial contagion. This is essentially the same position the Fed is in with respect to the global system.

1.1.3 The Global Dollar System — Including the Eurodollar and Shadow Banking Systems — Becomes Dependent on the Fed as a Global Lender of Last Resort, Including to Foreign Adversaries

The net effect of these "emergency" (now permanent) facilities and programs has been to substantially broaden the number of global counterparties (banks, shadow banks, and "other financial institutions"[43]) with direct or indirect access to the Fed's balance sheet. These monetary facilities — specifically the Overnight Reverse Repo Facility (o/n-RRP) and the Standing Repo Facility (SRF) — serve to provide a floor and ceiling, respectively, to money market and dollar funding markets, with an effectively unlimited ceiling at the FOMC's discretion to raise caps as needed.[44]

The Fed has also expanded its dollar liquidity and foreign-currency liquidity swap lines with foreign central banks to prevent obstruction in the key arteries in the global dollar system.⁴⁵ While typically limited to countries with a close relationship to the U.S. (e.g., U.K., Canada, the EU, Japan and Switzerland), a crisis like COVID-19 saw these broadly expanded to many others.⁴⁶ Former senior Bank of England official Paul Tucker has noted how geopolitically crucial these swap lines have become, and he bemoans the sometimes strategically myopic decisions to deploy them (or not).⁴⁷

The global dollar system consists of a network of interlinked private and public sector balance sheets that use dollar assets (mainly USTs) as collateral to make loans and secure financial transactions. When times are good and counterparty trust is high, these balance sheets expand and grease the skids of commerce and investment. However, this offshore system does not have direct access to the Fed discount window and so it is vulnerable to runs when growth falters or financial risks increase counterparty mistrust.

The function of swap lines is to provide dollar liquidity to friendly foreign central banks, who then lend those dollars on to stressed domestic financial institutions, and hopefully put out any nascent financial fires. As a result, the Fed has become the global financial firefighter in chief, with a chief de facto responsibility to backstop foreign banking systems, lest any run lead to a systemic event in western asset markets.

However, not all major foreign central banks have access to these facilities, most notably China. To cover this gap in its ability to manage global dollar funding markets, the New York Fed executes repo and reverse repo transactions⁴⁸ through its foreign and international monetary authorities (FIMA).⁴⁹ While not publicly acknowledged, it's understood that the dominant FIMA customer is China.⁵⁰

This facility allows China to borrow dollars directly from the Fed without selling Treasury holdings. In a time of Treasury market stress driven by foreign selling of USTs like that seen in March 2020, the Fed will print new dollars and give those to China in exchange for UST collateral. This adds a challenging monetary wrinkle to contingency planning⁵¹ by U.S. policymakers contemplating the potential for an acute crisis over Taiwan in the coming years.⁵²

1.2 Political Vulnerabilities

1.2.1 The FIRE and Tech Sectors Have Benefited at the Expense of the Manufacturing Sector, Leading to an Hourglass Economy and Acute Wealth Inequality

In the early 1960s, American economist Robert Triffin noted that to maintain the U.S. dollar as the global reserve currency, the U.S. would be forced to run structural trade deficits to keep a growing world economy sufficiently supplied with dollars. The effects of this "Triffin Dilemma" manifested slowly, over the course of decades, with the gradual erosion and elimination of wide swaths of our industrial base. The U.S. economy has evolved over decades to structurally absorb global surpluses by selling off its scarce and desirable assets to foreign investors, including major adversaries.

This has greatly benefited the Technology and Finance, Insurance, and Real Estate (FIRE) sectors who exist to create investable securities and help direct foreign dollar surpluses into them, often via opaque, tax-sheltered offshore structures. The U.S. is the money laundering capital of the world.[53]

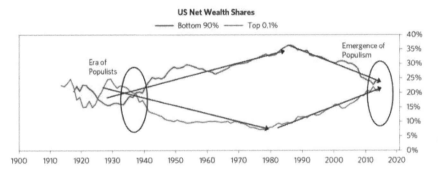

(Figure 6: According to Bridgewater, "the wealth of the top one-tenth of 1% of the population is about equal to that of the bottom 90% of the population, which is the same sort of wealth gap that existed during the 1935-40 period.)"

In hindsight, we can see a correlation between the systemic effect of the USD as the GRC, and the structural increase in income inequality, the rise of political populism, and the estrangement of working classes, all of which undermine trust in legacy governing institutions and civic trust.[54]

Our current system drives the population into debt, fosters inflation that erodes meager savings, incentivizes gig-work labor arrangements, and concentrates real wealth and hard assets among a small elite class. Scarce assets are mostly held by the already wealthy, who gain disproportionately from asset appreciation — partly the result of monetary policy.

An IMF study found that "an individual in the 75th percentile of wealth distribution who invested $1 in 2004 would have yielded $1.50 by the end of 2015 — a return of 50 percent.[55]

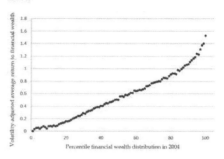

(Figure 7: The USD System Structurally Requires That The US Recycles Offshore Foreign Surpluses Into Onshore Financial Assets, Exacerbating Domestic Inequality And Undermining Democracy.)

A person in the top 0.1 percent would have yielded $2.40 on the same invested dollar — a return of 140 percent."

Meanwhile the Federal Reserve's 2022 Survey of Consumer Finances found that the top 1% of households owned 32.3% of all wealth in the United States, while the bottom 50% of households owned just 2.6%.[56] The top 5% of households owned 62.1% of all wealth, while the bottom 90% of households owned just 37.9%. This pattern of ownership has pathologically distorted the U.S. political economy and leads to social disaffection and economic alienation that threatens the stability of U.S. democratic institutions.

The well-known hollowing out of our national industrial capacity accelerated with the entry of China in the WTO, with the US losing five million manufacturing jobs in less than ten years. This same period saw a dramatic rise in opioid addiction, a crisis that killed almost 80,000 Americans in 2022.[57] Despite the hope of converting China towards the western rules-based liberal order, it's clear that Beijing is intent on expanding its "state-led, non-market approach to the economy and trade" that "cause serious harm to workers and businesses around the world, particularly in industries targeted by China's industrial plans", according to the US Trade Representative in a 2022 report.[58]

This has increased political polarization and the power of the existing economic elite, with the predictable result: undermined institutional legitimacy and manifest decay of democratic systems.

1.3 Geopolitical Vulnerabilities

1.3.1 Atrophy of the Defense Industrial Base is a Direct Consequence of the Dollar System

The dollar system has played a role in the gradual decline of the U.S. defense industrial base. As the cornerstone of the global monetary system, the U.S. dollar's position as the world's reserve currency encourages other nations to amass considerable dollar reserves. This enables the U.S. to sustain continual trade deficits, with imports often exceeding exports. This pattern has encouraged the offshoring of manufacturing processes to nations where production costs are lower. Among the industries affected by this trend, the defense sector has been significantly impacted.

The progressive shift from domestic production to reliance on foreign-made components has led to a contraction of the homegrown defense manufacturing industry. Over time, this erosion of the domestic defense industrial base has amplified concerns regarding supply chain security and the resilience to navigate geopolitical crises.

Weapons category	Total U.S. contractors			Current U.S.-based prime contractors
	1990	1998	2020	
Tactical missiles	13	3	3	Boeing, Lockheed Martin, Raytheon Technologies
Fixed-wing aircraft	8	3	3	Boeing, Lockheed Martin, Northrup Grumman
Expendable launch vehicles	6	2	2	Boeing, Lockheed Martin
Satellites	8	5	4	Boeing, Hughes, Lockheed Martin, Northrup Grumman
Surface ships	8	5	2	General Dynamics, Huntington Ingalls
Tactical wheeled vehicles	6	4	3	AM General, General Motors, Oshkosh
Tracked combat vehicles	3	2	1	General Dynamics
Strategic missiles	3	2	2	Boeing, Lockheed Martin
Torpedoes	3	2	2	Lockheed Martin, Raytheon Technologies
Rotary wing aircraft	4	3	3	Bell Textron, Boeing, Lockheed Martin (Sikorsky)

(Figure 8: Examples of the reduction of defense suppliers over the past thirty years for major weapons categories.)

As the Royal United Services found in their study:

> "A country must either have the manufacturing capacity to build massive quantities of ammunition or have other manufacturing industries that can be rapidly converted to ammunition production. Unfortunately, the West no longer seems to have either... If competition between autocracies and democracies has really entered a military phase, then the arsenal of democracy must first radically improve its approach to the production of material in wartime."[59]

The Pentagon is finding that a larger and larger defense budget (requiring more and more debt issuance and higher interest costs from rising rates) is going to a smaller & smaller number of DoD contractor performers, even as our defense leaders desire to radically transform a sclerotic and oligopolistic defense industrial base.

The DoD found that this consolidation and atrophy is a risk to national security, "Over the last 10 years, DoD spend is up 23%, but the number of small businesses involved w/ the DoD is down 43%, at large biz it's down 7%. We've completely lost the middle of the industrial base."[60]

As Ukraine[61] and numerous US-China war games[62] have shown, the winner in prolonged modern conflict between two near-peer powers is based on which side has the strongest industrial base. Such warfare just eats through massive amounts of munition, with Russia consuming four times the US annual missile production in just three months of combat.

Moreover, scaling up or turning shuttered production lines back on is very difficult for two reasons: First, these armaments require skilled (and aging) labor in scarce supply with a long training time. Second, the supply chain for subcomponents is very thin and fragile, with extensive foreign (including Chinese) dependencies.

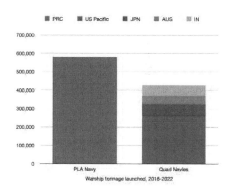

(Figure 9: The Chinese navy has demonstrated substantially more shipbuilding tonnage than the Quad's (Us, Japan, Australia, And India) Pacific navies, combined.)

The relationship between industrial atrophy and strategic military disadvantage is most manifest in shipbuilding.[63] A leaked analysis by the Office of Naval Intelligence showed that "China is the world's leading shipbuilder by a large margin", controlling "~40% of global commercial shipbuilding market" with a shipbuilding capacity 232 times greater than the U.S. Its projections show that the PLA Navy (PLAN) had 355 battle force ships (compared with USN's 296), but that this gap will grow substantially by 2035: 475 for China and ~310 for the U.S."[64]

The US still has the most advanced, exquisite technology, but quantity has a quality all its own. The shiniest toys may not bring a decisive advantage in many China conflict scenarios. Military leaders recognize this and are aggressively shifting to "re-shore" domestic manufacturing and "re-build" our defense industrial base. The structural monetary imperatives of the global dollar system, however, are a direct headwind blowing against these newly recognized strategic imperatives.

To put a finer point on this dilemma: the status of the USD as the GRC has led to the atrophy of the U.S. industrial and military capacity, while also driving political decisions that embed fiscal deficits. Just at the moment that defense leaders recognize the need to reverse decades of industrial decay, however, rising debt service obligations further constrain discretionary fiscal outlays.

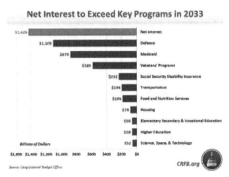

(Figure 10: Net interest expense will be larger than defense or any other US government program by 2023.)

By 2023 — over the same period that China will widen its shipbuilding lead and accelerate its military modernization across key domains — U.S. net interest expense is expected to exceed all other key government spending programs, including defense.[65] This is not a trajectory that bodes well for effective military deterrence or decisive advantage in the unfolding strategic competition between the U.S. and China.

1.3.2 The Global Dollar System Has Been Cleverly Exploited by the U.S.'s Principal Strategic Adversary, China, to Finance its Global Ambitions

As the U.S. has run ever deeper twin (current and capital account) deficits, we've handed China massive dollar reserves which, instead of recycling into refinancing our bonds, they've used to go on a spending spree around the world, buying up hard assets and taking large-scale positions in western equity and real-estate markets. China and a handful of other nations now own over $12 trillion in U.S. equities, up from $2 trillion in 2010.

As part of their exceptionally ambitious Belt and Road Initiative (BRI), China has made dollar-denominated loans to other emerging markets, usually with local infrastructure (ports, land, dams) as collateral.

China's strategy of recycling of dollar surpluses via the BRI has worked to help them secure strategic minerals and increase their geoeconomic sphere of influence across the Global South and the Eurasian periphery.

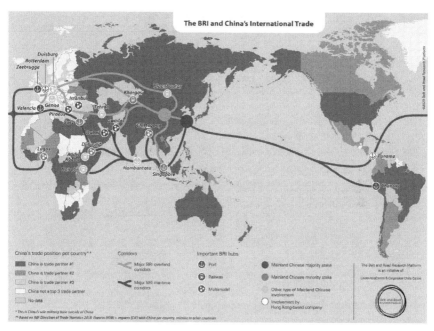

(Figure 11: The Belt and Road Initiative is the centerpiece of China's geoeconomic influence and security strategy, that was largely financed by redirecting dollar surpluses accumulated from China's structurally imbalanced trade with the west.)[66]

Just as one example of the scale of China's ambitions, their state-owned enterprises (SOEs) have built over 100 commercial ports and other facilities around Africa in the past 20 years, and own or operate 96 in 53 countries.[67]

Essentially, China has used this system to construct an elaborate, global series of leveraged hedges against the dollar system, knowing that the Fed will be forced to intervene in any systemic crisis, opening foreign swap lines and pushing whatever dollar liquidity is needed to prevent large-scale dollar defaults that could cascade across the interconnected global banking system. And, in the unlikely event the debtor nation does default, well China has a claim to the hard asset collateral it really wants in the first place. Heads they win, tails we lose.

Less well known, but equally pernicious is China's covert recycling of dollar surpluses via offshore money centers to control scarce western assets and influence and corrupt democracies. A synergy between transnational criminal organizations, state intelligence organs, and western middlemen operating in the "gray zone" of global finance have helped route trillions via shell companies into western financial and real estate markets.[68]

With this covert financial power comes covert influence power and covert geopolitical power. The result is the U.S. loses the capacity to credibly deter China while China increases its strategic position in the Global South and undermines western democracy.[69]

2. Strategic U.S. Challenges from Adversary Monetary Network Constructions

This section argues that, in concert with its Digital Silk Road Initiative, China is constructing alternative monetary arrangements and related technologies that challenge core instruments of U.S. geopolitical power.

China has certainly suffered substantial social and economic costs from their mishandling of the pandemic, and the whipsaw of capricious national policy. Against the backdrop of declining demographics, China now faces massive youth unemployment (officially >20%, but potentially pushing 40%), high local and provincial off-balance sheet debt loads, and a Ponzi-like financial system anchored on an extreme housing bubble.[70] It is likely that these issues will constrain (at least in the short run) China's economic prospects, but it is important to not be overconfident that these stumbles will knock China off its strategic course (See Figure 12).

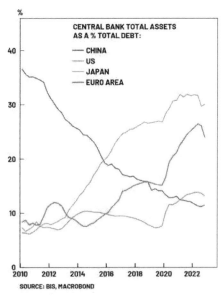

(Figure 12: China has more than enough central bank balance sheet capacity and off-balance sheet dollar assets to put out any financial fires, as it wields its dollar reserves in service of its geoeconomic grand strategy against the West.)

We argue that China's "block, build, expand" modus operandi for executing its grand strategy across key military, geopolitical, and technology domains also applies to the monetary sphere. The perceived zero-sum competitive logic of network power competition is driving the security dilemma shaping policies and strategies of the U.S. and China against one another.

In this context, we examine the strategic challenges facing the U.S. because of China's multi-pronged activities to 1) Block US Sanctions Power, 2) Build Its Own Independent Trading and Financial Settlement Network, and 3) Expand Its Geoeconomic Sphere of Influence.

2.1 The Sanctions Challenge

China is pursuing an integrated diplomatic and technical development strategy to construct alternative financial and digital network rails that act as a "systems bypass" to the incumbent western dominated financial infrastructure.

Beijing witnessed how easily the G7 nations were able to seize Russia's foreign reserves and severely restrict its access to the global financial system via broad-scale SWIFT bans, Russian entity-designations, blocking sanctions, export controls, and other forms of economic warfare.

As it eyes Taiwan hungrily and resents the constraint that the current Western dominated financial systems place on its strategic autonomy, China has developed three monetary-technical networks to bootstrap a nascent, but growing, alternative financial system.

The first, the Cross-Border Interbank Payment System (CIPS), is the most traditional and further developed. Created in 2015, CIPS functions as a settlement and clearance mechanism for yuan transactions, but also contains a participant messaging system. In this respect, it contains the endogenous capability to replicate the functions of the Clearing House Interbank Payments System (CHIPS) for settlement and the Society for Worldwide Interbank Financial Telecommunications (SWIFT) network for interbank messaging. While the infrastructure is there, current usage dramatically lags incumbent systems – "CHIPS has ten times as many participants as CIPS and processes forty times as many transactions as CIPS."[71]

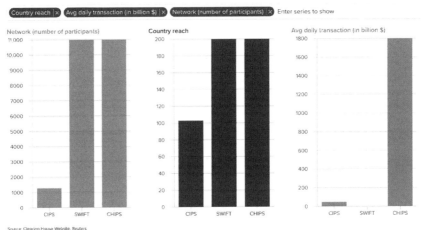

(Figure 13: "Yuan transactions only amount to 3.2 percent of all transactions using SWIFT. China's political goals to internationalize its currency, which led to the creation of CIPS, conflict with the capital controls on the yuan, making the yuan less attractive as a currency than the dollar.)"[72]

While CIPS usage is currently economically trivial, its growth and geographic focus is geopolitically significant. The total number of transactions on China's CIPS payments platform grew by ~60,000 from Q4 2022 to Q1 2023 and the total volume of RMB processed in the quarter fell slightly, down ~1 trn RMB ($140 bn USD). In addition, global bank participation in CIPS topped 1,400 financial institutions worldwide in Q2 2023, with 111 countries having at least one CIPS participant bank.

This growth is heavily concentrated in Asia and the Middle East, which are areas of intense geoeconomic focus for China's strategic influence and trade relations. Where trade goes, banking relations typically follow, and China is the dominant trading partner for nations in these regions. It is not a terrible strategy, historically, to bootstrap a financial and geopolitical influence network from a dominant trading network. After

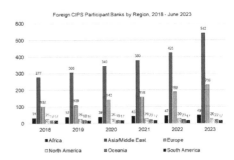

(Figure 14: Growth of China's Cross-Border Interbank Payment System is heavily concentrated in Asia and the Middle East.)

all, that is exactly what the legacy Western powers did over centuries of imperialism and post-war globalization.

For now, however, CIPS seems to be perceived by Beijing more as a back-up plan — a technical and financial network that can function regardless of western sanctions and continue to support China's global trade and settlement in extremis.

More exploratory and innovative are China's network power objectives by pushing its Digital Currency Electronic Payment (DC/EP) and Blockchain-based Service Network (BSN), both related elements of Beijing's Digital Silk Road strategy. DC/EP is the protocol and platform for the Digital Yuan, China's Central Bank Digital Currency (CBDC) project. China is currently in the process of rolling this digital currency system out at scale domestically. Even as it encounters some technical and adoption hiccups, the prospects for fine-tuned monetary and social control continue to drive accelerated implementation.

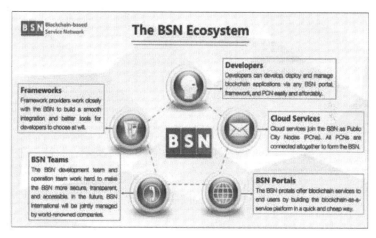

(Figure 15: The BSN platform is China's state-controlled, public "Internet of Blockchains" network, designed to be the backbone infrastructure for massive, cross-sector blockchain-based data interconnectivity across China, as well as the Digital Silk Road.)

BSN, however, is even more ambitious, as it aims to form an entirely new backbone infrastructure for digital exchange domestically and with China's global trade partners. It is a state-backed blockchain platform designed to shape emerging global norms around such digital infrastructure and direct development activities in its preferred direction.

Recognizing CIPS will never supplant CHIPS and SWIFT, China is looking to "leap-ahead" and capture first-mover advantage and structural network dominance over emerging global fintech and permissioned national blockchain systems.

As one DC strategic advisory firm wrote in their 2021 report:

> *"Beijing perceives its success in this endeavor as crucial not only to ensuring its long-term economic competitiveness in the global technology sector, but also to persuading foreign countries to adopt its norms for governing the internet and digital space more broadly. One important way that China is seeking to achieve this objective is through BSN, a state-backed blockchain system that Beijing is expanding both at home and abroad."*[73]

Beijing believes that global adoption of digital currencies is a strategic opportunity to "diminish the current global dominance of U.S. dollar-denominated banking and financial systems and reduce the exposure of China's global transactional data to the United States. It would also allow for a new global transaction system based on emerging digital infrastructure controlled by Beijing."[74]

Further, the gradual expansion of Beijing's technical-monetary architecture and CBDC protocols could force much of the world and western firms into begrudging adoption, which would provide Beijing the ability to fully monitor (and even constrain) in-network financial transactions.

2.2 The De-Dollarization Challenge

Project mBridge is a canary in the coalmine with respect to how China's geopolitical and digital monetary network ambitions are converging to potentially displace the dollar from its current role in energy and commodity trade. A joint collaboration between the Bank of International Settlements, Hong Kong Monetary Authority, the Bank of Thailand, the People's Bank of China, and the Central Bank of the United Arab Emirates, Project mBridge is a "multi-CBDC" arrangement that "directly connects jurisdictional digital currencies in a single common technical infrastructure."[75] The aim is to "improve the current system and allow cross-border payments to be immediate, cheap and universally accessible with secure settlement."[76,77]

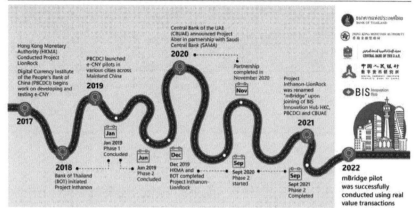

(Figure 16: Project mBridge is a strategic effort to connect the Asian and Middle Eastern economies via cross-bridged CBDCs.)

Rather than reconstruct the complex, hierarchical network of correspondent banking relationships that took the West decades to organically develop for G7 fiat settlement, Project mBridge (and its close cousin Project Aber between Saudi Arabia and UAE[78]) connects national banking systems to each other via CBDC networks maintained by each country's respective central bank.

The potential of these digital platforms to host real-time, peer-to-peer, cross-border payments and foreign exchange transactions on systems that are fully compliant and surveilled by these national authorities is very attractive to authoritarian-inclined governments that desire more control over their financial systems.

For China, scaling these systems with its major commodity and trading partners is a desirable mechanism to bypass the need to go through dollar-dominated foreign exchange markets that intermediate its massive international trade activities. Currently, most foreign exchange transactions use the dollar as a bridge currency in each leg of the swap.

China has continued to expand its extension of CNY swap lines with more countries, opened its onshore markets via Stock and Bond Connect, and further internationalized the Shanghai Gold Exchange to establish a weak quasi-peg between the yuan, oil, and gold. Cross-bridge CBDC arrangements would enable China and its partners to broaden and deepen these financial links, and conduct much more efficient currency swaps, and financial settlement activities that bypass the dollar system.

Further, this digital infrastructure lays the foundation for longer-term geoeconomic ambitions by Beijing to shift the denomination of (some of) its import bill from dollars to yuan. For example, paying just 10% of its commodity imports with yuan would free up ~$100-150 billion per year of its USD liquidity.

It is noteworthy that China and Saudi Arabia have increased their strategic partnership, as the erstwhile U.S. ally has become more geopolitically promiscuous under Mohammed bin Salman.[79,80] MBS — a millennial autocrat with no taste for democracy but extreme ambitions for domestic development — has found in Beijing the perfect source of both military support (e.g., ballistic missiles) and construction capabilities to drive his Vision 2030 objectives. Thus, it should not be surprising if we see the Saudis agree to accept yuan for its oil exports.

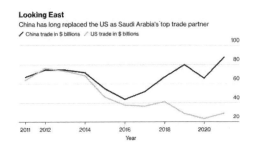

(Figure 17: Where trade relationships go, geopolitical alignments tend to follow.)

Now, while this helps China bypass dollar foreign exchange markets and potential sanctions risk blocking its oil payments, the question remains: what the Saudis do with those newly acquired yuan. Do they hold them as yuan reserves (invested in onshore yuan assets), sell them for dollars (invested in traditional dollar assets), buy gold (from China), or, more interestingly, use them to pay Chinese defense and civilian contractors for drones, missiles, Neom-style fantasy cities, desalination plants, nuclear reactors, and other advanced technology and infrastructure projects?

One sees a similar dynamic playing out with other "balancing" powers in the Middle East. The UAE is known to be very comfortable with "playing the geopolitical field", effectively renting out its national investment and technology firms to Chinese gray-zone entities that need a plausibly deniable middleman with western capital for strategic technology acquisition and elite political influence operations.[81]

2.3 The Geoeconomics Challenge

One can see the above efforts as deliberate elements of China's "Block, Build, Expand" strategy to block western financial coercion (via independent, "fail-over" monetary networks) and build its own RMB-based trading and settlement networks that improve the security of its critical energy and commodity inputs (via close strategic and technical links with major trading partners).

These are concerning but may be a mere prelude to the expanding geoeconomic challenge represented by China's Digital Silk Road and related internationalization of its digital networks, infused with its authoritarian ethos.

Network power is sticky power — it attracts and then traps.[82] Digital network power from controlling and influencing foundational information infrastructure is especially sticky. China recognized that it could secure strategic influence by shaping internet and telecommunications infrastructure around the world, writing in an internal publication:

> *"The internet needs governance, cyberspace needs sovereignty, but each country's technical competency and economic development exists with significant gaps, requiring an independent, self-controlled, shared internet governance structure, demanding each country improve its cyber infrastructure and internet management platforms. Today, China's internet and telecommunications infrastructure is in a global leading position. To improve economic integration in this domain international influence must increase, China needs to orderly promote the Digital Silk Road, and promote the Belt and Road Initiative alongside national and regional digitization competencies."*[83]

China is exporting (and finding strong demand for) a bundled techno-authoritarian "stack" consisting of dedicated fiber-optic cable networks, cloud hosting, "cybersecurity" services, 5G/Internet of Things digital infrastructure, surveillance equipment, cross-bridged CBDC platforms (built to integrate with the China's Digital Currency/Electronic Payment (DC/EP)[84] system of course), and sophisticated AI monitoring software, alongside onsite training, technical assistance, and customer support for would be autocrats across the globe.

This "Authoritarianism-as-a-Service" fulfills a strategic purpose given China's current geostrategic power projection gap. It doesn't have the blue water navy and overseas basing infrastructure (yet) to confidently secure its access to necessary strategic resources. Imperial aspirants of the past typically relied on in situ military capabilities to keep pliable governments in power (or replace them).

While its private military companies (PMCs) are growing alongside China's overseas energy and natural resource operations, these are still small-scale, and lack official reinforcement to be a credible strategic force in distant political capitals. Wagner Group has filled this gap somewhat in certain especially weak and unstable locales, but those mercenaries don't report ultimately to Beijing.

While China hopes to have the hard power necessary, eventually, to project force across Eurasia, the next best thing is to close the "virtual" distance by means of digital colonization. Foreign governments that rely on Chinese providers for their essential digital, telecommunications, and financial infrastructure will have essentially traded away a good portion of their sovereignty and become de facto captured in China's strategic sphere of influence. Such governments are very unlikely to renege on a contract with a Chinese firm or vote against Beijing at the UN or other international forum.

When a foreign power can read all your citizen's data, control all your domestic and international financial transactions, and run all your government services on their digital platforms, that foreign power effectively controls your country. Their strategic vision and political prerogatives supervene on your own, and China's are decidedly not liberal in orientation.

This is the scope and potential geoeconomic challenge posed to the West by China's Digital Silk Road ambitions (as well as the related Global Development Initiative, Global Security Initiative, and Global Civilization Initiative, the three new centerpieces of President Xi's global strategy).[85]

Cold War 2.0 will be fought in the Global South, as emerging markets and developing countries choose which model of techno-monetary governance they want to subscribe to. China's aggressive sales model is likely to attract many authoritarian and authoritarian-inclined customers.

Now, the West lacks a compelling alternative that respects its founding values and democratic ethos. Imitating China with an "authoritarian-lite"

G7 CBDC is doomed to fail. The West will not succeed by trying to "out-totalitarian" the CCP.

If the West can't develop an alternative, asymmetric strategy that respects our values and plays to our strengths, China will fill the vacuum and the prospects for freedom will dim around the world.

3. Potential Advantages and Risks of Emerging Non-Traditional Monetary Networks

Despite these challenges, the U.S. remains a strong, incumbent power with an open society and a claim to technological leadership (even if tenuous). To navigate the coming period of geopolitical turbulence and strategic competition, we will have to consider non-traditional approaches. We close this essay by offering a sketch of just such an alternative, asymmetric strategy premised on the following thesis:

Bitcoin and regulated dollar-based stablecoins may help the U.S. counter adversary efforts to challenge U.S. geoeconomic power while reinforcing liberal value systems around the world.

We will outline these potential advantages and highlight potential risks policymakers should address below.

3.1 Global, Organic Demand for Bitcoin and USD-Based Stablecoins May Help Counter China's Geopolitical Ambitions for the Digital Yuan and the Belt and Road Initiative

There is a reason China has been among the most bitcoin-hostile governments in the world, banning bitcoin mining and making all cryptocurrency transactions illegal. Bitcoin is a clear and present threat to China's strategic ambitions for the DC/EP as well as its efforts to enforce capital controls. The latter has been a worry for the PBoC, with stablecoins like Tether being a popular vehicle for mainland Chinese to bypass annual limits on overseas capital transfer. These moves on bitcoin coincided with a crackdown on other mechanisms for capital flight like gambling in Macau and the Hong Kong banking sector.[86]

The existence of bitcoin is a severe complication for China's CBDC ambitions, presenting an attractive store of wealth and effective cross-border payment system to those BRI nations that China seeks to entangle with the DC/EP.

Bitcoin and dollar-stablecoin adoption along the frontlines of Cold War 2.0 may serve as a bottom-up bulwark against China's geo-monetary network expansion strategy. China has banned bitcoin in its own country but cannot do the same across the rest of Eurasia, the Middle East, and Africa, many nations of which have relatively permissive cryptocurrency regimes.[87]

In fact, China's banning of bitcoin mining led to the U.S. almost immediately taking the hash power lead.[88] At the heart of the "new Silk Road," Kazakhstan and Russia now round out the top three nations for bitcoin mining, with Russia's Soviet-era overcapacity in hydro production and cold Siberian climate rapidly emerging as a prime destination for exiled Chinese miners.

The U.S. has a plurality (~37%) of global hash rate, followed by China (21%), Kazakhstan (13%), Canada (6.5%) and Russia (4.7%). Further, many African nations are looking to repurpose excess power generation (some even funded by Chinese BRI loans) for bitcoin mining (including operations run by or with U.S. firms). Bitcoin could thus serve as a potential "wedge" issue that divides China from its extended sphere of influence (and its domestic "rogue miners"), putting China's bitcoin hostility at odds with the domestic interests of its own miners and giving the U.S. an opening to re-gain on-the-ground influence in contested parts of the Global South.

To address these challenges, the United States can take special advantage of the dollar-based stablecoin ecosystem that has emerged to facilitate cryptocurrency trading, especially offshore. The top two largest dollar-pegged stablecoins hold a market cap exceeding $100 billion,[89] and are growing quickly. One can argue that these private stablecoins are winning the fight the U.S. should be fighting against the DC/EP, with market-driven transaction volume in just these two dollar-stablecoins vastly outpacing that of the PBoC's DC/EP efforts to-date.

The world needs dollars but wants autonomy. The yoke of dollar-debt service and import dependency will not be easily traded for a digital renminbi, but corrupt national-level deals are often made at the expense of social interest and driven by personal leadership interest.

When it comes to serving the demand for digital currency, China has a determined strategy to rope nations into its techno-authoritarian stack and trade dependency. Thus far, the U.S. has been able to free ride on private innovation, but continued success in this regard is not guaranteed.

No less an authority than the Vice Chair for Supervision at the Federal Reserve, Randal K. Quarles, noted in a 2021 speech, that "a global U.S. dollar stablecoin network could encourage use of the dollar by making cross-border payments faster and cheaper, and it potentially could be deployed much faster and with fewer downsides than a CBDC."[90]

The strategic benefits the U.S. accrues from increased global dollarization are highly significant. Given that the global economy suffers from a somewhat chronic "Eurodollar" shortage, stablecoins provide another rail to satisfy demand for dollar liquidity. While these "crypto-Eurodollar" issuers must come under some form of regulatory framework and risk management supervision, it is likely that domestically domiciled stablecoin issuers will be regulated into holding a large portion of their reserves in highly liquid, cash-equivalent instruments, just as money market funds do.

As a result, increased demand for these stablecoin issuance (mostly driven by increased demand for bitcoin, and its rising dollar price) will drive increased demand for U.S. bonds (and other U.S. corporate and municipal debt blessed as "money-good" High Quality Liquid Asset collateral). At a time where foreign demand for our debt is drying up, bitcoin-driven stablecoin growth can serve as another source of government financing. Again, given the global dynamics involved in stablecoins, this is essentially an international tax levied on dollar-bitcoin inflows that supports U.S. debt financing.

Note that while the foreign official sector is broadly trying to de-dollarize or diversify their FX exposure on the margin, the populations in these countries want dollars more than local currencies. The fact that ~99% of stablecoins[91] are dollar-denominated appears to demonstrate that, absent government forces, the high salability of the dollar[92] will win against other currencies.

Thus, even as governments seek to de-dollarize, stablecoins represent a way to maintain the reach of the dollar-system by going directly to the people, where they present individuals an enduring and accessible alternative to their local currency, weak property rights, and shaky banking institutions.

Further, countries often use capital controls to make it harder for their citizens to flee their local currencies and access dollars, but for tech-savvy citizens, stablecoins empower them to route around such controls more easily. This aligns with U.S. human rights objectives and our tech-driven democratization tool kit and should be a core component of international development programs going forward.[93]

3.2 If Bitcoin Were to Monetize to Reach Close Parity with Gold, the U.S. (Holding the Most Bitcoin) Would Gain Relative to our Adversaries and May Serve as an Asymmetric Hedge Against Tail Risks in the Treasury Market

Bitcoin is a novel synthetic, and scarce, digital commodity with global fungibility, limited counterparty risk (zero if self-custodied), large and growing liquidity, and unit scalability to settle any quantity of value. Its monetary properties offer a similar, if not better, scarcity and bearer profile than gold and other commodities. Its technical properties offer a similar, if not better, transactional and settlement profile than fiat-exchange system rails (e.g., SWIFT, FedWire).

As an open source, global software project it is undergoing continuous innovation, especially in the surrounding domain of interoperable second-layer protocols (e.g., Lightning Network and related applications) that extend its usability to everyday commerce in mobile-first environments around the world. It thus can serve as a "reserve asset for the people" that isn't naturally centralized by central banks or large financial institutions.

From the perspective of a FX reserve manager — especially one caught on the diplomatic fence and pulled between the rising East-West dichotomy — bitcoin, as a politically neutral reserve asset, may become marginally more attractive. It helps that this neutral reserve asset, being natively digital, comes with its own decentralized rails for trustless transaction and settlement.

Some nations may apprise the increasingly fraught geopolitical environment and seek to hedge their position with an outside money system that is mostly insulated from transactional interference. Nevertheless, bitcoin-to-fiat rails will be mostly subject to the political control of jurisdictions in which those rails are operational.

States will still seek to control and monitor bitcoin, and related stablecoin, flows as best they can, which will set up a technical arms-race between protocol development and chain-analysis. Some states may desire the benefits of holding bitcoin for themselves, but seek to limit domestic, individual engagement.

If U.S. adversaries attempt to overturn the global USD/UST system and related international monetary order to build their own competing bloc dominating Eurasia with gold, energy, and commodities at its heart, what is the western counter-response? We could agree to re-monetize gold, but given Russia and China's holdings, that would rebalance the monetary center of gravity in their favor.

We would benefit from the relief of the exorbitant burden, and the resulting shift in capital flows, and trade deficits would help rebuild our domestic manufacturing base. But it would mean accepting a much-diminished role for the U.S. in the world system, and a ceding of significant power to emboldened authoritarians dominating Eurasia. It's not clear that such a system would be inherently any more stable than the current one, and not lead to war eventually.

Many western technocrats see salvation in some combination of G7 fiscal reform, energy revolution, domestic CBDC tech, and a compromise monetary regime anchored more significantly to Special Drawing Rights (SDRs). In such a regime, the U.S. would use its incumbent power over institutions like the World Bank and the IMF to move towards a global system of interoperable CBDCs to support eSDR issuance (that may or may not prejudice or exclude compatibility with China's DC/EP). Under such a vision, these eSDRs may help sustain a version of globalization, balance and settle global trade, and accommodate rising powers without the west giving up too much control. Whether China (and OPEC+) would accede to such a system is an open question.

This system would help shore up nervous national governments' control over restive populations by concentrating key technical powers over savings and commercial transactions. It would enable more tailored forms of capital control and allocation to direct financing to politically preferred sectors (e.g., "green" industries) while squeezing disfavored firms out. One could see the West moving closer to a Chinese model of state-capitalism and a similar direction in national approaches to individual rights and political expression.

Bitcoin, on the other hand, offers an alternative. From a national security perspective, key decision-makers may realize the fact that allowing bitcoin to monetize alongside (or outpacing) gold would disproportionately benefit the U.S., whose citizens and firms hold potentially a majority of all bitcoin, and whose companies and capital markets would grow in tandem. That is, while China and Russia double-down on analog gold, the U.S. can countermove to digital gold.

As China faces intermittent power crises[94] and a mammoth energy import appetite,[95] North America's (and our close ally Australia's) prodigious energy abundance gives our states and locales a natural advantage to compete in the global, zero-sum proof-of-work hash race for the block reward. The unique demand characteristics of bitcoin may also help drive the transition to reduce the carbon-intensity of the grid without state subsidies and incentivize energy innovation[96] like in Small Modular Nuclear reactors[97,98] and hybrid bitcoin-battery wind/solar generation projects.[99]

A gradual shift to a global monetary system centered on a neutral reserve asset that we hold a large share of would allow the U.S. to reverse the structural trade flows which have eroded our manufacturing capacity and made us acutely vulnerable to Chinese supply chains.

Potential Risks

Inflexible monetary policy: With a declining role for the UST market, bitcoin's rise as an alternative neutral reserve asset will constrain monetary policy authorities and challenge their ability to control interest rates through open market operations or other Federal Reserve administrative facilities. Responsibility for economic intervention by the government will fall mostly to fiscal authorities, whose decisions on taxation and expenditure are subject to democratic mandate. This may impose limits on the scale of intervention in crisis situations and force more market adjustment for misallocation of capital. In a sense, this would involve trading off the long-term tail risk instability of the current system for more persistent, but hopefully manageable economic volatility.

Protocol changes: The bitcoin protocol is open source. Updates are made by rough consensus via a power balance between economic nodes and miners, within and across geographic jurisdictions. As such, U.S. authorities will have no decisive power or control over how the protocol may evolve, in ways that might limit future chain-analysis surveillance and financial monitoring. U.S. authorities will have to participate in these debates as a peer with other nations and their citizens and use soft power influence to help shape the future direction of the protocol. There is no guarantee that future changes will not constrain current instruments of national power like sanctions designations, even if the current design of the protocol makes tracking and designating public addresses relatively easy for law enforcement.

Domestic and international shifts in economic power: Any dramatic increase in the value of bitcoin will result in new power centers concentrated in those states and nations early to adopt. Domestically, this will manifest as an increase in the economic power of states that have abundant energy resources (especially excess renewables or stranded assets) and/or have attracted bitcoin holders and companies to their locales. Internationally, the story will be similar, with currently marginal states (like El Salvador, Singapore, and Gulf States) that are early to bitcoin seeing a relatively dramatic rise in their national wealth, and associated influence. This could have unanticipated effects on U.S. foreign policy and how we engage with changing power blocs built around an alignment with bitcoin and bitcoin mining.

Increasing reliance on overseas chip fabrication: Almost all bitcoin mining hardware is manufactured overseas and relies on microchips from a limited number of advanced semiconductor foundries in Asia. If bitcoin and bitcoin mining becomes systemically important to the U.S. economy, this reliance may present a strategic vulnerability. While there are ongoing efforts to re-shore this production, the geographic concentration of mining hardware supply chains will remain an area of strategic national interest, similar to how the DoD sees semiconductors in the DIB.

Unanticipated effects on domestic and international energy production: As a geographically independent and interruptible source of demand for low-cost energy, bitcoin mining may have a dramatic effect on energy markets and power systems. While the net effect of these changes is likely to be very positive (as noted above with respect to the incentives for renewables and grid stabilization), the resulting shifts could be disruptive if not well managed. Domestically, grids that offer ancillary services may attract bitcoin miners at the expense of other grid systems, which could have second-order consequences setting up a new form of competition among regional energy grids that are currently economically independent. Internationally, nations with large, stranded energy resources may become new loci attracting bitcoin mining, which given the global nature of the market will open up intense competition. If bitcoin mining becomes tightly integrated into the domestic grid, and are suddenly attracted to a new, more competitive jurisdiction or region, this may cause local disruption that authorities may seek to manage and mitigate.

Adversary attack: As a proof of work system, the rules of the protocol require all nodes to only accept as valid those blockchain histories that have the most demonstrated energy expenditure (i.e., the longest chain). Thus, the only way to double-spend a transaction or mine empty blocks or otherwise disrupt the normal functioning of the network is for an entity to acquire and deploy at least 51% mining "hash power". While such an attack will require immense resources and planning (and may end up being self-defeating), it cannot be entirely ruled out as impossible. Therefore, the game theory of such an attack requires careful analysis, and analytical red teaming, to identify scenarios in which the network would be vulnerable, assess the resources necessary to execute them, and determine the risk-weighted relative likelihood of their success, given potential future conditions of the network. This is an area that needs continued research and study, especially as adoption grows, hash power concentration changes, and mining hardware supply chains evolve.

Other, unanticipated risks: Bitcoin is a novel monetary asset, with just over a decade of market behavior and technical functioning under its belt. While it has been extraordinarily reliable as a network, and its decentralization makes it very difficult to manipulate, it is hard to rule out "unknown unknowns" that could emerge in the future and threaten the stability or functioning of the network. The bitcoin community as a distributed collective is always on the look-out for potential threats and risks, but completely unknown, unanticipated issues are possible.

Conclusion

In this essay we've reviewed:

1. **The strategic vulnerabilities emerging for the U.S. despite (and even because of) its current monetary network dominance.** We found that the global dollar system is generating increasingly acute financial, political, and geopolitical liabilities that present a potential systemic risk to U.S. national security and global power.

2. **The strategic challenges from ambitious adversary efforts to undermine and bypass existing global digital networks.** We found that China is executing a comprehensive (and thus far successful) strategy to block western financial coercion via sanctions-resistant settlement systems, build deep RMB-based monetary and trade relationships with critical geopolitical balancing powers, and expand

its technological and geoeconomic sphere of influence across Asia and the Middle East via the Digital Silk Road.

3. **The potential strategic advantages and risks from emerging non-traditional monetary networks like bitcoin and dollar stablecoins.** We found that bitcoin and stablecoins could help counter the expansion of China's digital authoritarianism, bolster U.S. sovereign debt markets, and foster individual autonomy in developing countries with extractive and oppressive regimes.

As the U.S. navigates this "decisive decade", U.S. policymakers should be attuned to non-traditional approaches to mitigate adversary asymmetric strategies with our own. The strategic benefits of a pro-bitcoin policy stance to U.S. national security and geopolitical advantage are worth serious further analysis.

QR Code to **Chapter 1** Endnote Links and Figures on the Bitcoin Today Coalition website:

Endnotes

1. Weaponized Interdependence: How Global Economic Networks Shape State Coercion – H. Farrell and A. Newman, Belfer Center for Science and International Affairs
2. Executive Order 12333 – National Security Agency/Central Security Service
3. Suspicious activity reports, explained – F. Shiel and B. Hallman, International Consortium of Investigative Journalists
4. End-Use Monitoring and Effective Export Compliance – Kevin Kurland, BIS
5. CYBER 101: Defend Forward and Persistent Engagement – U.S. Cyber Command
6. Sanctions Programs and Country Information – Office of Foreign Assets Control
7. Commerce Implements New Export Controls on Advanced Computing & Semiconductor Manufacturing Items to the People's Republic of China – BIS
8. The Fractional Preferential Attachment Scale-Free Network Model – R. Rak and E. Rak, NIH
9. "The estimation that by January 2001, 60% of the Presidential Daily Briefings were based upon SIGINT, a percentage that has surely increased over the last decade." National Security Agency has pushed to "rethink and reapply" its treatment of the Fourth Amendment since before 9/11 – Lauren Harper, UNREDACTED
10. The Contentious U.S.-China Trade Relationship – A. Siripurapu and N. Berman, Council on Foreign Relations
11. How the U.S. Stumbled into Using Chips as a Weapon Against China – H. Farrell and A. Newman, WSJ
12. 'We have survived': China's Huawei goes local in response to US sanctions – Qainer Liu, Financial Times
13. Exclusive: China plans $500 million subsea internet cable to rival US-backed project – Joe Brock, Reuters
14. Western companies take slow steps towards China 'de-risking' – Y. Yang and P. Nilsson, Financial Times
15. The Fraying of the US Global Currency Reserve System – Lyn Alden
16. Sanctions have frozen around $300 bln of Russian reserves, FinMin says – Reuters
17. EU bars 7 Russian banks from SWIFT, but spares those in energy – Philip Blenkinsop, Reuters
18. Hedging Sanctions Risk: Cryptocurrency in Central Bank Reserves – Matthew Ferranti, Harvard University
19. MERICS China Security and Risk Tracker 03/2023 – Helena Legarda, MERICS
20. Central banks of China and United Arab Emirates join digital currency project for cross-border payments – BIS
21. China uses commodities buying power to push yuan internationalization – Avery Chen, S&P Global Market Intelligence
22. How to Hide Your Foreign Exchange Reserves—A User's Guide – Brad Setser, Council on Foreign Relations
23. Networks, Crowds, and Markets: Reasoning about a Highly Connected World, Chapter 19: Cascading Behavior in Networks – D. Easley and J. Kleinberg, Cambridge University Press
24. Backfire: How Sanctions Reshare the World Against U.S. Interests – Agathe Demarais
25. Six New BRICS: Implications for Energy Trade – G. Baskaran and B. Cahill, CSIS
26. What the FinCEN leaks reveal about the ongoing war on dirty money – Matthew Collin, Brookings
27. The Untold Story Behind Saudi Arabia's 41-Year U.S. Debt Secret – Andrea Wong, Bloomberg
28. The 2023 Long-Term Budget Outlook – Congressional Budget Office
29. Federal Surplus or Deficit [-] – St. Louis Fed
30. Partnership Letter – Hirschmann Capital
31. An Update to the Budget Outlook: 2023 to 2033 – Congressional Budget Office
32. This Time is Different Chartbook: Country Histories On Debt, Default, and Financial Crises – Carmen Reinhart, NBER
33. Principles for Navigating Big Debt Crises – Bridgewater
34. Explainer: What is the 'Basel III endgame' and why are banks worked up about it? – Pete Schroeder, Reuters

35 Social Security Funded Until 2034, and About Three-Quarters Funded for the Long Term; Many Options to Address the Long-Term Shortfall – Carolyn Colvin, SSA

36 The Black Swan of Cairo: How Suppressing Volatility Makes the World Less Predictable and More Dangerous – N. Taleb and M. Blyth

37 Suppressing Volatility Makes the World More Dangerous – FS

38 U.S. Treasury Markets: Steps Toward Increased Resilience – Group of 30

39 Market Value of Marketable Treasury Debt – St. Louis Fed

40 Liberty Street Economics: From the Vault: A Look Back at the October 15, 2014, Flash Rally – M. Fleming, P. Johansson, F. Keane, and J. Meyer, The Federal Reserve Bank of New York; How did COVID-19 disrupt the market for U.S. Treasury debt? – J. Cheng, D. Wessel, and J. Younger, Brookings; Fedwire resumes operations after hours long disruption – Ann Saphir, Reuters

41 What did the Fed do in response to the COVID-19 crisis? – E. Milstein and D. Wessel, Brookings; Section 13. Powers of Federal Reserve Banks – Federal Reserve Board

42 Federal Reserve Board announces it will make available additional funding to eligible depository institutions to help assure banks have the ability to meet the needs of all their depositors – Federal Reserve Board

43 Other financial institutions explained – European Central Bank

44 Section 13. Powers of Federal Reserve Banks – Federal Reserve Board

45 Central bank liquidity swaps – Federal Reserve Board

46 Federal Reserve announces the establishment of temporary U.S. dollar liquidity arrangements with other central banks – Federal Reserve Board

47 Paul Tucker on *Global Discord: Values and Power in a Fractured World Order* – Mercatus Center

48 Repo and Reverse Repo Agreements – Federal Reserve Bank of New York

49 Central Bank & International Account Services – Federal Reserve Bank of New York

50 China Repo Facility – Joseph Wang

51 Chairman Gallagher's TTX Remarks 4/19 – The Select Committee on the Chinese Communist Party

52 Taiwan foreign minister warns of conflict with China in 2027 – Amy Hawkins, The Guardian

53 Can FinCEN Solve America's Money-Laundering Problem? – Peter Stone, The New Republic

54 Our Biggest Economic, Social, and Political Issue – R. Dalio, S. Kryger, B. Rowley, and N. Hannan, Bridgewater

55 How the Rich Get Richer – Davide Malacrino, IMF

56 Survey of Consumer Finances – Federal Reserve Board

57 Provisional Drug Overdose Deaths from 12 months ending in April 2022 – NCHS, CDC

58 USTR Releases Annual Report on China's WTO Compliance – United States Trade Representative

59 The Return of Industrial Warfare – Alex Vershinin, Royal United Services Institute

60 DOD Report: Consolidation of Defense Industrial Base Poses Risks to National Security – Todd Lopez, U.S. Department of Defense

61 Wargaming a Long War: Ukraine Fights On – J. Lacey, T. Barrick, and N. Barrick, Modern War Institute

62 The U.S. Industrial Base Is Not Prepared for a Possible Conflict with China – Seth Jones, CSIS

63 "But what about US allies and partners (e.g., "the Quad") across the Indo-Pacific. Surely our combined maritime power will continue to dwarf the PLAN! The Quad's shipbuilding tonnage (w/ the US Pacific Fleet's allocation)? A bit under 430K tons" – @tshugart3

64 Alarming Navy Intel Slide Warns of China's 200 Times Greater Shipbuilding Capacity – Joseph Trevithick, The War Zone

65 Net Interest Will Total $10.5 Trillion Over the Next Decade – Committee for a Responsible Federal Budget

66 New Map of the Belt and Road Initiative – Clingendael

67	China's Port Investments Are Raising Security Fears. How to Deal with Them. – L. Lane and C. Tang, Barron's
68	It's not about Tesla or Alibaba it's much bigger than that – Deep Throat
69	China's Growing Influence in Latin America – Diana Roy, Council on Foreign Relations
70	"The PBoC balance sheet now looks too small compared with China's gigantic debt load. As the PBoC has increasingly relied on claims on domestic institutions for BS expansion since 2015, essentially it means China has lagged other major economies in the game of debt monetization. – Shanghai Macro Strategist
71	The dollar has some would-be rivals. Meet the challengers. – A. Kumar and J. Lipsky, Atlantic Council
72	Ibid.
73	RWR Blockchain Report 6/2021 – RWR Advisory
74	Ibid.
75	Project mBridge: experimenting with a multi-CBDC platform for cross-border payments – BIS
76	Ibid.
77	Project mBridge Connecting economies through CBDC – BIS
78	Saudi Central Bank and Central Bank of the U.A.E. Joint Digital Currency and Distributed Ledger Project – SAMA
79	Saudi Arabia Considers Accepting Yuan Instead of Dollars for Chinese Oil Sales – S. Said and S. Kalin, WSJ
80	China-Saudi Trade is Booming… And Not Just Because of Oil – Eric Olander, The China Global South Project
81	US security officials scrutinize Abu Dhabi's $3bn Fortress takeover – A. Massoudi and D. Sevastopulo, Financial Times
82	America's Sticky Power – Walter Mead, Foreign Policy
83	"China's Digital Silk Road" by the China Electronic Information Industry Development Research Institute (Translated)
84	Understanding the adoption context of China's digital currency electronic payment – H. Xia, Y. Gao, and J. Zhang, Financial Innovation Full Text
85	Takshashila SlideDoc - China's Vision for a New World Order: GDI, GSI & GCI – Manoj Kewalramani, The Takshashila Institution
86	China's Casino Crackdown Part of Quest to Transform Macau – Shirley Zhao, Bloomberg
87	Legality of Bitcoin by country or territory – Wikipedia
88	U.S. overtakes China to become biggest bitcoin mining hub in the world – Adela Suliman, The Washington Post
89	Top Stablecoin Tokens by Market Capitalization – CoinMarketCap
90	Speech by Vice Chair for Supervision Quarles on central bank digital currency – Federal Reserve Board
91	Top Stablecoin Tokens by Market Capitalization – CoinMarketCap
92	Proof-of-Stake and Stablecoins: A Blockchain Centralization Dilemma – Lyn Alden
93	FACT SHEET: Advancing Technology for Democracy – The White House
94	China's power crisis: why is it happening and what does it mean for the economy? – Zhao Ziwen, South China Morning Post
95	China Is Buying Gas Like There's Still an Energy Crisis – Bloomberg
96	Greening Bitcoin With Incentive Offsets – T. Cross and A. Bailey, Resistance Money
97	Oklo to power bitcoin mining machines : Corporate – World Nuclear News
98	Going Nuclear: Bitcoin Mining's Potential Energy Future – Ben Strack, Blockworks
99	Bitcoin's Carbon Footprint Revisited: Proof of Work Mining for Renewable Energy Expansion – J. Ibanez and A. Freier, MDPI

CHAPTER 2

BITCOIN, AFRICA, AND U.S. NATIONAL SECURITY INTERESTS

By Ben Kincaid

Ben Kincaid *spent the first half of his career as a U.S. Diplomat, serving and leading teams in multiple countries in Africa, the Middle East, and South Asia. Ben worked across the U.S. interagency and with senior foreign officials to drive partnered approaches to pressing national security challenges in some of the world's most troubled places. Today, he's CEO of ReElement Technologies Africa, whose mission is to bring the critical mineral processing step to Africa, empowering nations to capture the value of their natural resources. Ben is also founding partner of Bridger Solutions, an Africa-focused bitcoin mining company. He serves as an advisor to Allegro Group, a Fargo-based talent and leadership transformation company. Ben lives in Santo Domingo, Dominican Republic where his wife is currently posted to the U.S. Embassy. He holds a BA in International Studies and Political Science from Virginia Military Institute and an MA in Latin American Studies from Georgetown University.*

Introduction

The rise of bitcoin in Africa offers a glimpse into future global trends and warrants analysis of its potential to bolster U.S. national security interests. A freer, safer, and more prosperous world is one in which African people and nations secure their political, economic, financial, and energy independence. This is a world in keeping with American principles of freedom and sovereignty, directly addressing core national security interests as they pertain to external threats, as well as securing and maintaining key allies worldwide. Still a nascent movement, the bitcoin ecosystem is quietly delivering such independence, supplying a lifeboat for people during crisis and in the absence of state capacity.

At the nation-state level, the bitcoin ecosystem, including bitcoin mining, is emerging as a "freedom alternative" to the Chinese Communist Party (CCP) and other external actors who seek to control and exploit through centralized surveillance technologies such as central bank digital currencies (CBDC). As America focuses on how to defeat the re-emergence of totalitarianism at scale, it is a national security imperative to identify and encourage organically occurring "freedom and sovereignty" movements wherever they exist.

Bitcoin is one of those movements and is achieving results in Africa which call for our keen attention in this regard, especially in the context of China's strategy of influence and control in Africa and the Global South. In stark relief to the Chinese model, bitcoin is an open economic system, controlled by no one, and Africans are increasingly opting in. A grassroots movement and ecosystem that advances security, stability, and freedom — without trillions spent or deploying troops — is particularly good news for America.

When one considers that, given demographic trendlines, Africa is the future of humanity, analysis of bitcoin's impact there to date becomes more critical still to geopolitical and security considerations for the U.S. We must also turn to the question of sovereignty and where it optimally resides for shared prosperity by nations and peoples through free-market commerce. As sovereignty advances for local communities and nation-states, many root drivers of hardship and violence — and which attract exploitative external actors — can be constructively addressed. I will describe how bitcoin is empowering Africans to maximize sovereignty and prosperity at a local community level, perhaps the most critical component of successful democracies. I will also argue that the bitcoin ecosystem — through bitcoin mining and the emergence of bitcoin as a neutral reserve asset — may strengthen sovereignty at the nation-state level, a critical development for countries to regain control from external actors seeking to extract and exploit.

What Is Bitcoin Doing Now in Africa?

The bitcoin ecosystem in Africa is active and responding practically to critical problems that have not been solved otherwise. A speculative hard asset to protect the wealthy from currency debasement? In the West, perhaps that is still the primary value proposition. Not in Africa. According to in-depth reporting from CNBC, bitcoin is "offering an onramp to the financial system for people who would otherwise be left out. In countries where the vast majority of the population is unbanked… a virtual currency that does not require an intermediary to approve transactions can be a vital lifeline for survival." The reporting also highlights the work of U.S. company Strike, partnered with Nigerian company Bitnob, to enable almost zero cost fiat to fiat remittance payments using bitcoin as the pipeline from the U.S. to Kenya, Nigeria, and Ghana.[100] Since this reporting, (and despite a months-long "bear market"), the service has expanded to several other African nations, reaching a total population of almost 400 million. Africa is testing the premise of bitcoin as global digital public infrastructure, and it is passing the test. China and other centralized autocracies are no doubt taking note.

In war-torn Eastern Democratic Republic of Congo (DRC), revenue from bitcoin mining saved Virunga National Park, Africa's oldest protected space and home to one-third of the world's mountain gorillas, from closure. These data mining operations secure the bitcoin network by monetizing stranded — otherwise wasted — hydroelectricity. The revenue in turn provides funding for park salaries and public infrastructure, helping to support over 10,000 jobs reliant on the park and its local power plants.[101] Without this economic activity and alternative, many more young men would be forced into the conflict that has killed millions (yes, millions) since the mid-90s.

Kenyan bitcoin mining company Gridless Compute is subsidizing renewable energy minigrids in three countries through bitcoin mining operations, resulting in the electrification of rural communities.[102] Minigrid operators throughout east Africa are quickly either becoming bitcoin miners or integrating mining operations, to optimally finance rural electrification. 600 million people in Africa, most residing in the countryside, still have no access to electricity — an outrageous figure to consider in 2024 — and one that contributes significantly to economic despair, political instability, and cycles of conflict that continue to bedevil state and external actors alike. And at the sovereign level, in 2024 Ethiopia and Kenya both announced they are working with bitcoin mining companies as part of their respective national strategies to develop renewable energy projects and most optimally leverage their vast energy resources.

A Protocol for Democratic Development

The tight-knit trust-based networks of African villages are marrying up with bitcoin as a decentralized and open public financial infrastructure. Open-source protocol Fedimint is fast empowering small to medium-size communities in Africa and around the world by conveying digital property rights and ability to transact value through bitcoin in a community context. While solving for transactions and secure custody challenges for communities, Fedimint's most profound insight is one that speaks to the heart of open and free societies everywhere, especially now in the West: vibrant localism is essential for democracies to flourish.

Community-empowering solutions such as Fedimint are tools yes, but also emergent local civic associations that not only solve human problems, but cultivate face-to-face interaction between neighbors, an essential bulwark against centralizing power that "hinders, restrains, enervates, stifles, and stultifies so much that in the end each nation is no more than a flock of timid and hardworking animals with the government as its shepherd."[103] This quote from Alexis de Tocqueville is a warning of what will follow democracy as we isolate ourselves from our fellow man and eschew the hard but vital work of building a world with our fellows in our local communities. Democracies need more "African village" ethos, and African villages need bitcoin to unleash their potential. The African village and bitcoin point to key components of democratic culture that are, arguably, on the wane in our western democracies, speaking to a core national security interest: defense of our liberal democracy, both abroad and at home. Fedimint's inspiration may be Africa; however, its application may advance global democratic development and ultimately address financial exclusion in many localities here in the United States.

Opportunity for African Leadership

As indicated above, bitcoin can achieve substantive results and meet the challenges that so far have been inadequately addressed by African governments or various external actors, such as China and the World Bank. This is because bitcoin is a decentralized, open-source, equitable, and accessible network which, like the internet before it, has tremendous potential for further adoption. Moreover, as populations increasingly use the network, nation-states will inevitably take notice. The winning strategy for a nation-state will be to embrace the movement; a losing strategy will be to embrace Chinese-style repression and centralized control of financial rails.

What is increasingly certain is that as bitcoin adoption increases, governments will be forced to make a choice. The United States has an excellent opportunity to use its good relations and its status as the world's champion of freedom, sovereignty, and self-determination to nudge African countries in the right direction. Many African leaders will look to America for guidance on this issue; in this context, U.S. state and federal legislation and policies will undoubtedly be examined closely.

A market-incented flywheel effect is needed to unleash Africa's energy potential, and to deliver energy and financial independence to both people and nations alike. Understanding the political dynamic of bitcoin adoption and use at the grassroots level, the savviest of African leaders will begin to grasp how the bitcoin ecosystem can induce sovereignty at the nation-state level. In fact, this is already happening, albeit without fanfare or public announcements. One country's state utility in east Africa is selling 300 megawatts of previously stranded hydroelectric power to host bitcoin mining data center operations. In this instance, the government is selling this power as an effort to service debt to the CCP, which financed the hydroelectric project years ago.[104] The US should encourage this as a positive development that helps African countries shirk their dependence on external actors, as such dependency restricts their ability to leverage natural resources for domestic economic development.

Given vast energy resources on the continent, bitcoin mining is the pioneer offtaker that will help countries monetize stranded energy, finance the development of renewable energy infrastructure, and attract additional paying customers of renewable energy such as cloud compute, AI, and traditional mining industrial consumers.

Framework for Analysis and Assessment

As part of a framework to evaluate bitcoin's development and prospects on the continent in the context of U.S. national security objectives, we will use the White House's five-year strategy for sub-Saharan Africa.[105] Not raised directly in the strategy document (although implicit throughout), is a treatment of CCP influence, strategy, and counter-U.S. initiatives on the march in Africa. We will address that issue directly throughout this chapter. Core pillars of the strategy follow.

1. Foster Openness and Open Societies: a key tenet of this pillar of strategy is to "foster a digital ecosystem built on open, reliable, interoperable, and secure internet and information and communication technology across sub-Saharan Africa." I will make the leap and call this the "counter malign CCP activities" element of the strategy. No surprise that this comes first.

2. Deliver Democratic and Security Dividends: Importantly, the strategy calls for "civilian-led, non-kinetic approaches where possible and effective."

3. Advance Pandemic Recovery and Economic Opportunity: a key tenet is to "leverage and streamline financing and co-invest to deliver game-changing projects to strengthen economies, diversify supply chains, and advance U.S. and African national security… to help close the global infrastructure gap and support resilient and dynamic economies."

4. Support Conservation, Climate Adaptation, and a Just Energy Transition: the strategy highlights that the U.S. "will work closely with countries as they determine how to best meet their specific energy needs"… and will "pursue public-private partnerships to sustainably develop and secure the critical minerals that will supply clean energy technologies needed to facilitate the global energy transition."

Focusing on prospects for the bitcoin mining industry to address strategic pillars three and four, we will analyze effects and impact in a section titled "Economic Opportunity and a Just Energy Transition."

US STRATEGIC OBJECTIVE 1:
Foster Openness and Open Societies

Bitcoin responds directly to this element of our U.S. strategy, presenting the most secure, decentralized, and censorship resistant digital financial infrastructure to reinforce "open, reliable, interoperable, and secure internet"[106] infrastructure on the continent. This is increasingly critical as digital authoritarianism — modeled by the CCP — is on the march in Africa, and throughout the world. A decentralized immutable ledger that enables peer-to-peer transactions without a third-party intermediary is even more important in regions of the world where a) huge portions of the population are unbanked; and b) where China is present and driving an authoritarian option.

Bitcoin Adoption

Chainalysis' 2022 "Geography of Cryptocurrency" reveals that the number of retail transfers of cryptocurrency under USD 1,000 are 80 percent higher in Africa than the next highest region, and that the number of open peer-to-peer exchanges are more than double than the next highest region in the world.[107] Although Chainalysis does not parse its data, bitcoin is the preponderant cryptocurrency throughout Africa. These figures are more remarkable still when one accounts for extremely low internet penetration and usage in the African rural countryside.[108] These statistics indicate that local Africans are voting (opting in) for open and decentralized solutions to their financial needs, which include a reliable store of value (savings mechanism) against inflating local currencies, and an effective and inexpensive way to transact cross-border. This is a blow to CCP-inspired digital authoritarianism; preference for bitcoin combined with the recent failure of the e-Naira (Nigeria's CBDC) advances an organic march toward digital freedom and is resisting state and external actor preference for authoritarian solution sets.[109]

Chinese Communist Party: The Authoritarian Tech Stack

However, the CCP has laid a formidable foundation over the last two decades in Africa. They have spent too much time and effort — and poured too many dollars into Belt and Road Initiative (BRI) projects — to roll over to any open, decentralized alternatives to their vision for Africa and the world. It remains an open question which direction African leaders will take, as they find themselves increasingly caught between Chinese influence and their populations' rejection (albeit uneven) of CCP and CCP-inspired centralized solutions. China's control over strategic physical infrastructure in Africa is a significant point of strategic concern, but so is their influence and control over technology and communication infrastructure which presents a threat to U.S. — and African — national security interests.

In short, China wields the most influence over the technology and communications infrastructure "stack" in Africa, and the U.S. is not going to dislodge it through the same brute force building and spending tactics. Nor should we. America should, however, look to decentralized protocols that are growing organically, such as bitcoin, and competing favorably vis-a-vis authoritarian alternatives because they do the job more effectively. It turns out that open economic systems simply work better, especially when given the freedom to flourish. Bitcoin's rapid growth benefits from top-down "freedom" via regulation to be sure; but it also is not dependent on it, which is a function of its decentralized security through the "proof of work" mechanism and its cryptographic defense. This promises to frustrate CCP and CCP-like efforts to no end, and — just maybe — will seep into the heart of the Chinese system itself, a topic we will return to.

Kenyan Michael Kioneki writes astutely on the competition between state and non-state digital currencies as African people and leaders seek solutions to cross-border (retail and commercial) transactions that currently impede the benefits of global commerce and trade to African people and nations. He writes, "Even though China is Africa's largest trading partner, only 7% of global foreign exchange transactions by turnover involved the Chinese Yuan... However, with China at the forefront of the global race to develop CBDCs, Beijing's odds look vastly better in Africa, where it can pull on its decades-old influence and more recent economic power. There are over 10,000 Chinese companies operating across the continent, with these firms having made over USD 300 billion in investments."[110]

Kioneki also notes that a majority of smartphones in Africa are manufactured by Chinese companies and a staggering 70 percent of Africa's 4G network is operated by Chinese state-owned enterprises. He highlights that the latest Huawei-series phones in Africa are equipped for interoperability with the Chinese DCEP (their international CBDC). That fact alone should give us serious pause. China, simply, is building on 20 years of physical, communications, and digital infrastructure development on the continent, along with the capture of select African elites that comes along with that activity. BRI increasingly connects Africa and China, and that trade corridor may be the "ideal test case for the digital yuan to act as a bridge to financial flows."[111] Thankfully, America will likely not present a centralized counter solution to the CCP, but it can and should encourage countries to consider bitcoin as a decentralized alternative to China's dystopian surveillance-enabled CBDC.

Bitcoin as an Emerging Alternative to the CCP

Bitcoin is emerging as a counter to a CCP or CCP-inspired CBDC, but also — potentially — as a viable neutral reserve store of value asset at the sovereign level. Although early, this should be welcomed, especially as African and other nations weigh options to diversify from U.S. Treasuries, some of whom seek to join the CCP-dominated BRICS bloc of nations. Bitcoin as a neutral reserve and sovereign savings asset — while not impacting the USD as global reserve currency — provides solutions to countries without ceding ground to a CCP-led economic bloc which runs counter to US interests in the world. USD as the global reserve asset is not going anywhere soon; however, a BRICS-bloc decision to transact with a gold-backed currency, with most of the gold under Chinese custody, is not good for the dollar, nor is it good for countries in a bloc dominated by the CCP.[112]

And while the Chinese are seeking to counter USD dominance, they have also greatly benefitted from a system which has allowed them to lend dollar-denominated loans through BRI over the last two decades to African nations, resulting in the construction of over 100 commercial ports and other strategic infrastructure projects.[113] China's weaponization of the USD to secure influence worldwide and to — paradoxically — counter U.S. strategic national security interests is nowhere more evident than in Africa.

Bitcoin's emergence as a gold-like neutral reserve store of value asset would be a strategic surprise to the Chinese, who have been re-positioning for the end of the US dollar system, primarily by adding to its gold reserves. The U.S. and other primarily free and democratic nations stand to disproportionately gain from adoption of a neutral reserve hard asset that the CCP will avoid due to their inability to control and manipulate it. This dynamic will only intensify as the CCP leverages its dominant position in the BRICS bloc and as more countries seek membership in BRICS to defend against financial vulnerabilities stemming from dependency on U.S. Treasuries. Finally, bitcoin as a neutral reserve currency alternative would insulate "BRI-indebted" African nations from compulsion by the CCP to transact in an internationalized "e-yuan", a development which would have profound top-down authoritarian effects on those nations and populations. As Pines points out, "Bitcoin is a clear and present threat to China's strategic ambitions for the e-RMB as well as its efforts to enforce capital controls [at home]."[114]

Bitcoin: A Strategic Dilemma for the CCP; Heeding Tocqueville

The CCP's 2021 crackdown on the bitcoin transactions and mining ecosystem, while allowing Chinese bitcoin companies to continue international operations in Africa and elsewhere, is also of strategic significance. Outside of bitcoin industry insiders and enthusiasts, this event went largely unnoticed. I contend it will be looked back on as a decision with massive impact, both geoeconomically and to the CCP regime itself. It is also a critical signpost for the U.S. foreign policy establishment as they confront the CCP now and in the years to come. It should be of no surprise that the CCP will not tolerate an open, free, decentralized, and censorship-resistant financial asset in Mainland China. It is antithetical to CCP ideology that bitcoin is an uncontrollable financial rail that facilitates capital flight. And although the CCP cannot stop bitcoin transactions, it can identify its users and jail them, as well as implement tactics of technological control similar to those used in suppressing a free and open internet. Simply put, what the CCP represses is probably good for an open and free society, and bitcoin is squarely in this category.

The resurgence of now-illegal bitcoin mining on the Mainland, combined with steady growth of Chinese bitcoin companies operating outside China, will increasingly test the CCP regime. Xi Jinping's tenuous balance between iron-fisted political and ideological control on one hand, and his social compact with the "capitalist" class on the other, will be tested by Chinese bitcoin entrepreneurs and industrialists. This tension will arguably play out most dynamically in African countries as organic, and eventually nation-state, demand for bitcoin-related services increasingly pits capitalists against their authoritarian regime. Perhaps more significant still is the fact that Chinese "bitcoiners" are immersed in the values and ideology of what bitcoin represents: freedom, openness, decentralization, and censorship resistance. Not to mention creating economic opportunities for themselves and their families they would not otherwise have. This is a dangerous dynamic for the CCP, and one the CCP may be forced to act against more aggressively as the bitcoin network grows stronger, especially given that Chinese bitcoin industrialists are headquartered in Mainland China.

The U.S. foreign policy interagency should consider the above dynamic in conjunction with the CCP's analysis of Alexis de Tocqueville's prescient writing. Former PRC Vice President Wang Qishan closely read Tocqueville's "Ancien Regime and the French Revolution," as he considered de-stabilizing social dynamics that could be at play in the surging and successful Chinese context. "It is almost never when a state of things is the most detestable that it is smashed, but when, beginning to improve, it permits men to breathe, to reflect, to communicate their thoughts with each other, and to gauge by what they already have the extent of their rights and their grievances."[115] Wang Qishan and the CCP elite are clearly not looking to Tocqueville to model a "Democracy in China" but are seeking hints at what they must head off at the pass if their authoritarian regime should survive. Growing Chinese participation in the bitcoin industry is increasingly a boon to Chinese prosperity and — potentially — a Trojan Horse for freedom, which is indeed a threat to the regime.

U.S. STRATEGIC OBJECTIVE 2:
Deliver Democratic and Security Dividends

The bitcoin ecosystem, and the equitable social movement it embodies, is such a powerful "democratic opening and opportunity" throughout Africa that it is capable of countering the influence of the CCP and other authoritarian regimes. Bitcoin's initial and most dramatic "use case" is as a lifeline for individuals in countries prone to property rights abuses, strict capital controls, autocratic regimes, and conflict. However, as adoption continues to grow across the continent, African policymakers are enacting favorable digital asset laws and regulation, many of them a reversal of prior policies. In Nigeria for instance, the Federal Ministry of Communications and Digital Economy announced in May 2023 a "national blockchain strategy," quite a dramatic turnaround after seeking to ban bitcoin in 2021.[116]

The embrace of the bitcoin — or an "open digital asset" — ecosystem by African leaders will be a signal that they are listening to populations and allowing an open, decentralized, and free mechanism of value communication to bloom. This is a good thing for democracy but not an easy decision by leaders under the sway of the CCP, or otherwise inclined to control their populations through monetary means. Absent a ubiquitous mechanism like the e-RMB, bitcoin offers African leaders a solution to problems without the need for state intervention. For states that lack the capacity to attend to their unbanked majority, the choice to embrace open digital assets — namely bitcoin — is becoming very clear. For countries that try to enforce against an open alternative, leaders will increasingly contend with freedom-seeking populations empowered with a censorship-resistant tool for financial transactions.

The Dilemma of Sovereignty: Central African Republic as a Case Study

Democracy, security, and economic development are intertwined, especially in Africa's poorest nations. States cannot advance democratically until their territory and populations are secure and real economic opportunities abound. Cheap substitutions for nation-state sovereignty, defined largely by a ruling elite captive to external powers, seek to exploit state incapacity, and countries suffer from the pernicious cycle that ensues. Bitcoin as an empowering, democratizing, and stabilizing force from below, combined with being a tool for weak states to claw back sovereignty should thus be considered as part of a better solution set. Short-cut solutions come in the form of debt trap diplomacy, development aid, and "free" security support that tend to entrench a corrupt elite and chisel away at nation-state level sovereignty.

Central African Republic is a case in point. In 2017, to stave off civil war and regime overthrow, President Faustin Touadera took the cheap and easy — and perhaps only — solution he had on offer: a Faustian bargain with Vladimir Putin and Russian mercenary group Wagner. In sum, he received vital security support from a capable and brutal partner — Wagner — in exchange for his natural resources, as well as a good chunk of political power. A play straight from Machiavelli's "The Prince," Wagner struck like a Cobra. They placed a Praetorian guard around the President, installed a Russian citizen as national security advisor, and went to work extracting diamonds, gold, and timber in payment. They will no doubt keep the regime "safe" as long as they are profiting from the enterprise.

In parallel, China stepped in to "support" CAR through the BRI, their own form of malignant debt trap diplomacy. We now know that even Iran got in on the action. Thankfully, a plot by the IRGC to build an anti-West terrorist organization in the ungoverned CAR hinterland was scuttled.[117] In 2021, three years after commencing operations in CAR, Wagner ran the same play in Mali, under the same general circumstances. But this time, to rescue the Malians from Al-Qa'ida-affiliated terrorists on the march. Libya, Algeria, Burkina Faso, Niger, and other African countries remain in the crosshairs. Western nations engaged in aggressive diplomacy to dissuade CAR, Mali, and others from pernicious alliances with adversary nations, but did not provide any real alternatives to what were existential challenges for African leaders in these weak states. The most critical takeaway: with the drawdown of French influence in their old colonial sphere, Russia and China saw a geopolitical opportunity to step into the gap with their particular and malign form of "neocolonialism." The most critical questions to come from this are: how does America shore up democracy and security in these vulnerable corners of the world without spilling blood and treasure? And how do African nations — in fact all nations — break the cycle of dependency on stronger external powers?

America and her Western allies, most prominently France, are unlikely to pursue a military campaign in northwest Africa to wrest nations and people from the clutches of Russia and China, or from terrorists for that matter. The removal of 3,000 French troops from Mali in 2021 after seven years of uneven results makes that quite clear, as does the July 2023 coup in Niger. Nor should Western coalitions go toe-to-toe with the Russians and Chinese by playing their game, one that continues to erode nation-state sovereignty in Africa and elsewhere. The US should, however, draw lessons from history to see that Wagner and China are seeking to perfect (arguably more brutally and repressively) a system of influence, extraction, and control that colonial powers commenced long ago.

Given that leadership in Paris and Washington have apparently — and rightfully — decided to pivot from direct intervention, this is a moment to focus on a more modest, effective, and longer-term solution: support for nation-state sovereignty vis-a-vis principal adversaries China and Russia. Sure, development and humanitarian support, trade initiatives, and traditional soft-power diplomacy can and should continue. But we must also identify asymmetric approaches that advance sovereignty and self-determination for people and nations now increasingly under the influence of our enemies.

The emergence of bitcoin presents an off-ramp for countries who are hopelessly indebted to international financial institutions and now to China. In West Africa, 14 "sovereign" nations continue to transact in CFA Francs, meaning their monetary policy is set in Europe and not by their own leadership. Over the last decade, China has spent hundreds of billions of dollars in this region of Africa to spread influence and gain access to strategic infrastructure. In parallel, France's influence in West Africa is diminishing. China's strategy is multi-faceted, but arguably their biggest strategic coup would be to build a military base on the Atlantic seaboard of West Africa, possibly in the Gulf of Guinea. This would be strategically untenable for the United States, given the potential for China to park submarines with nukes across the pond from the U.S. East Coast.

This is perhaps the most dramatic and chilling example of why geopolitics — and now Cold War 2.0 — will play out in Africa. And it is happening at a time the U.S. is re-focusing on domestic imperatives, but also on the China challenge.

Considering the above, the U.S. has no choice but to identify and promote tools for African countries to become — some for the first time in practical terms — more sovereign nation-states. Bitcoin as a freedom-alternative for the people is already on the march in Africa. And countries that recognize and embrace this movement will do well. Countries that also leverage bitcoin as a neutral reserve asset and employ bitcoin mining to monetize abundant natural resources — and in a sovereign manner — will do extraordinarily well. It is in the U.S. national security interest to encourage fragile countries to break the bonds of external manipulation (in particular, China and Russia) and grow increasingly sovereign by using an open protocol and ecosystem that has zero barriers to entry.

Addressing the Root Causes of Insecurity

Ungoverned spaces like the vast Sahara desert allow Al-Qa'ida to amass and centralize power through a warfare economy. Open economic and technological tools which can penetrate the world's closed off places — where evil finds safe haven — are urgently needed. Smart phones, Starlink-enabled data, and bitcoin represent the asymmetric alternatives for young men who seek livelihood and purpose apart from the only source currently available: a well-funded evil organization with a totalitarian and nihilistic vision.

Just as the internet democratized communication and knowledge, bitcoin can democratize the proliferation of productive economies in spaces that previously only produced terror and death. The pace of bitcoin adoption in ungoverned spaces that breed conflict such as in northern Mali, will be an important marker to monitor. The bitcoin mining project that saved Virunga National Park[118], combined with an increasingly vibrant bitcoin ecosystem in conflict-torn eastern DRC, is an early indicator and model for what may be effective in other places where desperation drives radicalization, such as ungoverned territory in the Sahel region of Africa.

Terrorists always find methods to transact and prefer cash, gold, or the hawala system due to untraceability. While not the point of this piece, bitcoin will unlikely develop into preferred means of transactions for these groups, although the intelligence community and firms like Chainalysis may wish that to be the case given their capabilities.[119] From an offensive — or constructive — optic, we should focus on how wider adoption of bitcoin in these terrorist-controlled regions may drive "market competition" in "Al-Qaida-INC" monopolies over the young, able-bodied labor force, and starve off the primary driver of this evil: the ability to effectively recruit and employ. Additionally, as the communications infrastructure needed for bitcoin becomes more ubiquitous in places like northern Mali, tactical options to counter terrorist leadership increase. Bitcoin and the internet can figuratively and literally cast light in dark areas to a) more effectively counter hardened terrorist leaders, and b) provide alternatives to societies held hostage by their evil. Mali, Burkina Faso, Niger, CAR, and other African countries need mechanisms to gain, not lose, sovereignty and self-determination. The recent transition to horrifically brutal Russian-led security operations as exemplified in northern Mali is a slide in the wrong direction.

The Need for a Westphalia 2.0

Africa needs more sovereignty, capacity, and self-determination at a nation-state level, a Westphalia 2.0 if you will. The Peace of Westphalia in 1648 planted the initial seed for the modern nation-state construct by emphasizing territorial sovereignty and non-intervention, principles which could potentially guide an empowered, self-determined future for African nations, steering them towards a Westphalia 2.0 era where autonomy and self-governance are paramount. The impact of colonialism, geopolitical exigencies of the 20th century, and great power interests have slowed this process, or prevented it altogether.

African colonies were initially just that, vassal states of great powers, and sources of cheap raw goods and human labor. Shortly following World War II, independence movements coincided with the Cold War, giving France an excuse to intervene in their former colonies to secure French interests, and secondarily, to aid the American-led anti-Soviet alliance of nations. America used all levers of power and influence to counter Soviet influence in Africa and elsewhere; nation-state sovereignty (and in some cases democratic governance) took a back seat to this overriding security objective: arguably, this was a necessary evil to win the first Cold War.

The fall of the Soviet Union in 1989 marked Fukuyama's "end of history," and enabled the West and international institutions to unleash the globalizing forces of the free market more fully. The stated objective: ensure democracies and capitalism flourished everywhere. China, in particular, industrialized faster than any country in history, but, as the world now knows, did not become freer. More than three decades of "globalization" hence, the US is dependent on Chinese production of goods for most everything, the American manufacturing base and middle class is hollowed out, and the US created the greatest disparity of wealth the world has ever seen. In Africa during this post-1989 era, Cold War imperatives muted into the "internationalist" one, and supranational institutions stepped in to "manage" the economies of the Global South, a dynamic that persists to this day. This very incomplete description of history is necessary to illustrate a simple point: historical and global dynamics — much of it in the 20th and early 21st centuries — impeded much of Africa the opportunity to develop into sovereign nations.

Today, with globalism on the wane in favor of multi-polarity, a super-empowered China (from an economic perspective) and Russia (from a security one) contend for control in Africa, and to supplant international institutions' debt-induced hold over "sovereign" countries. The antidote: more — not less — sovereignty and self-determination. In addition to attending to the China threat, this is especially critical when one considers that Africa — demographically — is the future of humanity. The tailwind of opportunity for Westphalia 2.0 in Africa is de-globalization; however, this trend will also bring considerable potential for peril. The empowering potential of bitcoin at a nation-state level of sovereignty development should be considered in this context.

Georgetown professor Joshua Mitchell coined the term "Liberal Triumphalism" to characterize the post-1989 global "mission," facilitated by US military might and directed by "international" managers — both corporate and governmental. This mission was a grand one: deliver democratic and market "norms" to the post-Cold war world, and to the Global South in particular, and with China being the prize. Multinational corporations saw a great moment to fuse politics with commerce in this new grand international project, initially under a veneer of liberalism and free markets for all. However, having vanquished communism and reached Fukuyama's end of history, the great final task before humanity became to address imperatives that supersede nation-state borders, such as climate change.[120]

A post-Cold War "consensus" provided the space for nations to more constructively focus on global issues of import. This is a good thing to be sure, but in the right measure as a salutary supplement to interaction between sovereign nations, and not as a substitute for the nation-state. In excess, a totalizing ideology can take shape, which drives centralized control, and to favor those entities which have the greatest stake in such an emergent system without proper checks and balances. Such a dynamic is decidedly un-American and is not good for the world. Unforeseen economic and geopolitical distortions, that hyper-empowered the CCP and weakened the industrial backbone of America, are forcing an equilibrium. Thankfully, we have a modicum of political unity around this now-critical task.

Where Sovereignty Most Optimally Resides

For many African countries, the post-1989 transition to "supranationalism" is the most recent in yet another geopolitical dynamic that hobbles development of nation-state sovereignty. Many African nations are locked into never-ending cycles of external debt refinancing, while losing autonomy over productive capacity and natural resources. Alex Gladstein of the Human Rights Foundation provides deep-dive analysis of this pernicious effect.[121] As the U.S. seeks to rebalance "globalism" — primarily due to the CCP threat combined with economic fragility at home — the question of where sovereignty most optimally resides re-emerges as a question of great national security importance, and always a question central to the liberal democratic project.

Thomas Hobbes, reflecting on the Peace of Westphalia and the nation-state order that emerged, warned that "supra" and "sub" state alternatives are "perennial temptations of the human heart… and that their defenders may promise much, but neither 'commodious living' nor justice are possible through them."[122] Hobbes advanced that Roman Catholics were guilty of 'false universalism,' because they vested sovereignty at the supra-state level, in Rome. In turn, Hobbes thought that the Presbyterians were guilty of what he described as a "radical particularism," because they vested sovereignty at the sub-state level, in private conscience.[123]

In 2023, "supra" alternatives to sovereignty are represented primarily through multinational corporations and international governmental institutions which transcend the nation-state. What is old is new. Today's "sub" state alternative finds expression through tech-enabled isolation and avoidance of face-to-face relations in a community context, always essential for consensus-building and for life to go well, especially in the context of local liberal democracy.

Two centuries after Hobbes, Tocqueville foresaw that a potential future threat to the then-fledgling democratic project would be citizens desirous of a "parental" authority to lighten our burden as citizens, while simultaneously collapsing inward, increasingly de-linked and separated from building a world with our fellow man.

The Democratic Strength of the African Village

Africa is therefore fascinating and essential to consider the question of sovereignty and democratic development. We must also consider where sovereignty most optimally resides, and by extension, how bitcoin supports sovereignty well-placed.

Counterintuitively, we should focus not on what Africa gets wrong, but on what Africa gets very right. While much of Africa and the Global South struggle to emerge as capable nation-state sovereigns, they boast populations with strong and enduring bonds at the family, village, tribal, and regional/local levels of society. It is in this context that bitcoin is fusing into an organic "bottom-up" solution to financial disempowerment, and in a decentralized community context.

The "African village" is based on familial, tribal, and local ties that bind and engender trust-based civility through face-to-face relationships, and in conjunction with traditions that remain despite homogenizing global trends. While not a viable substitute for state capacity, in the best of cases, a resilient and vibrant localism does help people survive despite the worst of conditions.

In essence, Africa has in spades what America and the "West" are losing: a growing population that is diffusely spread via decentralized localities that govern themselves in large part by culturally and communally enforced reciprocal obligations. Without a uniformly applied rule of law, enforced by a capable state, this tenuous social structure can be targeted by extremists and/or criminal syndicates seeking to exploit communities in economic distress. However, the social substrate in much of Africa is made of the stuff that Tocqueville instructed was essential for the "democratic soul" to flourish.

The great challenge, according to Tocqueville, would become the democratic temptation to withdraw into ourselves and voluntarily re-tether ourselves to our communities through private associations, vibrant local politics, and institutions of faith. However, even in 2023, family, village, and faith remain the bedrock of much of African society. What is missing is nation-state level sovereignty that can work in democratic consensus with otherwise vibrant communities to secure the common defense and rule of law needed to advance human flourishing. "Supranational" decisions out of New York, Geneva, Beijing, and Paris are supplements to, but poor substitutes for, real nation-state sovereignty in Africa.

"The African village" is a source of innovation for bitcoin as an open protocol to secure property rights, a store of value, and a method of exchange for communities that are otherwise without financial infrastructure. One such innovation is Fedimint, described as "a modular open-source protocol to custody and transact bitcoin in a community context, built on a strong foundation of privacy." Fedimint is expanding to communities internationally but draws its inspiration and innovation from the qualities of the tight knit African community. The key insight — which I would claim is very much a Tocquevillian one — is that economic and democratic flourishing in this relatively new "international democratic order" is fortified and given succor at the most local of levels.

Fedimint is a protocol that balances the inherent "trust" within local communities — people bound to each other through family, tribe, shared history, culture, language — with the "trustlessness" of the bitcoin network to scale local banking via the Lightning Network, at once creating local economic opportunities, but also connecting these local communities to an interoperable and globally liquid monetary network. A "federated" community protocol that appoints multiple "guardians" to securely custody community funds is a potential bridge between true community banking and property rights and scalable usability of bitcoin as a publicly accessible utility. This can deliver community banking, with decentralized community control, to potentially millions of small-to-mid-size communities in Africa and the Global South.

While early, this is a potentially extraordinary tool for democratic culture worldwide, as well as an innovation that makes the village more resistant to malign actors who seek to exploit communities without alternatives or hope. Open, decentralized, layer two innovations such as Fedimint are the kind of "civilian-led non-kinetic approaches" that the U.S. government should recognize and support to achieve national security interests in Africa and elsewhere. In terms of where the liberal democratic project stands in 2023, we would do well to draw lessons from what Africa does well, and how we in the U.S. should consider the implications of waning localism, growing secularism, and centralization of politics on liberal democracy at home.

There is no more important national security interest than preservation of our bedrock democratic principles, values, and behaviors. In this vein, we must learn from Africa's strength: its people and its communities. Striking the balance between Tocqueville's "democratic man" who can act on the world without encumbrances and on equal footing (meritocracy) but who also remains "tethered" to salutary constraints (families and tribes and houses of worship) has never been more essential than now. Africa is not only the "future of humanity" due to demographics, but it may unlock the key to a democratic revival of spirit desperately needed in the lands from which democracy originally sprang.

U.S. STRATEGIC OBJECTIVES 3 AND 4:
Economic Opportunity and a Just Energy Transition

The key to financial and economic independence at the nation-state level is energy, and bitcoin's unique incentive structure can unlock Africa's energy potential. There is no lack of raw energy in Africa, be that measured in humans or joules. But the legacy of colonialism, postcolonialism, the Cold War, and now a new Cold War has stymied Africa's ability to harness natural energy resources, thus inhibiting their nation-state sovereignty. The retreat of globalism, or "supranationalism" as we have described it, will result in international relations increasingly defined by bilateral and multilateral relationships among sovereigns. African countries' ability to control, develop, and utilize their ample natural resources — starting with energy resources — provides not only a path toward a more prosperous future, but can stem the red tide of CCP neo-colonialism, disincentivize Russian PMC Wagner, and provide new opportunities for U.S. direct investment. African energy development is also essential for U.S. manufacturing to "friend-shore" as part of a broader strategy to reduce our dependence on the Chinese for, well, almost everything. We postulate that the fast-growing bitcoin mining industry and the Proof of Work mechanism is a key catalyst to unlock this much needed transition.

As The Economist published recently, Africa is just behind the Middle East with 13% of global gas reserves, and supercharging efforts to develop that capacity for export could be the answer to Europe's energy crisis in the wake of the Russia-Ukraine war. Only a fifth of this capacity is currently under construction, but energy majors in countries like Namibia, Senegal, Mozambique, and Mauritania are moving at pace to the opportunity.[124] While promising for pockets of Africa, and for Europe, it remains to be seen if the billions of dollars of investment needed to develop capacity will commensurately benefit Africa's acute need for domestic electrification. It also remains to be seen if large energy companies will allocate capital needed given the inherent political, economic, and security risks.

600 million Africans lack access to electricity.[125] This is the case despite Africa's vast renewable energy resources, the majority of which are undeveloped. Renewable energy production infrastructure that is in place often runs well under-capacity due primarily to dislocation from consumer demand. Africa boasts the world's best hydro, solar, and wind power, but the transmission infrastructure needed to deliver that energy to distant offtakers makes development at scale untenable. Hydropower is the primary renewable electricity resource, accounting for 70% of the renewable electricity share, which corresponds to 16% of total electricity production on the continent. The continent has the most untapped hydropower potential worldwide, with only 11% utilized.[126] While there is significant potential for wind and solar power, hydropower is generally the superior source of renewable energy given its high uptime of close to 100%, unless there is a drought.

International financing efforts, public and private development aid, and bilateral initiatives such as the CCP's BRI have all resulted in renewable energy infrastructure buildout across the continent. However, due to the dislocation of demand from many of these projects, it is not uncommon to find medium and large-scale projects (50 to 600 MW) operating at half or less of their capacity, in some cases close to zero, because of dislocated demand and lack of transmission infrastructure. While solar and wind power in the Sahara in theory supports all of Europe's electricity demand twice over, the transmission infrastructure — if technically feasible — would cost tens of trillions of dollars.

Not to mention that China manufactures and controls most of the inputs for solar and wind power production.[127] Most energy experts agree that beyond oil and gas, Africa's vast natural renewable or "green" energy resources represent the most untapped potential for Africa to connect its own population to electricity, and also to be a part of a meaningful energy transition worldwide to more renewable sources. For Africa, the challenge is how to achieve this without sacrificing sovereignty, but by taking control of natural energy wealth and using it to enhance opportunity and common prosperity for their people.

Bitcoin Mining: An Asymmetric Advantage for the U.S.

Enter bitcoin mining, a flexible computational capability which monetizes electricity into a decentralized globally liquid currency in a way that is interruptible, and location agnostic. If the market trajectory of the last 15 years is an indicator, bitcoin will change energy markets the world over and solve challenges that to-date have been insoluble.

Even financial behemoths such as Fidelity and BlackRock[128] and energy majors such as Exxon[129] and Shell[130] have recently taken notice — and action. There is nowhere on earth where this energy revolution will play out more impactfully than in Africa. At the sovereign level, we see this beginning in Ethiopia and Kenya. In early 2024, Ethiopia's sovereign wealth arm announced a partnership with a data center and bitcoin mining company, potentially unlocking hundreds of millions of dollars of investment into the country. This formalized a process that had been underway since 2022 between Ethiopia and private bitcoin mining companies to unlock to generate precious hard currency (USD) revenue from an enormous amount of otherwise stranded energy. The Grand Ethiopian Renaissance Dam, which generates gigawatts of excess (stranded) energy, is remote from traditional offtakers (populations and industrial consumers). So it would be ideal for bitcoin mining operations and could generate approximately 4-6 billion dollars of revenue per annum (at 50K bitcoin) with just one-tenth of that dam's current excess capacity.[131] That is revenue that can be used in a sovereign manner to include financing transmission infrastructure to get more energy to more people. If Ethiopia chose to take revenue in bitcoin, they would be in essence self-generating a neutral reserve asset from their energy resources like gold — but one they could self-custody as a digital bearer asset.

Ethiopia's neighbor Kenya followed suit in May 2024 by signing an MoU with public bitcoin mining company Marathon Digital which could bring 80 million USD of investment dollars to the country from that company alone. Notably, the Kenya-Marathon partnership was formalized during President William Ruto's state visit to the White House, and with Ambassador Meg Whitman and President Ruto in attendance. Such deals are clearly a boon to important bilateral relationships such as Ethiopia and Kenya, especially in the context of strategic competition with China.

In another east African country, there are near-term plans for bitcoin mining to monetize 300MW of a 600MW hydroelectric facility financed by the CCP's BRI. Also remote from demand, this hydroelectric project produces much-needed energy, but is dislocated from offtakers without any mechanism (transmission) to get it to them. This resource-rich country is otherwise left with a large bill to repay the CCP, and yet another infrastructure project that promises much but delivers little, continuing the cycle of debt-driven dependency on external actors.

In this instance, an enterprising U.S.-based Chinese company is developing a project to host miners at the site, advertising primarily to western bitcoin mining companies, a tangible example of Xi Jinping's dilemma described earlier.[132] Having been pushed outside of Mainland China, Chinese bitcoin industry-related companies continue — paradoxically — to be a vibrant part of proliferating a decentralized and free open protocol alternative to a CCP-styled CBDC. And in this case, the company is using bitcoin as an innovation to solve the original economic distortion caused by CCP debt trap diplomacy.

As we re-shore and friend-shore, could a U.S.-led bitcoin mining industry, in coordination with energy majors and friendly African sovereigns, present a viable alternative to the CCP's grand project for Africa? With a market incentive at its back and Africa's strong desire for U.S. investment and partnership — as well as preference for a liberal vs. illiberal future — U.S. company-led bitcoin mining operations may present an asymmetric advantage. In this framing, bitcoin mining could be levered as a free-market tool to build out cheap renewable energy capacity needed for U.S. manufacturing in friendly nations as we aggressively wean ourselves off dependence on the CCP for strategically critical inputs. Simultaneously, a public-private plan to relocate manufacturing in friendly African nations would effectively counter our adversaries while building strategic alliances. As bitcoin mining scales, it would serve as the market-driven pioneer species to build out energy lily pads for other industrial off-takers of energy that favor U.S. strategic objectives and reduce dependency on adversaries.

Due to the neutral protocol design and block reward incentives, bitcoin miners are the first data centers to seek stranded (cheapest) energy in challenging markets such as in Africa. While the economic incentives are not strong enough to make them first movers, manufacturers and big tech data centers will not be far behind bitcoin mining "pioneers" as they prove out the viability and stability in Africa and Global South markets. This dynamic stands to greatly benefit America, but we must move on this opportunity early to optimize strategic advantage. Building on the work of James McGinniss, the next 5-10 years is the time to push given the "gold rush" phase of bitcoin mining underway. "Are miners rushing to cheap spots on the power grid so different than so many laborers and entrepreneurs flocking to San Francisco in 1849 for the gold rush or to Texas for oil production in the late 1800's, rather than using their labor and talents to actually make something that could be traded for gold or required oil to produce? Like then, the "bitcoin mining rush" won't always be the case."[133] On its current trajectory, bitcoin mining is driving down the cost of energy. As it does so in Africa, more people get more access to cheaper electricity.

Such a concerted national "friend-shoring" strategy may unlock opportunities for adjacent industries to better secure America's supply chains for the critical inputs that ensure future American prosperity, innovation, freedom, sovereignty, and national security. A deflationary effect on local energy prices creates new opportunities for a localized industrial base and new opportunities for local labor emerge accordingly. This has powerful economic implications for Africa, but also for the U.S., as it can ease a transition to re-establish a manufacturing base in the United States. In sum, bitcoin mining as a catalyst for securing supply chains for critical minerals through sustainable mining operations in Africa should be examined in depth.[134] This is a function of bitcoin mining being the first industry in the world incentivized to locate and then build-out low-cost energy, creating a structural decrease in the cost of energy production. Combined with efforts underway by bitcoin mining that incentivize minigrid buildout at scale, bitcoin mining's potential impact in Africa, prospectively, is staggering.

Bitcoin Mining:
Toward a Just Energy Transition

It is increasingly clear, albeit not broadly recognized, that bitcoin mining is incentivizing the buildout of renewable energy minigrids, helping to meet the demand of 600 million Africans currently without access to electricity. It is clear not because of well-articulated theory, but because we are watching this dynamic take place in real time. In fact, minigrid operators are now becoming bitcoin miners because of how mining solves demand risk as a flexible, interruptible, and location agnostic first and last resort buyer of power. These unique characteristics enable minigrid projects to pencil out financially for investors, providing a market incentive for minigrids to scale to meet the enormous need for electricity.

As miners scour the earth for the lowest cost sources of energy to secure the bitcoin blockchain — and through its immutable protocol design — they are increasingly using renewable energy sources that are otherwise wasted and incentivizing the buildout of more of the same. This generates climate positive externalities.[135] Bitcoin mining data centers are also converting otherwise polluting methane (CH4) emissions into electric energy. The protocol does this by providing a mechanism that makes it economically viable to tap into stranded electrical and chemical energy.

The United Nations Environment Program (UNEP) recently stated, "Cutting methane is the strongest lever we have to slow climate change over the next 25 years." This is the case because methane unburnt is over 80 times more warming than carbon dioxide.[136] Given current and prospective bitcoin mining operations that convert methane into electricity, bitcoin mining becomes a powerful "climate positive" technology tool.

Companies are already moving to this opportunity through waste-to-energy to bitcoin landfill remediation projects on the African continent and elsewhere given economic incentives. Such a project in one African country alone would have an outsized positive impact on the environment, as well as provide clean energy, employment opportunities, a tax base, and improve overall well-being in communities negatively impacted by poor waste management. While not all African countries have the same raw energy potential from oil and gas, hydro, wind, and solar, they do all have landfill and biomass that can be converted into an asset with sovereignty-enhancing monetary value. This is very good news for Africa, America, and the world at large. It is also an industrial enterprise where U.S.-based innovation can leapfrog China's BRI-related projects through private sector-based foreign direct investment. These projects create real value, as well as a market incentive to reduce emissions, as opposed to CCP statecraft fueled by debt and enabled by elite capture, resulting in distorted economic outcomes.

Current capital raises are underway to deploy hundreds of millions of dollars to catalyze maximum emissions reduction in the most rapid and cost-effective manner possible. The investment thesis for these funds identifies the problem (methane emissions) and drives the innovative solution as on-site data centers at landfills to convert the methane into clean, usable, and low-cost electricity. Given free-market incentives, bitcoin mining data centers possess superior economics to drive rapid development of landfill emission mitigation operations. It seems that bitcoin mining is the missing link to unleash (finance) the buildout of already-existing technology to mitigate methane at scale. Importantly, the economic incentives of the protocol make bitcoin miners the ideal stranded renewable energy offtakers of first resort, especially in emerging markets, thus paving the way for the next wave of offtakers — and builders — of renewable energy.

It is critical that relevant U.S. agencies like EXIM, USAID, MCC, Power Africa, and Prosper Africa partner with the private sector and host countries to identify opportunities and execute as quickly as possible at target landfill sites across the African continent. Africa is well-positioned to model this climate technology for the world and is a rare example of a free market-driven — and thus sustainable — path to Environmental, Social, and Governance (ESG) impact investing. Additionally, bitcoin mining monetizes, thus measurably eliminating, methane emissions (vented and flared gas) at oil and gas sites worldwide, and will increasingly be paired with the burgeoning oil and gas industry on the continent, vital for not only Africa's energy needs, but also for Europe's, especially in the context of the Russia-Ukraine war.

In sum, bitcoin mining is quickly showing the world how the industry can help humanity accomplish two critically important objectives: 1) unleash more, not less energy, to help developing nations and 2) reduce emissions as we grow our energy supply for the world. According to African energy analyst Mbae Mutegi, "Africa has some of the fastest growing economies in the world. Access to clean, affordable, and reliable electric power is a key ingredient for faster economic growth and development of any economy."[137] The still-nascent bitcoin mining industry is paving this path.

Conclusion

As I write, there is breaking news of regime change in Niger via a coup d'état. A recent darling of Western countries in the Sahel region, the United States and France in particular had hope for the ability of the regime in Niger to hold the line against a surging regional jihadist threat, while favoring U.S. and European partners over Russia and China. Hundreds of millions of dollars in development aid, U.S. troops, international forces, a desert Air Force construction project without precedent... yet the cycles of violence, state incapacity, and economic despair continue. The situation in Niger is the latest example of African "crisis" that the international community has been unable to solve through traditional guns and butter diplomacy — despite political will, budget, and the courageous work of military and civilian national security professionals on the ground. While not a silver bullet, bitcoin and bitcoin mining are sovereignty-enhancing tools for the people and the state in places like Niger where traditional tools of statecraft have fallen short. Where tactical "outside-in" solutions have had, at best, very uneven results, we must support tools that can address the root causes of disorder, violence, and despair.

It is critical to recognize that bitcoin's adoption and use throughout Africa is a popular vote in favor of American values, as well as a vote against the CCP's totalitarian vision for the world. Bitcoin's impressive growth is taking place despite the statistic that 75% of Africans do not have reliable internet access.[138] Therefore, public-private efforts to get more reliable internet to more people — such as Starlink in Nigeria — will also result in banking the unbanked through bitcoin and its layer two open protocols. Growing adoption and use of bitcoin in turn signals the people's preference to Africa's leaders, a critical factor as CCP-styled CBDCs become more widely available as tools for centralizing control and enabling autocratic regimes. While bitcoin adoption and use locally constitutes a powerful social movement for freedom, it is bitcoin mining that leaders will increasingly leverage to enhance nation-state sovereignty. Bitcoin mining's emergence as climate technology, as well as a market incentive to deliver electricity to millions without access responds directly to the White House's most recent strategic policy imperatives for Africa.

The U.S. should support bitcoin's adoption as well as the burgeoning mining industry, recognizing that U.S. and western companies will lead industrial expansion and private sector investment that favor U.S. strategic, political, and economic objectives. Bitcoin's emergence also provides Africa's leaders a viable alternative to never-ending debt traps, to include those most recently laid by the CCP.

African countries most ensnared by the CCP's BRI project have the most to gain from bitcoin as a surging alternative financial rail, although they will need encouragement from the U.S. to embrace this path. Still early (think internet in 1993), a creative and coordinated strategy by the USG interagency will yield outsized gains, especially in the regions of greatest strategic importance to our interests, given entrenched CCP influence.

Like organic "freedom movements," such as the solidarity movement in Poland, that chiseled away at the USSR's centralized authoritarian control, bitcoin is a freedom movement on the march that was neither invented by the USG, nor does it depend on the USG for its survival. However, as Cold War 2.0 accelerates, the USG should use its power and influence to provide succor and support for a historic innovation that advances the cause of liberty and freedom. As the future of humanity — and democracy — there is no more important region than Africa to support this freedom technology.

QR Code to **Chapter 2** Endnote Links and Figures on the Bitcoin Today Coalition website:

---

100   Bitcoin is poised to blow up Africa's $86 billion banking system – MacKenzie Sigalos, CNBC
101   Gorillas, militias, and Bitcoin: Why Congo's most famous national park is betting big on crypto – Adam Popescu, MIT Technology Review
102   Jack Dorsey's Block backs bitcoin mining company that wants to bring 25-cent electricity to rural Africa – MacKenzie Sigalos, CNBC

103	Democracy in America Volume II - Alexis Tocqueville, 1840
104	Author's professional contacts
105	U.S. Strategy Toward Sub-Saharan Africa – The White House National Security Council
106	Ibid.
107	The 2022 Geography of Cryptocurrency Report – Chainalysis
108	Internet use in urban and rural areas – Internet Telecommunication Union
109	The Nigerian Election and Naira Crisis are Fueling Bitcoin Adoption – Abubakar Khalil, Forbes
110	Digital currencies may break the US Dollar's hold over Africa's cross-border trade - Michael Kioneki, Medium
111	Ibid.
112	See Matt Pines' Chapter 1 Great Power Network Competition and Bitcoin for an in-depth assessment of this topic
113	Bitcoin and U.S. National Security - Matthew Pines, Bitcoin Policy Institute
114	Ibid.
115	Tocqueville In China: The Communist Party Studies 'The Old Regime' – Sheila Melvin, Arts Journal
116	These 3 Countries Explain Why The IMF Stance On Bitcoin Changed – Javier Bastardo, Forbes
117	Iranian terror network exposed in Central Africa – Maariv Online, The Jerusalem Post
118	Gorillas, militias, and Bitcoin: Why Congo's most famous national park is betting big on crypto – Adam Popescu, MIT Technology Review
119	The Chainalysis Crypto Myth Busting Report – Chainalysis
120	Age of Exhaustion – Joshua Mitchell, The American Interest
121	Structural Adjustment – Alex Gladstein, Bitcoin Magazine
122	A Renewed Republican Party – Joshua Mitchell, American Affairs
123	Ibid.
124	Why Africa is poised to become a big player in energy markets – The Economist
125	New IAEA Publication on Climate Change and Nuclear Power Highlights Potential in Africa – Lucy Ashton, International Atomic Energy Agency
126	RePP Africa – a georeferenced and curated database on existing and proposed wind, solar, and hydropower plants – Rebecca Peters, Jurgen Berlekamp, Klement Tockner, & ChristianeZarfl, Nature
127	China dominates solar, does the U.S. stand a chance – Wall Street Journal
128	Fidelity joins the rush for a bitcoin ETF, following BlackRock, Ark Invest and others – Jesse Pound, CNBC
129	Exxon is mining bitcoin in North Dakota as part of its plan to slash emissions – MacKenzie Sigalos, CNBC
130	Oil and Gas Industry Giant Shell Forays Into Bitcoin Mining Industry – Pratiksha, The News Crypto
131	Suppressed by world superpowers, Ethiopia should turn to Bitcoin – Project Mano, Bitcoin Magazine
132	Author's professional contacts
133	Age Of the Electron Part IV: The ElectroDollar, a Possible Answer to the Fraying US Global Currency Reserve System – James McGinniss, Substack
134	See James McGinniss' Chapter 4, "Securing America's Future in the Age of the Electron" for more in-depth analysis
135	Bitcoin Network To Reduce More Emissions Than Its Energy Sources Produce – Mickey Koss, Forbes
136	Methane: A crucial opportunity in the climate fight – EDF
137	Energy Trilemma: A Case for Africa Power Utilities – Mbae Mutegi, Power Magazine
138	The path to a Bitcoin standard in Africa – Charlene Fadirepo, Bitcoin Magazine

CHAPTER 3

BITCOIN AND THE MIDDLE EAST: AN EPOCH BEYOND THE PETRODOLLAR

By Robert Malka

Robert Malka *is a Board Member for the Bitcoin Today Coalition, where he has built relationships with dozens of offices on The Hill. He has also helped design the first required bitcoin certification program at a public high school in the world under Mi Primer Bitcoin, a nonprofit in El Salvador. He is co-founder and COO of a company that provides 24/7/365 interpreting services for the deaf in the United States, Canada, and the Middle East, and has also built socratic-centered alternatives to K-12 schooling. He has written on Deafness, the philosophy of Nietzsche, and bitcoin's relationship to culture. He has a Bachelor's in Philosophy and the History of Math and Science from St. John's College, Santa Fe.*

Introduction

In 2023, the following companies stated that they intend to base elsewhere, leave the United States, or invest internationally thanks to a lack of regulatory clarity or stubborn enforcement actions: Coinbase;[139] Gemini;[140] and Kraken.[141] Binance.us is struggling against the SEC, and has lost many of its executives.[142] According to a statement made by Nic Carter in the

New York Times, whether to leave the US is "the number one thing crypto startups are talking and thinking about".[143] Bitcoin miners continue to flock to parts of the United States, notably Texas, but many of those same companies are seeing incentives elsewhere, including Marathon, the largest bitcoin mining company in the United States.[144]

Counterintuitively, it is after the FTX scandal, in which one might think interest in bitcoin would have dropped, that the largest players in finance have shown interest in bitcoin. This includes traditional asset management companies such as BlackRock, whose CEO, Larry Fink, believes bitcoin will come to "transcend any one currency".[145] In line with this bullish view, BlackRock has successfully received a spot market bitcoin ETF after approval by the SEC, alongside eleven other firms, an auspicious overture for 2024.[146] To no one's surprise, US bitcoin ETFs saw $4.6 billion in volume in their first day of trading. This is in parallel to the Silicon Valley leadership who have shown great enthusiasm for the technology, such as Apple CEO Tim Cook.[147] Reversing course to alienate such a base, and making it unpalatable for them to work with and on the bitcoin network, would darken American horizons with businesses big and small.

Many bitcoin and crypto-centric companies, including Marathon and Gemini, are seeing opportunity in the Middle East, where governments are warm to their presence. It is not unreasonable to suspect that multinational companies will flock to easier places to do business, particularly if they also have access to cheap electricity made from renewables. This should be concerning to American policymakers and regulators in general, but particularly with respect to this space, since bitcoin is a significant revolution in finance, energy, and technology. Not being at the center of such a revolution has negative implications for the future of the United States.

Bitcoin as a Public Good

The bitcoin network is a public good similar to the internet. It is fundamentally decentralized in nature, peer-to-peer, and accessible to everyone, day or night. It settles transactions without intermediaries, and its layer two protocol, the Lightning Network, settles transactions at the speed of a text message. Indeed, with bitcoin, the money is the message. Because it requires no intermediaries, value and information at last share nearly identical properties. Such a shift will affect multiple industries.

A global financial tool allowing instant payment settlement can change the way energy is bought and sold, where settlement often takes several days. It is easy to imagine that Gulf countries see the inefficiencies in selling their oil and natural gas, preferring to settle transactions in a frictionless and politically expedient manner. Companies like Strike let businesses use bitcoin rails to settle in dollars at the speed of the bitcoin network, keeping the advantages of quick settlement while remaining currency-agnostic.[148]

The smartest people go where innovation is happening. The Silicon Valleys of the next tech revolution will experience an influx of the smartest, richest people in the world, who generally want to be at the center of things. Closing the United States' doors to bitcoin will lead to brain drain at a time when the United States cannot afford it. Such people also generally invest in the infrastructure of that tech revolution — leading the charge on bitcoin, for example, will also mean leading on innovations in energy, cryptography, finance, hardware computing, and more.

Bitcoin lets people save what they earn, improving the lives of ordinary citizens. In our current inflationary economy, wealth is preserved only if it grows at a rate that matches or outpaces inflation, since it has to combat a decreasing purchasing power. This forces investors and citizens to seek higher-risk investments to achieve returns year-over-year.

Companies, governments, and citizens using a deflationary money focus less on spending and cheap consumer products, since one's purchasing power increases over time the more one saves.[149] This lets citizens think outside of month-to-month or annual goals, and more towards decades-long initiatives, such as developing a legacy to bequeath to grandchildren. This mentality ripples outwards over time, towards neighborhood, state, and country. While countries such as China manage to think in decades by means of a centrally-planned regime, bitcoin allows it to occur from the bottom-up with little top-down enforcement.

Bitcoin also reshapes how governments run their economies. It makes remittances to other countries seamless, blurring borders. It allows even the unbanked to be their own banks, pulling them into the economic system and letting them grow their wealth — without overdraft fees, obscure rules, and intermediaries. This has been famously detailed in El Salvador,[150] and this book's previous chapter discusses bitcoin's effects in Africa, where one such benefit to Africans is precisely the above.[151] Bitcoin's transparent monetary policy makes strategies such as quantitative easing more irrelevant. Fractional reserve banking also becomes more difficult — in a more bitcoin-centric world, people will prefer to be loaned real, rather than paper, bitcoin, which can only be minted according to the halving rate and the difficulty adjustment. Currencies getting their purchasing power from their governments' bitcoin reserves will struggle to be inflated far beyond the country's possessions, which can be reviewed on the pseudonymous ledger. In the longer-term, this stabilizes currencies tethered to bitcoin and eliminates those which do not, giving the former a geopolitical advantage over the latter. Countries that adopt or support bitcoin first will receive the compounding benefit of greater long-term stabilization.

Because Bitcoin exists independently of national politics, it can coexist alongside the dollar and any national CBDC. This gives countries in disadvantaged regions an option besides relying on the support of their regional power. While this means American allies in Africa and Asia can trade with the United States in bitcoin, even as China and Russia impose economic pressure, it also means that the United States will develop new economic dependencies with allies. We consider the Gulf allies who, by means of their oil, have maintained American hegemony through the petrodollar, which is in visible decline. Given that Gulf countries are diversifying their economies away from oil and the petrodollar, the United States must navigate discussions on energy and money carefully to come out on top in the next decades. Thankfully, an investment into bitcoin mining also means an investment into renewables and grid stabilization.

Bitcoin miners have already stabilized energy grids, with Texas's ERCOT grid being the most prominent example.[152] Mining makes it profitable to build power plants which would not otherwise be economically feasible to build, encouraging more abundant, and therefore cheaper, energy.[153] Its encouragement of renewables also facilitates this, as renewable energy is often cheaper than fossil fuels.[154] It has massively reduced the waste of power plants required to run at peak level year-round by picking up otherwise-wasted or stranded energy.[155] Miners are energy buyers who can also stop consuming energy in seconds without penalty during peak hours, returning that energy to the grid for other consumers. Getting paid for energy that would otherwise be wasted means energy producers can carry that over to consumers, also leading to cheaper energy.

Energy is a US national security issue — not having enough of it is a threat; not having a stable grid is a threat; and not having enough efficient, renewable energy, and being energy-dependent on foreign countries, is a threat. Insofar as climate change is a looming threat, bitcoin promotes the production and development of green energy. It is already primarily powered by renewable sources, which are often cheaper but more intermittent and prone to waste. Bitcoin miners help by taking advantage of this otherwise stranded energy, improving overall efficiency.[156]

Bitcoin is just fifteen years old, so these are the limited changes we can envision from our youthful vantage point. It is not dissimilar from the limited vision we had in 1995 of how the internet would change the world. Technologies are value-neutral, with the internet having done much good, and some ill. It is believable that bitcoin, too, will not be a utopian technology. Its transparent and pre-programmed monetary policy can be a double-edged sword for nations locked in geopolitical struggle: they will no longer be able to manipulate their monetary supply or the cost of capital within their economies to stabilize certain commodities or industries. If Larry Fink of BlackRock is right that bitcoin will transcend any one currency, this means that sovereigns will be unable to manage business cycles, a great adjustment for economies whose money supplies have been centrally managed for decades. We expect that fiat currencies will exist alongside bitcoin for precisely this reason.

Whatever comes of bitcoin, it promises to exceed our wildest expectations just as the internet has.

As Vital to the American Economy as the Internet

Today's world is unthinkable without the internet. Production since the mainstream implementation of the internet in 1993 has increased roughly 50% and much of that growth has been centered around the United States and American companies.[157]

Russia, in contrast, was unable to take the lead after the collapse of the USSR, and the difference in economic condition between both countries' GDP is stark. Countries that took the lead on the internet became the hubs of the new economies, while those that didn't were left behind, forever playing catch up. The same will likely be the case for bitcoin.

It is, of course, terribly easy to speak about the importance of the internet with hindsight. We live now in a world saturated with it, where virtually everything we buy, from refrigerators to cars, are connected to it, let alone watches, telephones, and televisions. But the skepticism was just as intense towards the internet in the mid-1990s. Newsweek famously published an article headlined, "Why the Internet Will Fail,"[158] and the New York Times published an article at the height of the dot-com bubble describing the "overload of useless information" on the internet as a reason for its future failure.[159] This remains true, but the internet lives on: we are more overloaded with useless information and TikToks than ever.

This reminds us of the assurances that bitcoin will fail — already, it has "died" over 470 times and counting.[160] In both cases, American pluckiness has tipped the scale in favor of these new technologies. Of the largest one hundred internet companies in the world, over 70 are American or have headquarters based in the United States.[161] Being at the forefront of internet adoption allowed the United States to harness its capabilities early on. Internet companies today generate trillions in revenue globally, with U.S. tech giants like Apple, Microsoft, Amazon, Alphabet (Google), and Facebook capturing much of the value. The internet economy constitutes roughly 9% of U.S. GDP today.[162] Compare that to Russia, where the rough equivalent available to view, IT and digital economy, comprises just 3.8% of its GDP.[163]

Ambitious countries and peoples have followed the cutting edge. In bitcoin's case, El Salvador has boldly declared it legal tender, yielding compelling results.[164] Greatness and technological innovation are far from inevitable or an historical certainty, being rather the outcome of good decisions made while a technology is still nascent. Economists increasingly point to bitcoin as possessing similar transformative potential as a network technology. While still early, data suggests it is triggering a shift toward decentralized systems and peer-to-peer exchange of value. The 800+% increase in bitcoin's value over the past 5 years indicates growing mainstream adoption.

If historical patterns hold, being a leader or laggard matters. The nations that recognize bitcoin's possibilities early can shape its norms, integrate it into existing systems, and build companies and talent to capture newly generated wealth. Those discounting it may find themselves in 20 years far behind in the new internet of money.

For another analogy, we can review South Korea versus North Korea:

Data from the UN for 1996 (value of GDP in millions)

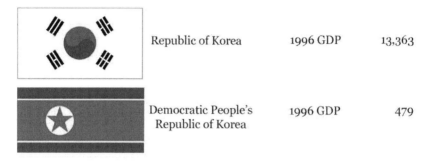

	Republic of Korea	1996 GDP	13,363
	Democratic People's Republic of Korea	1996 GDP	479

(Figure 18: Data from the UN for 1996 - value of GDP in millions)[165]

Today's contrast between the two economies is stark: South Korea's economy is nominally 57 times greater than North Korea's when viewed through the lens of GDP.[166] In comparison, the UN numbers indicate that in 1996, post-USSR collapse, South Korea's economy was almost 27 times bigger than North Korea's, and it may be fair to suggest that the internet has played a part in the growth of South Korea's economy, relative to North Korea's. Not to mention the other benefits of being at the cutting-edge of the internet: higher tech industry development, thorough access to digital education, and so on. One is curious to see what would happen if a country such as North Korea adopted bitcoin, and how it might reduce or close the gap between the two countries.

It is hard to quantify the impact of the internet on our economies, but McKinsey attempted to do so in a 2011 report. In that report, it suggests that the internet constitutes 3.4% of GDP in large and developed countries — likely an underestimation today given the rapid advance of the internet-enabled economy and supporting technologies since this study was conducted. Such an underestimated amount still constituted a greater GDP than agriculture or utilities. If the internet had been a country in 2011, it would have had a larger GDP than Spain.[167] Lagging behind on the internet would have rendered the United States helpless against its adversaries in a multipolar world. As it stands, the United States was the sole superpower for almost thirty years, from 1991 to 2020.

Bitcoin and the Middle East

While individual states within the US, such as Texas, are driving the bitcoin network forward,[168] the federal government and its regulatory bodies threaten to slow that progress. In contrast, the United Arab Emirates, and Abu Dhabi specifically, is the focus of the new Middle East, and at this rate will be (one of) the Silicon Valleys of the bitcoin revolution.

The UAE is made up of seven emirates (states run as kingdoms), each with its own local ruling family. Abu Dhabi is the largest, most energy-rich Emirate, and the ruling Nahyan family is driving innovation within it. The local population has numerous mining setups for bitcoin, thanks to subsidized electricity tariffs.[169] As noted by Hashrate Index, multiple mining companies are already in Abu Dhabi.[170] Phoenix Technology is running a 200-megawatt (MW) facility, and Marathon Digital Holdings is building one with a 250 MW nameplate capacity. All major initiatives are partnered with the sovereign wealth fund of Abu Dhabi, Zero Two. Abu Dhabi is further committing to the space, so that over 600 MW are expected to run in Abu Dhabi by year's end, and a gigawatt of power dedicated to mining in Abu Dhabi is not so far away. Given its intention to further rely on renewables,[171] it is fair to assume that reliance on bitcoin mining will only increase, since renewables are inflexible with regards to demand. Nuclear is similarly inflexible, and bitcoin miners help enable much-needed flexibility as demand-flexible energy buyers. Note that the largest solar project in Abu Dhabi will provide 5 GW of power by 2030 — an enormous amount for solar. As Hashrate Index makes clear, it is a certainty that the solar farm will produce excess electricity that can then be monetized by bitcoin miners.

At present, about 3.7% of the bitcoin hashrate comes from Abu Dhabi, which is estimated to hold roughly all of the mining operations in the Emirates, making them the biggest miners in the Gulf region by far. In contrast, roughly 35% of hashrate is produced in the United States.[172] About 14% of the global hashrate is produced in Texas alone according to Foundry, the biggest mining pool in North America.[173] Considering that miners have been mining in the United States since 2010, this is an impressive differential — only a few years ago, there were no mining operations in Abu Dhabi. Companies such as Marathon have openly stated their interest in investing further into the country.

Few countries in the world are both politically stable and friendly to businesses. The UAE has made itself one such country, and there is no reason to believe that the Nahyan family will introduce or allow any instability in the near future. This is highly attractive to companies seeking geographic diversity as they expand, or seek better business conditions.

The UAE has excelled at encouraging foreign direct investment, with over 30 free trade zones having no corporate tax, VAT, or import duties. The Abu Dhabi Global Market is one such free zone, particularly focused on attracting digital asset businesses. When it comes to regulatory policy, the ADGM has three regulatory bodies that collaborate to produce optimal business conditions, and the Financial Services Regulatory Authority (FSRA) oversees digital assets.[174] Their policy, developed in 2018, is clear and transparent: products that have the characteristics of a security are treated as securities, and may make an offer of securities to the public.[175] They may also apply for an exemption under the Exempt Offers regime. Issuers are allowed to raise capital with the approval of the FSRA, with significant investor protections, and transparency on decisions, designations, and reasoning is clear. Financial services entities are required to meet specific resource requirements to do business, and to prove that they meet such requirements. The ADGM even advises on physical office space on Al Maryah Island, where the ADGM is located, should the company want a physical presence in Abu Dhabi.

The ADGM follows English Common Law, and has made multiple parts of their infrastructure frictionless, such as supporting e-Courts, strong enforceability of judgment, 0% taxation, and a full ecosystem of business needs, from accounting to legal. The guidance document for digital assets, which is helpful, albeit not exhaustive, comprises a mere 32 pages.[176] Fiat tokens (known as "stablecoins" in the United States) are licensed and regulated as "Providing Money Services." Bitcoin, considered a "utility token", is understood as a commodity and is not regulated.[177]

This framework also regulates intermediaries, "including custodians, broker-dealers, asset managers, and advisors, similar to their conventional counterparts with a particular focus on the risks relating to financial crime, consumer protection, technology governance, and custody arrangements, where applicable".[178] This degree of clarity leaves very little economic inefficiency — or crime in the vein of FTX — to be had. If US regulators borrowed from the UAE's clear approach to regulatory policy and legislators re-emphasized the importance of energy and continued diversification of its economy, including in manufacturing, the United States would be formidable indeed.

There is little question that, particularly on the federal level, the United States is moving counter to its historical openness to public goods and new technologies with bitcoin. The Obama and Biden administrations have not shown warmth to a technology that promises to uplift the poor and disenfranchised, and combat climate change — both foundational tenets of their campaigns.

Operation Choke Point 2.0

We begin with the history. Operation Choke Point — also known as OC 1.0 — began in 2013 and lasted until 2017, and was a federal crackdown on financial criminality, including money laundering. One of the well-known results of Operation Choke Point in the crypto community was the end of the Silk Road, a digital black market that allowed users to buy and sell illicit goods.[179] Its creator, Ross Ulbricht, is famously serving a double life sentence plus forty years. The Department of Justice, in trying to distance itself from bitcoin and digital assets, has sold over nine thousand bitcoin it received from shutting down Silk Road, out of a total of 51,352 BTC.[180] Whether intended or not, the effect of such a sale was to put a temporary downward pressure on the price of bitcoin to make it less palatable in the short term, something that has occurred during Operation Choke Point 2.0 (OC 2.0) as well.[181]

The goal of OC 2.0 seems to have been to cut the cryptocurrency industry off from the banking sector. Banking enforcement has been targeting legal crypto businesses, and a number have lost the ability to keep accounts with big banks, forcing them to open bank accounts offshore.[182] Banks were targeted for shutdown, leading to the demise of Silvergate, Signature, and Silicon Valley Banks, and causing greater instability within the traditional banking system.[183] Smaller banks are getting swallowed up by the larger ones. To add to this, in March of 2023,[184] President Joe Biden proposed a 30% tax on electricity used in cryptocurrency mining, claiming that it is causing "excessive energy use" in his budget blueprint for Fiscal Year 2024, though it hasn't been politically viable. Still, OC 2.0 sets a dangerous precedent that legal industries an administration doesn't like can be throttled or shut down by aggressive regulatory action, further creating a business-unstable environment.

There is also an ongoing regulatory battle between the SEC and the CFTC.[185] The issue is what to call a security — putting the product under the purview of the SEC — and what to call a commodity — putting the product under the purview of the CFTC. Bitcoin is widely understood to be a commodity, but there are regulatory uncertainties around, for example, approving a bitcoin spot ETF, which falls under the SEC. The SEC has taken aggressive actions against companies and put pressure on exchanges. There is little clarity within existing law, and Congress is currently in gridlock, leading to regulatory creep.[186] Congress could help regulators by "clearing up how decentralization plays a role, providing the CFTC and SEC with 'particular triggers' that delineate when an asset can shift from being a security to a commodity".[187]

There are yet promising signs that American states see a future with bitcoin. The Texas legislature proposed a bill in March of 2023 attempting to support bitcoin businesses and prevent any penalties towards miners.[188] Florida's Ron DeSantis is pushing against CBDCs, by implication allowing for bitcoin to thrive.[189] Other states such as Kentucky and North Carolina are warm to bitcoin mining, and have considered legislation to support it. Where the federal government is making efforts to close the door on bitcoin, we see that some states opt to be sanctuaries within the bitcoin ecosystem. It is uncertain how this dynamic will play out, and whether the federal government will change its official position.

In the meantime, bringing the United States financial ecosystem into the 21st century also means bringing financial literacy to United States citizens. America needs an informed populace to navigate and engage these new assets. Such literacy would include a helpful overview of digital assets in general, and bitcoin in particular, for youth, other citizens, and even government officials who are orthogonal to the key players engaged on these issues. Luckily, several free, open-source solutions are widely available. An informed populace, and a streamlined government, are helpful foundations in the shared goal of securing the United States against its enemies.[190]

Bitcoin and National Security

There are three great concerns for US national security with respect to bitcoin: 1) that America's energy grid is not stabilized, supported, and expanded by bitcoin mining; 2) that America's economy and financial system are not driven by the next technological revolution; and 3) that America experiences a brain drain towards the Middle East and potentially its geopolitical competitors.

To the first: our grid is in danger. Certain areas of the United States are at elevated risk of blackouts over summers, from California to Kentucky,[191] on top of being exposed to harsher weather throughout the year. There is also a greater strain on grids from electric vehicles and the broader electrification push associated with the Energy Transition.[192] To develop new power plants, particularly high-energy ones such as nuclear, will take years or decades to develop, in part thanks to overregulation. Guaranteed energy buyers can facilitate the development of such plants while also managing the stranded (wasted) energy that comes with some of these plants being built at a great distance from population centers.[193]

To the second: complacency breeds mediocrity. Our financial system has a competitor in bitcoin. If bitcoin is allowed to thrive in the United States, our financial system will adapt and create better products. Our economy will be further supported by bitcoin's development, and not always in obvious ways. For example, if people's homes are heated by small bitcoin rigs, as some products allow, the mined bitcoin can help to pay off people's heating bills, cutting their costs.[194] Industry could similarly supplement costs by using bitcoin mining, in addition to the other ways bitcoin can facilitate industry.

This does not factor in the jobs we already have through bitcoin, for example, the first-order jobs of maintaining bitcoin mining rigs, and the second-order service, marketing, coding, and other jobs that make up the ecosystem.

To the third: we have worked hard to keep the world's best and brightest with top universities, a friendly business environment, and the promise of success if one works hard. So long as they stay, worldwide talent will continue to come here, ensuring our success well beyond the 2020s. The only question is, will they make their home in the greatest country in the world, or will they settle elsewhere?

Avoiding the End of US Hegemony

For centuries, the West has been viewed as a dream destination for millions. The United States has carried the mantle of this effort as the world's dominant power for almost ninety years. Should the United States regress into further recessions and political instability, and allow China and Russia to become dominant global powers, the West itself will be at the cultural, economic, and geopolitical mercy of those who do not share its interests.

Simultaneously, we face the emergence of the Gulf countries, particularly the UAE, as competitive hubs for technological innovation and financial services. While these nations have traditionally aligned with U.S. interests, we must maintain our technological edge to ensure that these developing tech hubs remain aligned with Western values. Without this edge, we risk losing strategic influence over the future of global finance and technology, potentially letting the Gulf states gravitate towards China's sphere of influence.

To maintain our position and values, the U.S. must proactively engage with these emerging realities, fostering innovation at home while partnering with like-minded nations. Encouraging a better understanding of bitcoin and how bitcoin mining encourages the development of renewables is necessary, particularly for policymakers and regulators. Incentives for mining, along with investment and development from government entities such as ARPA-E, should be welcomed. Incentivizing data centers to adopt the energy-saving innovations developed through bitcoin mining would improve our energy grid. Letting miners open new power plants and restore old ones would maintain and revitalize our struggling infrastructure, particularly as regional grids experience greater stress from electric vehicles and AI. Abundant energy drives down electricity prices, letting us innovate, invent, and build economic and cultural capital, the kind that brings meaning to our lives and solves problems.

Regulatory clarification will be essential in the coming years. A streamlined application process for companies interacting with the SEC and CFTC is essential. Regulatory and legal clarity delineated by Congress is long overdue. Consumer protection laws being applied to companies that are obviously shilling scam products is much-needed common-sense legislation. Allowing the bitcoin spot ETFs was a great decision to kick off 2024, giving this new asset class a chance to fully blossom with institutional support. Giving consumers the ability to store their savings in bitcoin without taxing them for it, similarly to how one's savings are not taxed just because they are saved in dollars, or exchanged from euros, will further incentivize engagement with the technology. Not attempting to penalize citizens for having private wallets, and freedom of financial movement, will show how deeply we embody our love of freedom in this country.

Finally, there will be states, such as Texas, inclined towards creating bitcoin hubs akin to Silicon Valley, and the federal government should enable this to happen. Many of our best and brightest minds are interested in decentralizing technologies, cryptography, and finance, and our deepest problems of late center around inequality and the disadvantages of traditional banking.

But it goes further than that. China is building a breathtaking twenty-one nuclear power plants,[195] in addition to the 3,100 coal plants already built,[196] in order to make up for their current dependence on imports for their energy – over 67% of their crude oil supply is imported as of 2019.[197] The United States, meanwhile, is fortunate to continue exporting more energy than it imports, but is struggling to maintain low costs for gasoline,[198] let alone keep up with the millions of electric cars joining the grid by 2030.[199] In our shift to renewable energy, we have shut down pipelines, and our shift to renewables is happening too slowly, unevenly, and without proper consideration to the negative externalities to grid stability and power prices that come with them. Given that we are not a dictatorship, we will need market incentives to compete with China's intention to have abundant energy. Being energy-disadvantaged against regions with abundant natural resources, let alone an adversary possessing five times the population of the United States, has stark national security implications.

Despite these challenges, there is reason for optimism. The United States remains at the forefront of bitcoin and energy, positioning us to shape their development. Proactive policies that embrace innovation and leverage our advantages will maintain our leadership, harnessing the potential of bitcoin to improve our infrastructure, drive economic growth, and maintain our technological edge. The choice is ours: to embrace this opportunity, or cede our advantage to more agile competitors. American strength over the next fifty years is ours to keep — or lose.

QR Code to **Chapter 3** Endnote Links and Figures on the Bitcoin Today Coalition website:

139 Coinbase CEO says SEC is on 'lone crusade,' dials back on suggestion exchange may relocate – Ryan Browne, CNBC
140 Gemini to Exit the US Market – Iaroslava Kramarenko, GN Crypto
141 Kraken Agreed to Shutter US Crypto-Staking Operations to Settle SEC Charges: Source – Nikhilesh De, CoinDesk
142 Binance.US CEO Leaves Embattled Crypto Exchange – Vicky Huang, WSJ
143 Crypto Firms Start Looking Abroad as U.S. Cracks Down – David Yaffe-Bellany, New York Times
144 Bitcoin Mining Around the World: United Arab Emirates – J. Mellerud and E. Vera, Hashrate Index
145 BlackRock CEO Larry Fink: Crypto Will 'Transcend Any One Currency' – Mat Di Salvo, Decrypt
146 BlackRock and Grayscale among 11 firms approved for spot Bitcoin ETFs in long-awaited SEC decision – Leo Schwartz, Fortune Crypto
147 Apple is 'looking into' cryptocurrency, says CEO Tim Cook – Sarah Perez, TechCrunch
148 How to Use the Strike Mobile Payment App – Krisztian Sandor, CoinDesk
149 See the book The Price of Tomorrow for a more thorough review
150 A review of remittances through Bitcoin using El Salvador's Chivo wallet as of July 2022 – Gareth Jenkinson, Cointelegraph
151 See Ben Kincaid's Chapter 2: Bitcoin, Africa, and U.S. National Security Interests for a more thorough review.
152 See Lee Bratcher and Pierre Rochard's Chapter 5: Bitcoin and Energy Security: How Bitcoin Stabilizes and Reinforces the Grid and Why It's a Matter of National Security for a more thorough review.
153 Gridless Is Extending Power to Rural Africa – George Kaloudis, CoinDesk
154 Green energy is cheaper than fossil fuels, a new study finds – Laura Allen, Science News Explores
155 Bitcoin Mining Is Good for the Energy Grid and Good for the Environment – Dennis Porter, CoinDesk
156 Stranded no more? Bitcoin miners could help solve Big Oil's gas problem – Richard Mason, Cointelegraph
157 The Productivity–Pay Gap – Economic Policy Institute
158 Newsweek in 1995: Why the Internet will Fail – Zee, The Next Web Newsweek in 1995: Why the Internet will Fail – Zee, The Next Web
159 Skeptics Cite Overload Of Useless Information : Internet Arrives At a Crossroads – Sharon Reier, New York Times
160 Bitcoin Obituaries Bitcoin has died 476 times - 99 Bitcoins
161 List of largest Internet companies - Wikipedia
162 Tech sector as a percentage of total gross domestic product (GDP) in the United States from 2017 to 2022 – Statista
163 IT industry in Russia - statistics & facts – Statista

164 El Salvador's Bonds Have Skyrocketed Alongside Bitcoin in 2023 – Ryan Gladwin, Decrypt
165 Per capita GDP at current prices - US dollars – UN Data
166 Comparison of the nominal gross domestic product (GDP) between South Korea and North Korea from 2010 to 2022 – Statista
167 The great transformer: The impact of the Internet on economic growth and prosperity – J. Manyika and C. Roxburgh, McKinsey Global Institute
168 See Lee Bratcher and Pierre Rochard's Chapter 5: Bitcoin and Energy Security: How Bitcoin Stabilizes and Reinforces the Grid and Why It's a Matter of National Security for more information on mining in the United States.
169 Bitcoin Mining Around the World: United Arab Emirates – J. Mellerud and E. Vera Hashrate Index
170 Ibid.
171 Ibid.
172 Bitcoin Mining by Country 2024 – World Population Review
173 New York & Texas gaining popularity among mining firms after China crackdown – VasiliyKoshkin, LA Moments
174 Digital Assets – ADGM
175 Capital Markets – ADGM
176 Financial Services Regulatory Authority – ADGM
177 Ibid.
178 Digital Assets – ADGM
179 U.S. Government Sold $216M of Seized Silk Road Bitcoin This Month – Oliver Knight, CoinDesk
180 Ibid.
181 Ibid.
182 'Operation Choke Point 2.0' Is SEC's 'Chemotherapy' for $14B Ponzi Problem, BCB's CEO Says – Aoyon Ashraf, CoinDesk
183 Brian Brooks: U.S. Government Using Crisis to Choke Off Crypto Access to Banks – Fran Velasquez, CoinDesk
184 Biden administration proposes 30% crypto mining tax, closing wash-trading loopholes – Danny Park, Forkast
185 Lawmakers Say Crypto Turf War Between SEC and CFTC Is an 'Industry-Fueled Narrative' – André Beganski, Decrypt
186 Ibid.
187 Ibid.
188 Texas legislature introduces bill to attract Bitcoin-related businesses, protect interests of same – Valida Pau, Forkast
189 Ibid.
190 My First Bitcoin's English website: www.miprimerbitcoin.io/en/
191 These areas of the US at 'elevated' risk of blackouts this summer – Jeremy Tanner, The Hill
192 Why the electric vehicle boom could put a major strain on the U.S. power grid – Katie Brigham, CNBC
193 Everything You Need To Know About Bitcoin And The Environment – Jonathan Buck, Forbes
194 Heating a home with a Bitcoin miner: Staying warm with sats – Joe Hall, Cointelegraph
195 How China became the king of new nuclear power, and how the U.S. is trying to stage a comeback – Catherine Clifford, CNBC
196 Number of operational coal-fired power plant units in China as of January 2023, by province/municipality – Statista
197 How Is China's Energy Footprint Changing? – CSIS
198 What types of energy does the US produce and consume? How much energy do Americans use? – USA Facts
199 Why the electric vehicle boom could put a major strain on the U.S. power grid – Katie Brigham, CNBC

CHAPTER 4

SECURING AMERICA'S FUTURE IN THE AGE OF THE ELECTRON

By James McGinniss

James McGinniss is CEO and Co-Founder of David Energy. David Energy is a USV-backed software-enabled retail electricity provider building an innovative VPP offering. Its software saves customers money directly on their power bill by connecting to and controlling their devices like battery storage, electric vehicles, smart thermostats, (eventually bitcoin mines), and more to charge, discharge, and avoid usage when power is most expensive. James is a rare voice in the climate and decarbonization community that is avidly pro-bitcoin. He developed his passion for bitcoin in 2016 at the same time he was starting his work on building distributed power grids, and  has written extensively on the intersection between grids and bitcoin in his free time since. He is also a founder and leader of the DER Task Force, a Substack podcast and community for distributed energy enthusiasts. Guests are primarily builders in the DER space, but also range to bitcoiners at the intersection of energy and bitcoin like Troy Cross. James holds an M.S.E. in Mechanical Engineering from UT Austin and graduated Magna Cum Laude from Georgetown University with a B.S. in Physics and Math.

This piece is for the patriots who want to build a future with a more prosperous, resilient, and flourishing nation than our current reality, irrespective of whatever present powers that be it may challenge.

Introduction

Since WWII, the global economy has undergone a period of rapid globalization backed by the US dollar, enforced by American military might, and powered by fossil fuels largely extracted or traded by American companies. Petroleum was the lifeblood of this global economic system and America's dominance, marking this era as the Age of Oil.

That's changing fast. Decarbonization and electrification of the economy mean that not only will we move away from fossil fuels, but that electricity will become the most important global commodity, ushering in the Age of the Electron. Contrary to what most may believe, this transition is primarily technologic in nature: an electricity driven world will be superior to the petro-system. Past energy transitions have traditionally disrupted incumbent superpowers, but the transition to electricity uniquely offers America the opportunity to successfully reposition itself globally while improving the domestic economy.

And it couldn't come any sooner. It's possible that the current petro and USD backed institutions that run America and the world are not worth saving. At the very least, the present system of an interconnected web of global corporations, bankers, and consultants has metastasized to the degree that it's begun, in many ways, to work against the interests of the American people. If this is true, then all we can hope to do is build new institutions. If there is no "soft landing", there may at least be a way to build a lifeboat stable enough to get people off the ship and safe before it sinks.

Much in the same way that the petro-dollar — and the dominance of the USD with it — emerged from the techno-economics of oil, so too will new currencies and institutions emerge in the Age of the Electron. In a strange push-pull dynamic, this era will be defined by both the hyper-local and the hyper-global: because electricity is a deglobalizing force, the physical world will contract from its presently hyper globalized state to the local. And yet at the same time, the internet will continue to act as a countervailing force that makes the globe more interconnected than ever. But if we are transitioning to electricity in a digital era, then where is the electro dollar?

Perhaps it is bitcoin. Bitcoin, while far from a clear "victor" in the dominant emergent technologies of the future, does demonstrate and possess many of the qualities of what this eventual victor will be. While our present institutions have reacted to bitcoin mostly with disdain, that should not be a surprise. Bitcoin is a direct threat to the foundation on which they stand. But we must remember that while it is the American spirit and its principles that builds these institutions, they are not themselves America, nor were they ever. We can even understand the urge to perpetuate them, but it is time to ask: what is our plan B?

Thesis

As we leave the Age of Oil and progress towards the Age of the Electron, there are four converging phenomena that America and its institutions must contend with:

1. A transition to electricity as the lifeblood of the economy is a deglobalizing force due to how expensive it is to transmit. As a result, access to cheap, local energy resources will be more important than access to cheap labor pools, the opposite of the globalized Age of Oil where access to cheap oil was ubiquitous through trade.

2. The USD as a global reserve currency is now undermining the strategic goals of the US by preventing the on-shoring of crucial supply chains, particularly of clean energy technologies, while making us a victim of our own success in global energy markets.

3. Bitcoin as a currency is native to a digital world driven by electricity, which maps well to the Age of the Electron. Its creation produces a clearing price for what is actually a productive use of electricity, incentivizing only real GDP growth.

4. On top of the US' weakness as a manufacturer, China is emerging as dominant in solar and battery supply chains, which spells trouble for US global positioning in an electricity-driven era.

As electricity now fast becomes the most important commodity in the world, it makes sense to explicitly tie our money to its production. Energy consumption is the most important pillar of any modern economy, and our money systems have already taken note. Namely, since the 1970s the dollar has been backed by oil. Prior to the modern era, gold and silver were the most valuable commodities, and thus made sense as a backer of currency. Similarly, in the near future an electrodollar construct offers us a way out of the petrodollar system and towards new institutions. It is imperative that the US begins building these new institutions and reorienting foreign and domestic policies around them.

The energy transition holds massive opportunities. In this piece, we will explore the history of the petro-industrial order and cement the argument that much of today's domestic social ills are directly downstream of our energy problems. Leaning into decarbonization, electrification, and digitalization will reinvigorate domestic labor by rapidly on-shoring manufacturing while making our supply chains and global position more resilient.

Across almost every metric that matters — natural resources, internal trade routes, external trade routes, defensive borders, and military force — the US remains dominant, despite the current precarious state of the empire. This means that the only real enemy is ourselves. By doubling down on the energy transition, we can fix domestic labor issues and reduce wealth inequality, rebuild our industrial base and government balance sheets, and emerge a more resilient, unified nation.

What is the Age of the Electron?

While our dominant fuel source over the past few centuries has changed, one thing has remained constant: combustion, or heat, acting as the prime mover in energy consumption[200] and conversion. Boilers, turbines, and internal combustion engines all involve igniting fossil fuels to heat our homes, power our grid, or move our vehicles. These underlying technologies have required an approach to building infrastructure that maximizes thermodynamic efficiencies. But the rules of the game are changing, and thus the ways in which we build and interact with our world will as well.

Despite the ubiquity of the power grid, it still only constitutes 38% of end-use energy consumption. Transportation, all from fossil fuel engines, constitutes 37% of end-use energy consumption, and commercial and residential are 10% and 12%, respectively, primarily from combustion-based space heating.[201] Converting just these two to electricity driven processes — heat pumps and vehicle AC or DC motors — will lead to more than doubling of electricity consumption as a proportion to all energy consumption during my lifetime. The pace of the adoption of these technologies is accelerating, and shows no signs of slowing down.

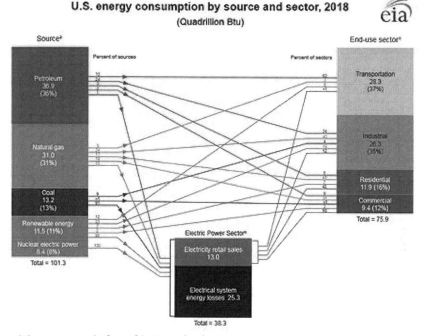

(Figure 19: Despite how ubiquitous the electricity grid has become, it still constitutes a minority of total energy consumption. This will rapidly change.)

The reason for this is simple: electricity-driven processes are just better and cheaper. Electrons generated from solar and wind are proving to be some of the cheapest energy we've ever created, and the conversion from electricity to work has long been the most efficient. If electricity is to become the fuel of the future, then the "steam engine" of this transition is lithium ion batteries. They already propelled the digital revolution in the form of batteries in our phones and computers, but they're just getting started. Because of the invention of the lithium ion battery, we can do something we never could before: store electricity at a reasonable price. One day, they'll be as ubiquitous, cheap, and useful as all varieties of gas tanks, from jerry cans to the propane tanks buried in yards.

It is hard to overstate the stunning implications this will have for the way in which we build and interact with not just electricity grids, but the world around us. The Age of the Electron means that more and more end-uses will rely on the electricity grid, from residential consumption to large industrial processes. But in the Age of the Electron, what matters is not so much that electricity will increasingly be generated by non-fossil fuel based feedstocks, rather that the drastic change in how energy is produced and consumed will alter the dynamics of global political and economic systems. This will have far-reaching consequences for the world around us, and it isn't the first time this has happened.

How Did We Get Here? Hydrocarbon Man and the Petro-Industrial Complex

In the modern world, one institution rules them all: the US petro-industrial complex, rooted in the petrodollar system. This new order emerged out of the chaos of World War II; fossil fuels, particularly oil, are the lifeblood of that system.

The feedstock for the US's economic might was access to cheap oil and formed the foundation of US hegemony. As early as the 1920s after WWI had demonstrated how important oil would be in warfare, securing oil supply became the primary national security interest of the US and other Western countries. Originally, the US controlled the global oil trade because the US was the largest producer of oil by far, with Standard Oil alone dominating 80% of global oil supply in the late 1800s and early 1900s.

Over time, new oil sources threatened to dethrone the US's production primacy, predominantly emerging from the Middle East, while concurrently the American appetite for oil began outstripping its own supply. This problem drove a strategic need for exploration and access abroad. Meanwhile, throughout the 1920s and 30s, oil was discovered in Saudi Arabia, Iran, and Iraq. Because the US and US-based companies were the dominant oil force in the world, these emerging producer nations had to rely on them for development. Only the large oil companies had the capital and expertise to get Middle Eastern oil out of the ground, so they received concessions from Middle Eastern governments often negotiated with the help of the Western governments. In exchange for royalties on oil extracted, the producing nations gave Western oil companies leases on their land.

These deals in the Middle East in the 40s and 50s created the foundation for the modern system in which we still operate. However, as the importance of Middle Eastern oil increased, the power of these emerging nations grew. Gradually, they began taking more and more of the profits generated and asserted greater control over their own industry, constantly threatening to nationalize production — which did happen. Eventually, OPEC consolidated and emerged as the largest producer of oil, and with it the US became the global distributor and protector of this system, not the major supplier as it had once been. What remains is an interconnected web of multinational corporations and banks: big auto, defense, aviation, and oil and gas companies, as well as consolidated farming operations dependent on fertilizer and many more. It is hard to imagine a sector where this complex doesn't grow roots; the petro-industrial complex is the very ground we stand on in the modern world.

The Petrodollar System

What emerged out of this was the US petrodollar system, a currency system that tied it all together. For a complete history on this, read Lyn Alden's magnificent Fraying of the Petrodollar System:[202]

> *"With the petrodollar system, Saudi Arabia (and other countries in OPEC) sell their oil exclusively in dollars in exchange for US protection and cooperation. Even if France wants to buy oil from Saudi Arabia, for example, they do so in dollars… In return, the United States uses its unrivaled blue-water navy to protect global shipping lanes, and preserve the geopolitical status quo with military action or the threat thereof as needed. In addition, the United States basically has to run persistent trade deficits with the rest of the world, to get enough dollars out into the international system. Many of those dollars, however, get recycled into buying US Treasuries and stored as foreign-exchange reserves, meaning that a large portion of US federal deficits are financed by foreign governments compared to other developed nations that mostly rely on domestic financing.*
>
> *The petrodollar system is creative, because it was one of the few ways to make everyone in the world accept foreign paper for tangible goods and services. Oil producers get protection and order in exchange for pricing their oil in dollars and putting their reserves into Treasuries, and non-oil producers need oil, and thus need dollars so they can get that oil.*
>
> *This leads to a disproportionate amount of global trade occurring in dollars relative to the size of the US economy, and in some ways, means that the dollar is backed by oil, without being explicitly pegged to oil at a defined ratio. The system gives the dollar a persistent global demand from*

around the world, while other fiat currencies are mostly just used internally in their own countries.

Even though the United States represented only about 11% of global trade and 24% of global GDP in early 2018, the dollar's share of global economic activity was far higher at 40–60% depending on what metric you look at, and this gap represents its status as the global reserve currency, and the key currency for global energy pricing."

This didn't have to be the case. The oil trade actually saved the USD reserve status when Saudi Arabia agreed to sell its oil in dollars in 1974. Under Bretton Woods (from 1944–1971), the USD was backed by gold. But as US debt mounted, French gunships actually showed up on our shores demanding to exchange USD for gold. Nixon was forced to decline the request, effectively ending the Bretton Woods system and putting the USD in an extremely precarious situation. Thus, this agreement with Saudi Arabia — and soon, all of OPEC — maintained global demand for USD despite not being backed by anything, as oil was the most important commodity. The petrodollar was born.

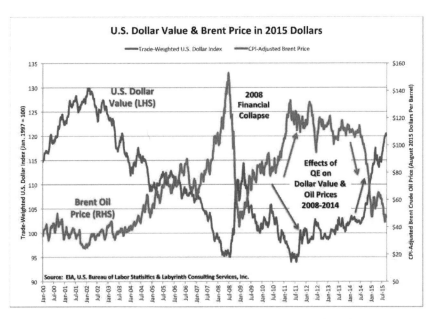

(Figure 20: As oil prices rise, the demand for oil drops and demand for the USD with it. Thus, the USD and oil have always been directly linked... until recently)

While some say the above description of the petrodollar system has been supplanted by the eurodollar (dollars deposited in European banks), that doesn't make it any less significant. The eurodollar argument is something like: US dollars and strength are now so ubiquitous — the de-facto plumbing of the global economy — that the oil trade is insignificant, thus a shift away from oil won't negatively impact the US position.

However, what's missed here is that the petrodollar was an explicit quid pro quo: use USD and get protection. This explicit trade is not the case with the eurodollar. Furthermore, access to cheap oil was of national strategic importance, whereas now the USD system and US aims can come into direct conflict.

The USD Reserve System is Unwinding

A new world monetary order is emerging that doesn't require the USD as a reserve currency, and that's a good thing long term. Or as Zoltan Pozsar says, we are witnessing the birth of Bretton Woods III.[203] The onset of COVID-19 in 2020 brought to a head the dynamics that had been brewing for decades in global energy and currency markets, which have now accelerated with Russia's invasion of Ukraine. This has come with some surprising realizations, most notably that the USD's global reserve currency status can explicitly hinder our aims. More important, however, is recognizing that the US's ability to react to these new realities with forward-thinking policies will define us for decades to come. Central to our reaction ought to be prioritizing energy policy above all others, with the understanding that manufacturing supply chains, dirt cheap energy, the rebuilding of the US working class, and the currencies we use are all deeply intertwined.

By seizing Russia's FX reserves after they invaded Ukraine, the US sent a clear message to the world: the USD is only a global reserve currency if you do what the US wants. How can other countries, especially those with lukewarm relations with the US, rely on USD as a reserve currency if it is now clear those reserves can be seized at any moment?

Furthermore, as we'll soon learn, it's no longer clear that the USD as a reserve currency is good for the US itself. Why should we care if USD is used in trade between France and Russia? In the case of Russia, the answer seems to be that we can use the USD itself as a weapon. But is that worth the continued cost of keeping the system running?

Regardless, as the US's role in global trade declines, its position will become less central globally. Countries will increasingly move away from the system toward inter-regional currency trading pairs (e.g. EUR/RUB), and it is becoming clear that the US has limited recourse to stop it. It would be far more prudent for US leaders to start focusing on securing supply chains of national strategic significance and reinvigorating the domestic economy than maintaining a system that used to do such, and does not any longer. Unfortunately, as we'll soon find, the system itself acts against those aims.

What Has it All Meant for the US?
Stagnation: What the Hell Happened in 1973?

While the causal direction is murky, the correlation is clear: the US has faced an economic stagnation — or rather a "divergence" — since the early 1970s, wherein bankers and international corporations win and domestic blue collar workers lose. An important driver of all of this was that energy got expensive.

While some argue the computing revolution and birth of the internet prove we never "stagnated", the fact remains that we have completely gutted the American middle class. If there was growth, it was not evenly distributed: it both diverged between classes and slowed in the world of atoms. For more on the latter, view the classic Thiel vs. Andreesen debate.[204] For convenience, I will use stagnation as a term to reference this widening gap. And if we are to steel-man a causal direction for this phenomenon for the purpose of this article, it would look something like this:

(Figure 21: Causal Chain - Stagnation)

The driver of the divergence from the Henry Adams' curve[205] is pretty simple: energy got expensive as global demand for oil finally caught up with supply in the early 70's, so the US started using less of it. What the American Order established was that any nation protected by the Order could trade with any other country within the Order. Thus, if all nations had the same cost of energy and access to global markets, then the areas with cheap labor would be the cheapest places to produce goods, creating a countervailing deflationary force in the face of energy inflation. This ended the "Henry Adams Curve" in America, as we started offshoring energy-intensive industries, lowering our overall consumption. That is, as energy prices increased due to the growing demand from industrializing nations like Japan and Germany, the US sought cheap labor to blunt the effects of their not-so-cheap-anymore energy. Labor and energy can be exchanged to a degree but are certainly not identical.

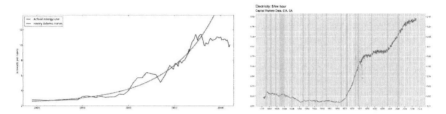

(Figures 22 and 23: The driver of the divergence from the Henry Adams' curve is pretty simple: energy got expensive, and we started using less of it, which can largely be described by offshoring industry. While since the 1970's, inflation-adjusted prices for energy haven't shown such a drastic increase, there was a clear step-change jump from pre-1970's energy crisis prices, as indicated in the chart on the bottom (in real-prices). They never recovered post oil-shock, despite being flat or deflationary since the turn of the century.)

While exporting our industrial base may not have been the intent of the petrodollar system, it is what happened. The phenomenon is described by the Triffin Dilemma which, in brief, establishes that in order to get enough dollars into global circulation, the US has to run structural trade deficits. That is, the only way to fund the system with enough dollars was for the US to buy more goods abroad than we sold. This made it very hard for domestic manufacturers to compete when selling abroad, as it effectively strengthened the US dollar against all other currencies, making our exports — our domestically made goods — more expensive against imports. Usually this would result in a weakening of the currency in question and a re-balancing for domestic manufacturing.

But this is not so in the case of the USD because it is the global reserve currency, keeping demand for it elevated as described in depth in Alden's piece. The result of this was "globalization", which is a nicer term for exporting the US industrial base. US consumers gained access to cheap goods, but US workers saw job opportunities disappear and wages compress.

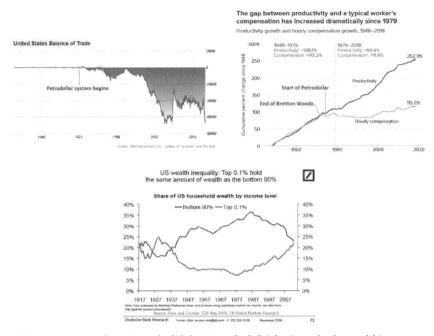

(Figures 24, 25, and 26: Not only did the US trade deficit begin at the dawn of this system, but so did the divergence in wealth of the top 1% and the bottom 90%. There are dozens of charts like this that demonstrate this inflection point in different ways, from obesity and fertility to incarceration rates. Whatever it was, something went very wrong with the US economy in the 70's.)

While it has led to an enormous increase in prosperity and quality of life globally, the USD reserve system seems to be, at this point, a root cause of America's domestic woes. It may be silly to reduce the complexity of our current political situation to energy, ignoring class, race, culture, etc., but it is the case that economic growth can alleviate much of the social pressures we currently face. In a sense, 1973 was the year the economy became a zero sum game domestically. A lot of intricate narratives were spun to make this change politically palatable, but the result is the same: the rich got richer at the expense, to a certain extent, of everyone else in the US (but not abroad). Domestic labor lost, while the executive suites and managerial layers of multinational corporations and banks that could manage the complexity of expanding supply chains, as well as international labor pools, won. So did the professional class of those that supported them, and anyone wealthy enough to own assets denominated in USD. While entrepreneurs could still find the "American Dream" of upward mobility, particularly in tech, all boats certainly did not rise with that tide.

If we accept that expensive energy led to a structural need for cheap labor to counterbalance inflation, then the way out of our current dilemma is to find cheaper sources of energy. Oil and gas cannot provide this for us. We have reached fossil fuel's theoretical thermodynamic efficiency limit, and, in a Malthusian sense, its role as a resource to spark growth. While the fracking boom allowed us to find cheap oil and gas reserves again, barring any large technological breakthroughs, oil and gas extraction will get harder and more expensive over time. For decades, we've always sought to find the cheapest resources first, so eventually our luck will run out.

Fortunately, the Age of the Electron offers us not only cheaper energy inputs, but also new engines and more efficient, more productive outputs. It is not necessarily the case that we need to consume more energy and return to the Henry Adams curve, but the point remains that oil and gas as a driving force of economic prosperity has plateaued. What we can do is use insanely cheap energy to break this domestic "stagnation".

Thus, another way of looking at our current economic stagnation is we have simply reached the global equilibrium between labor and thermodynamic conversion of oil into other productive uses, and we need something with a greater energy return on capital invested to reach the next cycle in generating humanity prosperity. It in turn makes sense that instead of money being backed by oil, the most important commodity in the world at the time, it will be backed by electricity, the most important commodity of the future.

Humans have an uncanny ability to turn tragedy into opportunity: a prime example being that as we realized the whales we were hunting for whale oil were going extinct, we invented a superior, more sustainable light source in the form of kerosene. There is a way out; The Age of the Electron is arriving just in time.

The Age of the Electron

The US must rebuild its balance sheet. In a way, there are three resources that matter in this regard: secure access to raw materials, a robust industrial base to turn those materials into goods, and hard currency on the government balance sheet from the surplus of production to aid in financing strategic needs — as well as a robust military to defend what's on the balance sheet. Post WWII, the US was dominant in all regards. We had the most gold, the biggest industrial base, endless access to food and raw materials, and the most powerful military in history by many orders of magnitude. This is why Bretton Woods effectively used the US balance sheet to rebuild the world economy in the wake of the destruction of WWII. But with the world around us brought into modernity, the US can now step back in certain ways from its role and focus inwards.

While the American Order led to the largest boom in human flourishing the world has ever seen, our balance sheet is now effectively vaporized in all three dimensions. First, the Triffin Dilemma essentially moved our industrial base off-balance sheet into foreign countries. One way to understand this is in how many 100s of billions — if not trillions — of dollars of equipment financed by American corporations sit in countries like China. In a conflict, what if those factories are nationalized? We cannot just bring those assets back home — they're stranded. At the same time, instead of focusing on securing access to raw materials, we've been focusing on securing shipping lanes of already produced goods from places like China.

Luckily, the US has enormous amounts of resources at home or nearby, but we must focus again on extracting these resources as China has, for example, in their growing dominance of the African continent. We need secure access to materials for inputs as we onshore our industrial base.

Lastly, what if foreigners want to stop holding their foreign reserves in USD and buying USTs? We would have no ability to finance anything at home, and would have to drastically reduce military spending and other entitlements. We need to unwind our over-levered 130% debt/GDP ratio and we need hard currency on our balance sheet to prepare for financing strategic future needs.

Resilience is about lessening dependence on foreign nations. Much in the same way foreign countries rely on the US for security, we in turn rely on them to finance the entire operation. Despite how powerful we appear, the US is essentially incapable of doing anything without others' help. And in the face of de-globalization and escalating tensions abroad, it is imperative that the US is able to domesticate large swaths of our economy.

People may view this as being a doomer, but that's far from the point — we're all expecting the music to keep playing, but it's time to start asking, "what if it stops"? Luckily, cheap electricity, bitcoin, and a gutted working class searching for a brighter future can converge into a new paradigm. We can move away from the eurodollar and petrodollar, embrace the electrodollar, and emerge a stronger and more resilient and unified nation in the process.

Energy is Getting Insanely Cheap

Unwinding the trade we made for cheap, globalized labor in the face of rising energy prices is simple: we need energy that is cheaper than fossil fuels — which clearly is not getting cheaper. Luckily, solar and wind are getting mind-blowingly cheap and are abundant in pockets of the country, despite a recent COVID-induced supply chain crunch that saw prices momentarily rise. And while it would be great to include nuclear in the discussion, the reality is it's not cheap enough yet to compete with solar, wind, and gas, most obviously in deregulated energy markets. This piece is not meant to explore how to kickstart our nuclear industry, but suffice to say that we need to cut red tape and fund R&D aggressively. Regardless of form, cheap energy breaks the "stagnation" cycle with a positive feedback loop that runs exactly counter to the negative one presented above:

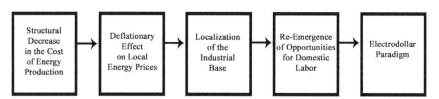

(Figure 27: Causal Chain - Energy is getting insanely cheap)

Unfortunately, the current paradigm traps us between a rock and a hard place. First, cheap imports of clean energy are essentially financed by a fossil-fuel driven economic order as described in the petrodollar section of this piece. So as the petro-industrial complex and the USD's reserve status wanes, our ability to secure cheap imports does too. This means we must start to manufacture these technologies at home cheaply.

However, the Triffin Dilemma concurrently makes it hard to manufacture anything at home — since domestic products are expensive compared to imports. So, while cheap imports of solar panels means the Triffin Dilemma helps create a deflationary effect on domestic energy prices and technologies and thus incentivizes local manufacturing of electricity-intensive industries, the Triffin Dilemma at the same time inhibits our ability to manufacture anything with the cheap energy.

Cheap imports are a blessing and a curse, and at a certain point this tension will snap. It's sort of like eating ourselves to death. But like the Ouroboros, where the snake devours his own tail, this process of eating the old way will also create the new.

Only absurdly cheap energy at home can overcome the labor arbitrage we receive by manufacturing abroad. This is the silver lining in the Triffin Dilemma— some sort of weird Ouroboros when it comes to clean energy supply chains that goes as follows…

(Figure 28: An Ouroboros snake eating its tail.)

We currently use the globalized supply chains to import cheap solar and storage. These resources provide cheap energy inputs and the infrastructure for its usage for 25 years or more. As the global economic order breaks down, we may see inflation in the price of imports. However, we'll have already benefited from deployment, so we can then use the cheaply deployed energy from imported solar to domesticate manufacturing. Dirt cheap energy allows more expensive domestic labor to win out. We ought to make an effort to help this natural process along, as the risk is that we see inflation in solar and storage technologies before deploying all that much of them could prove to be catastrophic.

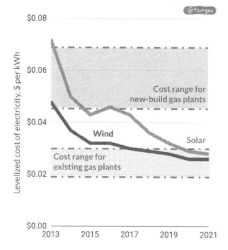
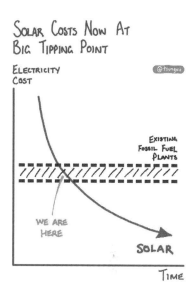

(Figures 29 and 30: While we should be funding SMR nuclear deployments, there is a strange phenomenon in the tech community that believes nuclear, which has only seen costs increase over the following decade, is somehow superior to solar, wind, and batteries, which has seen one of the most drastic reductions in costs (that continues) of any technology in modern history. The growth rates should make any tech investor's eyes pop, and is discussed at length in Tsung Xu's excellent piece)

Thus, we need to find a way to concurrently avoid inflation in solar and storage through imports today, while incentivizing the manufacturing of them in the US for tomorrow. The problem with our current policy of only focusing on tax subsidies to spur deployment of panels and batteries is that it ignores this risk. We need to onshore solar and storage supply chains by any means necessary — among other strategic technologies like semiconductors.

One way to do this would be adding subsidies to manufacturing that would make them competitive with imports, then gradually ratchet up tariffs as we reduce the subsidies. Effectively, we'd be leveraging the USD's reserve status (while it still exists) to spend heavily on on-shoring strategic industries like semiconductors and clean energy. The downside of this tactic would be that, despite creating actual domestic labor demand, spending can lead to further printing by the Fed and inflation, furthering the wealth inequality gap discussed prior. It may not be evenly distributed, which escalates domestic tensions. However, over time, the cheap energy at home should spur onshoring of all sorts of supply chains.

Regardless, the irony of this entire dynamic is that the more solar, wind, and electric vehicles get deployed, the more the petro-industrial complex wanes and thus our ability to continue importing these technologies. It's that very complex that is allowing for cheap imports in the first place. That is, we're essentially financing imports of solar and batteries on the back of a fossil fuel-driven economic order, and at a certain point the trade will break.

Thus, we must prepare for a time when the USD is no longer the global reserve currency and an end to the Triffin Dilemma, as we cannot indefinitely import solar panels on a trade deficit financed by the petro-industrial order. If we don't start making these technologies, eventually we won't be able to buy them. The hope is that, one way or another, the death gasps of one order may just create the foundations of the next.

The Ethics of Money Production

It is easy to forget in our fiat-dominated world that money is produced, just like any other commodity. While it may seem that the USD lacks a cost of production, this is not the case — especially if we accept the assumption that the USD is backed by oil and gunships that run on oil. This idea is important to understand as we build a framework for the future of the global money system, so let us establish some basic principles.

In "The Ethics of Money Production" by Jorg Guido Hulsman,[206] the author establishes plainly a few overlooked, but crucial ideas. The first is that:

> "To be spontaneously adopted as a medium of exchange, a commodity must be desired for its nonmonetary services (for its own sake) and be marketable, that is, it must be widely bought and sold. The prices that are initially being paid for its nonmonetary services enable prospective buyers to estimate the future prices at which one can reasonably expect to resell it. The prices paid for its nonmonetary use are, so to speak, the empirical basis for its use in indirect exchange."

In the case of the petrodollar, the "non-monetary service" provided by the US dollar was US military protection. As our ability to enforce global waterways recedes, so too will the global desire for this non-monetary service. However, this still does not explain the production of US dollars. The second idea that Jorg points out is on the nature of money production:

> *"How much money will be produced on the market? How many coins? The limits of mining and minting, and of all other monetary services are ultimately given through the preferences of the market participants. As in all other branches of industry, miners and minters will make additional investments and expand their production if, and only if, they believe that no better alternative is at hand. In practice this usually means that they will expand coin production if the expected monetary return on investments in mines and mint shops is at least as high as the monetary returns in shoe factories, bakeries, and so on."*

Put simply, there is no sense in using gold to invest in producing more gold when you can get higher returns elsewhere. But as monetary demand increases (through trade), it creates an incentive for minters and miners to invest in the production of money itself.

The cost of producing money made sense in an era of gold and silver coinage, but how would that apply to petrodollars? An extension of Alden's argument would be that US dollars were produced in relation to the production of oil. That is, the ebbs and flows of the oil trade and how much oil producers decided to invest in production dictated the amount of dollars needed to fund that system. In this sense, despite being a "fiat" system, US dollars from 1973 until 2008 have actually been produced in accordance with the dynamics of global energy markets.

Despite the focus of this piece being on bitcoin, this does introduce a slight wrinkle to the thesis. The jury is still out on whether or not it's the right currency for the electrodollar paradigm at scale, even if proof of work seems to have staying power for all the reasons soon to be described.

In the "Ethics of Money Production", it's clear that the author believes that "ethical" money production is market-driven. Meaning, as demand for the currency increases — as it is used in trade — the price of that money will increase against other goods and commodities. Thus, miners and minters will receive a signal to mine and mint new money to maintain balance between the currency and the goods and commodities people trade with it. Said another way, money should have supply/demand dynamics in producing the money itself, and it should also compete with other monies.

Ironically, bitcoin's supply was established by "fiat" by the creator, Satoshi Nakomoto. Only 21 million coins will ever exist. The argument for this is that any new production of money is theft against savers of that currency. This is a reasonable argument in the face of our current fiat system that is tyrannical in the other direction: when money can be printed at will, it is effectively wealth transfer from savers to producers. Particularly when it is the only currency in town, and its usage is enforced — militarily (just ask any petro-dictator that wanted off the petrodollar) and societally. A fair point.

The counterpoint, however, is that fixed money supply introduces a new tyranny: the price of money will continue to rise against other goods and commodities, essentially turning savers into a landed aristocracy. As bitcoin gets more expensive against other goods, it will be impossible to invest bitcoin to create more bitcoin given its fixed supply. In Hulsman's framing, this means bitcoin would not be an ethical money supply at scale, despite its effectiveness against the current inflationary tyranny. It effectively says that savers do not need to reinvest their savings into the economy to continue receiving gain. More important than any ethical argument, however, is the simple point that if bitcoin becomes too expensive against other goods, and its price cannot be lowered through new supply, it will not be an effective medium for trade, and market participants will turn away from it.

This is a bit of a moot point as it is not an actionable perspective for decades as this transition takes place. Bitcoin functions as a deflationary force against the inflationary regime for now, and is not yet a medium of exchange and trade. If bitcoin doesn't course correct as it begins being used for trade, it will simply get too expensive.

In a truly free-money system — where the currencies themselves compete — the only way for the price of bitcoin to drop is through decreased demand. So if bitcoin gets too expensive against other goods, and there is no way to reduce the price through new supply, market participants may freely look for other mediums of exchange. As long as bitcoin has to compete against other monies, there is nothing "immoral" about its pro-saver bent. New cryptocurrencies will continue to be freely made and used to the extent that they can outcompete bitcoin, and that's a good thing. Or, bitcoin itself will be forced to adapt in order to survive.

The Electrodollar: Bitcoin and the Grid

Unlike the petrodollar, the relationship between energy and money in bitcoin is explicit from day one. What is key to understand is that in the Age of the Electron, end use of energy will convert primarily to electricity away from fossil fuel-based combustion as an input. Concurrently, we see emerging a powerful property of bitcoin mining that it creates a clearing price on what we actually consider productive use of electricity. This in turn would incentivize only real GDP growth, something that we seem to be losing track of in the petrodollar construct.

Meanwhile, miners are incentivized to mine using the cheapest power, which already comes from renewables in many parts of the world, like Texas. The electrodollar thus offers us a potential way out of the stagnation inherent in the petrodollar system and a new institutional order that can better support increased productive capacity while ensuring our decarbonization efforts succeed. Climate-concerned detractors of bitcoin need to take note of the fact that, by railing on bitcoin in support of the USD, they are by extension supporting the petro-industrial complex.

While a return to "hard money" via bitcoin is an attractive idea in the context of our fiat excesses, the most interesting property of bitcoin is that it creates an explicit signal to what "productive" means for power consumption. Recall Hulsman's words quoted above:

> *"As in all other branches of industry, miners and minters will make additional investments and expand their production if, and only if... the expected monetary return on investments in mines and mint shops is at least as high as the monetary returns in shoe factories, bakeries, and so on."*

While many complain about bitcoin's energy intensity, it is actually its greatest feature. This is the case primarily in the security it brings the network, but secondarily in the incentive structure it creates. If you can create more economic profit using power to mine the currency that enables trade than you can create by producing a good to trade for the currency, then you probably shouldn't be using power to produce whatever that good is. That is, bitcoin mining acts as a filter by disincentivizing economic activity that will not lead to actual growth in productive surplus. This is unlike the fiat currencies we have today that, through cheap debt and targeting 2% annual inflation, drive us towards spending, mindless consumption, and creating companies that are oblivious to true value creation.

This is not just theoretical, as we can see this play out in real-time today, as described in "Leveraging Bitcoin Mines as Flexible Load Resources".[207] It does come with some caveats, however. Bitcoin miners are indeed flocking to the cheapest sources of power (and thus best places to mine) around the world, and manufacturers are not far behind.

In the US, this is primarily Texas due to a wealth of cheap domestic wind, solar, and natural gas production (and yes, areas like Kentucky are using bitcoin to try to prop up coal, but bitcoin is not going to save coal so it is merely a short term concern). However, the dynamic of the price of bitcoin setting the clearing price for productive output described above is likely far off. Still, in places like Texas, we can get a glimpse into what the future holds.

First, the bad news. At a reasonable price for bitcoin of ~$40,000, the hashrate of the network, and using a brand new ASIC miner, the opportunity cost of mining bitcoin in energy price terms is, as of 12/9/2023, roughly $170/mwh.[208] For older, less efficient miners, it can be as low as $100/mwh. Meanwhile, the average price of power in places like Texas is as low as $30/mwh. This means mining is still profitable well above the average cost of power, and thus could sap up supply and inflate prices for other productive uses (however, many industrial processes still have opportunity costs of production well above $170/mwh). This is where the overblown concerns that bitcoin is an energy hog and will push costs for "productive" uses comes from.

Now, the good news. First, hashrate (the amount of computing power being used on a cryptocurrency network to secure the network and propagate transactions) has consistently increased as prices increase. A higher price per bitcoin incentivizes more miners to enter the network, which in turn requires miners to expend more energy to earn the same monetary reward as global mining competition increases. This, in turn, compresses the price

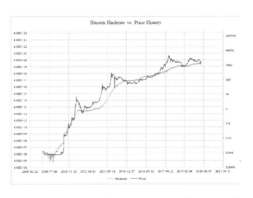

(Figure 31: The number of miners in the network increases as price increases. There is nothing to suggest that bitcoin would act any differently than any other commodity, where producers compete until the prices are driven to the marginal costs to produce.)

at which it's profitable to mine (the well-known phenomenon of margin compression in competitive markets). If bitcoin is to become a widely used currency, eventually the price must stabilize, and with it the hashrate will also, such that there is a reasonable (much lower than today) spread between the reward received for mining bitcoin and the marginal cost to produce it.

Second, miners in Texas and elsewhere are already proving to be rational economic actors and are shutting down mining as the price of power exceeds their marginal cost to mine — such as Riot Platforms.[209]

Third, the demand for power from bitcoin mining is driving the build out of new power plants, which will drive power prices for these new builds lower. When you put these three things together, you see that bitcoin mines could lead to net new cheap capacity and a reduction in average prices of power at scale. This is because when power supply is constrained, each mine shuts off at its marginal cost to produce, freeing up mining capacity for other productive uses.

An interesting hypothesis emerges out of these real phenomena: assuming in the Age of the Electron that all processes are run on electricity, bitcoin creates the strike price determining what is actually valuable to the economy. Today, bitcoin mining's profits are the spread between the price of power and its opportunity cost to produce, say $30/mwh to $170/mwh, so you make $140/mwh of power consumed (and need to pay off the cost of your miners). That means, you are better off producing any goods whose spread is greater. As bitcoin mining profit margins compress, this spread will be smaller too. Only those goods that can be traded for more bitcoin than the equivalent value of the electricity needed to produce them will be produced.

As Hulsman points out, this has been a property of money for thousands of years that we have forgotten only over the last fifty. So while there is the caveat pointed out above that no new supply of bitcoin is actually being "produced", bitcoin still looks and feels like energy money for the time being.

However, this is a potential problem down the road; independent of the miner rewards dynamic described here. If bitcoin cannot be produced as a function of energy input, it is possible that its price will spiral upwards against the goods being produced with that power, and lose efficacy as a medium of exchange. In Hulsman's framing, once the network has matured sufficiently in the far future, bitcoin production should actually be a function of hash rate, as hash rate is directly correlated to energy input. This of course runs counter to the very design (in the form of the difficulty adjustment and halvings) that was necessary to bootstrap the network. Still, it would create an explicit connection between electricity input and bitcoin production that does not exist today, and create the necessary dynamic for an Electro Dollar paradigm.

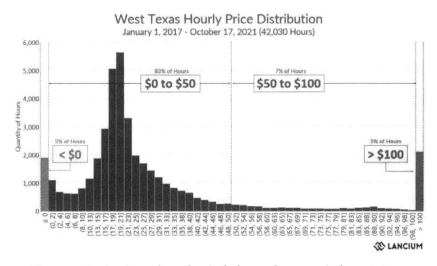

(Figure 32: Bitcoin mines only produce in the hours when power is cheapest. As new energy infrastructure is built to meet growing bitcoin demand and the bitcoin networks stabilize, the entire supply curve will shift to the right, helping all consumers of power. Source: Lancium.)

One popular concern that emerges out of these properties is a fear that bitcoin will use up all of the cheap power, but the truth is quite the contrary: the fact that bitcoin is the floor for economic activity creates an incentive to build power plants as cheaply as possible, which benefits all productive uses of power that create goods at prices above the floor. The marginal cost to produce bitcoin will settle at the lowest possible average cost to generate electricity, and only enough mines needed to secure the network will be built. An upside to the fixed supply is that, in its present state there will be a plateau of new mines built, leaving lots of excess capacity for cheap power to go towards other uses. If bitcoin truly incentivizes net new generation capacity on the grid, then its presence will lead to far lower average energy prices than in networks without bitcoin mines. This requires of course letting these incentives play out: if mines rush in and inflate power prices, it will create a signal to build more capacity.

As you'll explore further in the next chapter, bitcoin mines thus act as a stabilizing force for power grids. Ultimately, this means that industrial loads will either follow the bitcoin mines or build proprietary bitcoin mining business lines themselves. Over time, an equilibrium will be reached between creating money (mining bitcoin) and creating goods, the long-standing property of money and the economy that we have diverged from only since 1971.

And because electricity is so expensive to transmit, we will move production of goods to where power is cheapest, too — not just production of bitcoin. This is a meaningful difference from the petro-industrial complex, where we went to where oil was cheapest, extracted it, and then sent it to where we created goods. We could do this because shipping oil was comparatively cheap. In cheap energy networks, bitcoin mines will move in first and industrial centers will not be far behind. That is, cheap labor pools may not have access to cheap power, disrupting the globalized dynamic that exists today.

Of course as alluded to above, bitcoin mining is not purely driven by price. Hashrate cannot increase indefinitely because it requires ASICs, which require manufacturing capability of microprocessors. When looked at this way, bitcoin mining is a particularly potent currency for the digital age: it finds the equilibrium between electricity generation (power input), manufacturing of microprocessors (power transformation) and allocation of microprocessors to productive tasks (server load).

In the coming era of microprocessor scarcity, bitcoin, and its SHA-256 Application Specific Integrated Circuit microprocessor, also creates a clearing price for the production of all other types of microprocessors. Thus, in a digital world, bitcoin creates an equilibrium on productive capacity between electricity generation capacity and server capacity. If we're lucky, it may mean a future in which fewer social media and adtech companies use computationally expensive processes to sell cheap goods no one actually needs.

However, because we are so early on in bitcoin, maybe the electrodollar does not wind up tied to bitcoin. But the dynamic remains the same. Are miners rushing to cheap spots on the power grid so different than so many laborers and entrepreneurs flocking to San Francisco in 1849 for the gold rush or to Texas for oil production in the late 1800's, rather than using their labor and talents to actually make something that could be traded for gold or required oil to produce? Like then, the "bitcoin mining rush" won't always be the case. As the network matures and price escalates, reducing the upside potential of early adopters and yet inviting more miners in because of the high reward, the marginal cost of production of a bitcoin and the price of bitcoin will converge.

This happens with all commodities and there is nothing that suggests bitcoin would be any different. On the grid, this implies the strike price at which miners shut down will decline substantially as well. Said another way, mining will only be profitable when electricity is cheapest, and will not block other, more productive uses of power. Said another way, bitcoin will only be mined when the value of a bitcoin outstrips the cost to produce it (energy), which will get lower over time.

Ironically, climate-focused detractors of bitcoin often argue in favor of the USD and thus in support of the petro-industrial complex, which is not only driven by oil, but also incentivizes malinvestment, consumerism, and "growth at all costs" through inflation — or lots of energy waste. Sure, you could conceivably shift USD to be deflationary and renewables focused — or the electrodollar is just the dollar — but it would be naive to write-off the decades of institutional inertia preventing this, and described in detail in this piece.

Meanwhile, solar and wind are the cheapest sources of power we now have, and that's exactly where bitcoin mines are headed. Solar prices in Texas are headed towards $10/mwh (maybe even $5), and mining revenues will likely be driven down to $30/mwh or lower over time — down from ~$100-200mwh today depending on certain operational factors. Bitcoin and solar thus share an inseparable fate, creating a strategic need for the US to focus on not only deploying solar, but manufacturing it as well. And that's exactly what we're starting to see play out in places like Texas.

An Industrial Renaissance

The dynamics of electricity generation described above, wherein it is cheaper to move production to power than it is to move power to production, will (luckily) lead to the rapid re-onshoring of supply chains, without us doing much else at all. If 1973 was the year that energy prices irreversibly increased, forcing industrialized nations to start globalizing in order to find cheap labor to replace the access to cheap oil they had for decades prior, then 2021 is the year that this changed. Electricity production, due to solar, wind, and natural gas, is now so cheap that choosing to manufacture where the cheap energy is rather than where the cheap labor is is starting to pencil out.

This inherently means that the domestication of supply chains to areas where cheap electricity is abundant is a feature of the energy transition and the Age of the Electron. Transmission of electricity, while important, gets outrageously expensive even shipping it 1,000 miles. We can somewhat reasonably send Panhandle wind to California in the future, but certainly not to Taiwan.

This dynamic is very different compared to the global oil trade, where production of Saudi oil ($2/barrel) plus the costs of shipping it to end users in the US is still radically cheaper than producing in places like Texas ($40/barrel) right next to end users. Said simply, building high voltage power lines from here to Saudi Arabia is inconceivable compared to the ease of using oil supertankers.

Applied to the US, cheap electricity generated by solar, wind, and natural gas is enough to overwhelm even the powerful dynamics behind the Triffin Dilemma. On cue, something beautiful is emerging in Texas, the Midwest, and the Southeast: an industrial renaissance that not even the inertia behind the petro-industrial complex can stop. Why are semi-conductor and electric vehicle manufacturers alike suddenly flocking to Texas?

In electricity intensive manufacturing processes, the cheap energy inputs and lack of shipping costs can actually win out over the cheap labor that globalization provides access to. It seems we are starting to wake up to the importance of this to some degree, but we are likely 15–20 years behind our rivals in starting the on-shoring process. And we've yet to fully confront the massive threat of where we get the electricity generators of the future.

Domestic Battery and Solar Manufacturing is a National Security Issue

China is the Standard Oil of solar panels and batteries, two of the most important technologies in the Age of the Electron. Despite the fact that the Lithium-Ion battery was invented by an American and solar PV was invented at Bell Labs, we do not make any of these homegrown inventions in the US. That is a huge problem and was certainly not inevitable.

In much the same way we developed a strategic political focus on the Middle East because of access to oil, we need to start focusing on the energy supply chains of the future. Today, US leaders have no such focus and are letting an emerging China dominate where it matters—namely solar PV and battery production. And although that is luckily starting to change, it's not yet the mainstream, bipartisan view that it must be.

While we benefit from an abundance of cheap natural gas and our aging manufacturing giants like GE show prowess in wind turbine manufacturing, we are embarrassingly lacking in two of the most critical technologies of the future. We must make them on US soil, or at least on those friendlier than China's, something Ben Kincaid also explores in Chapter 2 in his essay about US strategic opportunities in Africa.

If solar, wind, and natural gas are the power sources of the Age of Electron, then batteries are the motor. Batteries are to electricity what the internal combustion engine was to oil, or the steam engine was to coal. Of course, batteries are not a motor whatsoever, but they are the fundamental technology that enable the motor, so we can treat them the same. Compared to the internal combustion engine, batteries benefit from economies of scale despite being small and modular. Because they are storing work already done from, say, a Natural Gas Combined Cycle power plant at 67% thermodynamic efficiency, and with a round-trip efficiency of 90% on their own, they are exceptionally more efficient than a 35% efficient traditional combustion engine sitting in a car. Batteries break us out of the Malthusian stagnation that combustion processes alone lock us into, and the Age of the Electron wouldn't happen without them.

(Figure 33: Chinese CATL, a battery manufacturer, dwarfs our tech giants in growth rates.)[210]

Furthermore, solar panels are marked by their remarkable ability to provide resilience to a centralized energy system. In fact, they represent the only mechanism we have to independently produce energy in a distributed manner. Natural gas, propane heaters, diesel, gasoline, and more all require extensive distribution networks, unless you happen to have an oil derrick and refinery in your backyard.

Despite only producing when the sun is out, once you own the panels, solar will generate power wherever it is for 25+ years. And paired with a standalone or electric vehicle battery, they can provide power at night (the Ford F-150 for 3+ days). We are still collectively underestimating how transformational a technology rooftop solar is in scaling human flourishing. As developing countries leapfrogged landlines for mobile, so too will they leapfrog centralized grids for solar and storage driven decentralized ones. Interestingly enough, a similar debate exists in the bitcoin community about at-home mining, decentralizing mining control, and onshoring miner production.

And yet, China manufactures 70%+ of solar panels and battery storage, including the raw materials supply chains leading up to the manufacturing process. If we're to rely on these resources, that needs to change. Projecting into the future China's dominance of clean energy supply chains in both solar panel and battery manufacturing — which mirrors that of Standard Oil and the US's early dominance in oil the late 1800's — coupled with the US's waning industrial might and the fraying of the US Dollar as the reserve currency spell trouble for the US. However, it is not too late for us to act— we've already found rich lithium deposits in friendly neighborhoods like Chile, Australia, and even our own backyard.

Not only is our access to critical technologies for our own needs in jeopardy, but our ability to provide value — and therefore wield influence — with others is also at risk. Developing nations will turn to Chinese manufacturers of these technologies, not to GE for engines or to Exxon to develop oil fields, as they did in the past. Batteries and solar, while critical, are only one example of the myriad ways in which the US offshoring manufacturing is a terrible strategy. The same could be said of semiconductors, steel, aluminum, pharmaceuticals, medical devices, or literally any basic necessities and infrastructure. Aside from our navy, which cannot be financed as the petro-industrial complex unwinds, what will future trading partners actually need us for?

So if there is one thing to take away from this piece, it is this: the structure of the USD as reserve currency prevents us from making anything at home. There is no keeping the system as is, and also bringing home manufacturing; you are for, or against. We must transition to a neutral reserve asset world, and prepare ourselves for the inevitable decline of the petro-industrial complex.

The dynamics of the Age of the Electron are drastically different than those of the Hydrocarbon Era, and our current position as global hegemon does not necessarily help us step into this new environment, precisely because the "exorbitant privilege" of our past has become the burden of our present — wielding the global reserve currency no longer helps us.

But there are plenty of advantages to exploit, if only we could stop the infighting and look to the future. Of them, access to cheap electricity is the single most important weapon we have, a deflationary force in an inflationary world.

Conclusion

This is not an energy transition, it is an energy revolution. Institutions of old will eventually break, and they will not go quietly into the night. This fact demands a certain vigilance in the approach to building new ones; the incumbents are not our friends, despite speaking as if they are, and are not to be trusted. Because when push comes to shove, the incentive structures are what they are, and the petro-industrial complex wishes only to perpetuate itself. And its perpetuation now exists in conflict with America's strategic aims.

Going forward, we must rely on our own minds and think from first principles, for that will be the only way to know what is what and carve a path into a more optimistic future. We cannot rely on what worked in the past.

So above all, this is a call to action. It is my personal belief that whether it's criminal justice reform or converting to clean energy, Americans actually agree on 70% of major issues. But it's in the interest of incumbent power structures to keep us divided by fanning the flames of our domestic culture war in order to distract us from their attempts to perpetuate a system that's now clearly failing us, and serving only them.

American corporate interests have diverged from those of its people, and US national security over the next decade is undermined by the interests of our very own petro-industrial complex. This is also true of the USD's status as the global reserve currency, as it actively prevents the onshoring of vital technologies and reinvigorating domestic labor.

In order to defend the interests of America, we may just need to reimagine its institutions.

QR Code to **Chapter 4** Endnote Links and Figures on the Bitcoin Today Coalition website:

200 Today in Energy – EIA
201 Ibid.
202 The Fraying of the US Global Currency Reserve System – Lyn Alden
203 Bretton Woods III – Zoltan Poszar, Credit Suisse
204 Peter Thiel and Marc Andreessen debate – Youtube
205 Where is my Flying Car – J. Storrs Hall
206 The Ethics of Money Production – Jorg Guido Hulsman
207 Leveraging Bitcoin Miners as Flexible Load Resources for Power System Stability and Efficiency – N. Carter, S. Connell, B. Jones, D. Porter, M. Rudd, SSRN
208 Bitcoin Mining Stats – Braiins
209 Texan Bitcoin miners profit by using less electricity; advocates say all Texans should get the same chance – K. Vu and E. Foxhall, The Texas Tribune
210 A guide to the energy transition – Tsung Xu, Materially Better

CHAPTER 5

BITCOIN AND ENERGY SECURITY: HOW BITCOIN STABILIZES AND REINFORCES THE GRID AND WHY IT'S A MATTER OF NATIONAL SECURITY

By Lee Bratcher and Pierre Rochard

Lee Bratcher is the President and Founder of the Texas Blockchain Council. The Texas Blockchain Council is an industry association with more than 100 member companies as well as hundreds of individuals that seek to make Texas the jurisdiction of choice for bitcoin and blockchain innovation. The TBC has helped research two pieces of blockchain legislation that were passed in the 87th Legislative Session and an additional two bills in the 88th Session, signed into effect by Governor Abbott. Lee and the TBC team have a specific focus on the regulatory environment around bitcoin mining in Texas. The TBC hosted the first and second Texas Blockchain Summits in Austin where speakers like Senator Ted Cruz, Senator Cynthia Lummis, and SEC Commissioner Hester Peirce have addressed sold-out audiences. Lee is a Captain in the US Army reserves working as Tech Scout for the 75th Innovation Command that supports Army Futures Command. Formerly, he was a political science professor at Dallas Baptist University teaching international relations with a research emphasis on property rights. Lee was awarded a Master's Degree in International Relations from St. Mary's University and is in his sixth year as a Ph.D. candidate at UT Dallas with a research emphasis on blockchain land registries. He lives in Richardson, TX with his wife Becca and their three daughters.

Pierre Rochard *has served as Vice President of Research at Riot Platforms since July 2022, after initially joining the company in 2019 as an Advisor. Pierre has researched and written about bitcoin since early 2013 and co-founded the Satoshi Nakamoto Institute in 2014 to curate the best primary source literature. In addition to developing open-source bitcoin software and launching the Lightning product at Kraken, he is a widely respected advocate for bitcoin's decentralized governance and value. Pierre also co-hosts the Noded Bitcoin Podcast and the Bitcoin for Advisors Podcast.*

Bitcoin Mining and the Electricity Grid

The growing prevalence of bitcoin mining on electrical grids presents both challenges and opportunities. By fostering strategic partnerships and adopting innovative practices among grid operators, electricity providers, and bitcoin miners, we can bolster the grid's resilience and increase its flexibility. Yet, if not carefully managed, the swift rise in large-scale power usage can jeopardize grid stability.

Bitcoin's proof-of-work mechanism, "mining", is the first decentralized clock in human history. A block every ten minutes provides the bitcoin ledger with a temporal ordering of transactions to prevent spending the same BTC twice.[211] This timely transaction finality and irreversibility makes bitcoin the world's first successful P2P electronic cash protocol. Bitcoin mining's decentralized nature enables the compute process — hashing — to be highly interruptible. Many individual miners can turn off and the bitcoin network can still reliably be used.[212]

Bitcoin mining, the computer process that secures the bitcoin ledger history, can be a highly energy-intensive activity when the mining reward is valuable. The real-world resource consumption enables the network to add new BTC to the ledger with a competitive process that prevents monopoly issuance profits, called seigniorage. In 2023, Coin Metrics estimated the total power draw of bitcoin mining around the world has reached between 12 and 14 GW.²¹³

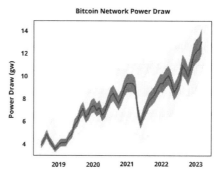

The energy consumption of bitcoin mining is closely tied to the exchange rate between bitcoin (BTC) and the US Dollar (USD). Simply put, an increase in the value of BTC means that mining bitcoin becomes more profitable, leading to more mining activity and consequently more electricity consumption.

(Figure 34: Bitcoin network's power draw. Source: CoinMetrics.)

If the price of bitcoin stabilizes around $60,000 USD, estimates suggest that the electricity consumption of bitcoin mining would reach its zenith between 2026 and 2028, consuming around 100 GW. On the other hand, if the price of bitcoin were to increase tenfold, hitting around $500,000 USD, the peak electricity consumption of bitcoin mining would be significantly higher, expected to reach around 700 GW in the same timeframe.²¹⁴

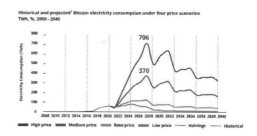

However, it's important to note that these are peak levels. After reaching these points, the electricity consumption for bitcoin mining is expected to decline. This is due to the scheduled "halving" events in bitcoin's protocol, which reduce the amount of new BTC rewarded to miners by 50% approximately every four years. Post halving, all else being equal, miners would need to spend twice as much on electricity to produce the same amount of bitcoin, leading to a decrease in total network electricity consumption as inefficient miners shut off or upgrade their ASIC fleets.

(Figure 35: Based on 2020 IEA Sustainable Development Scenario; 2021 electricity consumption value based on annualized July 2021 data. Source: NYDIG analysis)

In essence, these halving events act as an automatic "governor" on the resources consumed by bitcoin mining relative to the overall value of bitcoin.

Despite periods of increased activity and energy consumption when the BTC/USD exchange rate rises, the inherent mechanics of bitcoin ensure that, over time, the system becomes more efficient and uses less energy per unit of value. In the long run, transaction fees will be an increasing share of bitcoin mining revenue, though the future aggregate value of these fees is a topic of ongoing research.

The industrial-scale electricity demand enables bitcoin mining to play a transformative role in the energy sector, particularly in terms of stabilizing the energy grid, enabling renewable energy adoption, and stimulating innovation. Bitcoin mining's unique flexible load profile was recognized as a benefit to the ERCOT grid by the Texas Work Group on Blockchain Matters Report.[215] Bitcoin mining's fundamental electrical engineering and end-use make it the most interruptible, flexible large load on the grid along many criteria.[216]

	Cost of Reacting	Reaction Time	Availability	Granularity
Bitcoin Miner	Low	Quick	High	High
Data Center	High	Quick	High	Moderate
Steel Plant	Moderate	Slow	Low	Low

(Figure 36: Interruptibility: bitcoin miner v. data center v. steel plant. Source: Arcane Research.)

National Security and Grid Stability

A robust and reliable domestic electricity grid underpins national security due to its foundational role in supporting key societal and defense functions. Without stable electricity, infrastructure from communication networks to transportation systems, healthcare facilities, and defense installations could be severely compromised, leaving a nation vulnerable to both internal disruptions and external threats.

In an era of increasing digitization and interconnectivity, the electricity grid powers the very fabric of information exchange, be it civilian internet usage or secure military communications. It sustains the operations of data centers, intelligence agencies, surveillance systems, and advanced weaponry, all crucial for maintaining a nation's defense capabilities.

Furthermore, the electricity grid's resilience can impact the economic vitality of a nation, which in turn influences its geopolitical standing and military prowess. Energy instability can induce economic shocks, eroding a nation's ability to sustain a strong defense.

Moreover, a secure domestic grid reduces dependence on foreign energy supplies, insulating a nation against strategic vulnerabilities or foreign manipulation. Thus, ensuring the reliability of a domestic electricity grid is a strategic imperative for preserving national security.

Bitcoin miners can play a significant role in ensuring grid reliability[217] in times of high demand on the grid or during periods of low renewable energy output. By scaling down their operations, they can act as a 'virtual power plant' that reduces its power consumption when the grid is under strain, freeing up more energy for other consumers.

This kind of demand response strategy can be a powerful tool for maintaining grid stability,[218] especially during peak load periods. Texas' ERCOT grid operator illustrated this inverse relationship between electricity prices and bitcoin mining electricity consumption during the December 2022 Texas freeze:[219]

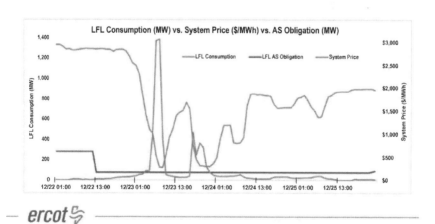

(Figure 37: Inverse relationship between electricity prices and bitcoin mining electricity consumption during the December 2022 Texas freeze. Source: ERCOT.)

Bitcoin mining, by its very nature, presents an effective mechanism for driving bitcoin revenues into the domestic economy. As a decentralized, globally distributed process, mining does not geographically limit the creation of bitcoin. Instead, it incentivizes the development of operations where conditions are most favorable — this can include the United States — provided the right infrastructural and regulatory environment.

Incorporating large-scale bitcoin mining operations into the U.S. grid system can bring significant economic benefits, including inflows of bitcoin revenues, job creation, and increased investment in energy security. These benefits can extend beyond the immediate financial gains, contributing to the country's strategic positioning on the global stage.

From a national security perspective, encouraging domestic bitcoin mining helps ensure that revenues associated with the creation and management of this digital asset stay within the U.S. economy, rather than potentially flowing to geopolitical adversaries. By doing so, the U.S. not only strengthens its own economic resilience but also reduces the risk of adversaries using these revenues to finance activities against American interests.

Ancillary Services

Bitcoin mining's role as a stabilizing force on the grid, demand response, happens through several different mechanisms. The first is ERCOT's Ancillary Services products,[220] which ERCOT procures through competitive auctions. Ancillary Services enable ERCOT to achieve their grid reliability mandate. The objective of these services is to provide ERCOT with an option — a right but not an obligation — to direct control over power generation and load to harmonize supply and demand on the grid. This is of critical importance since any imbalances can result in significant grid failures, including brownouts and blackouts.

Market and Operations

- ERCOT ensures that there are enough resources and resource flexibility available on the system to meet net load, net load changes, and uncertainties by using Ancillary Services and Reliability Unit Commitment.

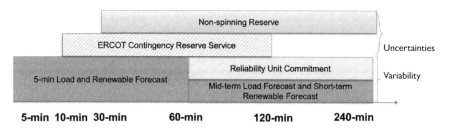

(Figure 38: Source: https://www.esig.energy/event/webinar-ercot-contingency-reserve-service-ecrs/)

The first product is called Regulation Service. Bitcoin miners' participation aids in maintaining a constant grid frequency. By adjusting their energy consumption every four seconds, miners can help balance supply and demand between five-minute dispatch intervals. This fine-tuned regulation assists ERCOT in ensuring a stable and consistent power supply.[221]

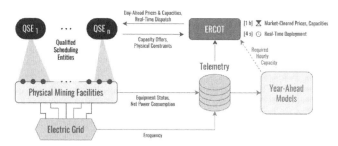

(Figure 39: Physical and economic interaction between ERCOT and the mining facilities participating in frequency regulation.)

Secondly, through the Responsive Reserve Service (RRS), bitcoin miners can bid to provide a buffer against sudden frequency excursions. Miners can decrease their electricity use in real-time to respond to unplanned unit outages, thus adding an additional layer of security to the grid's stability.

A new Ancillary Services product is ERCOT Capacity Reserve Service (ECRS). It's used to manage rapid net load ramps when the sun is setting, or clouds cover large solar installations. These decreases in electricity production can happen faster than peaker plants can turn on to balance the grid. ECRS adds additional capacity to the grid within a short 10 minute time frame and helps avoid blackouts or other serious issues that could arise due to solar intermittency.[222] Bitcoin miners will be able to bid into the ECRS auction to help balance the grid. This net load ramp is often referred to as the "duck curve":

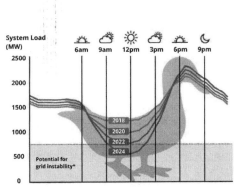

The Non-Spinning Reserve Service (Non-Spin) represents a longer-term safety net for the grid. By offering capacity that can be started or interrupted within 30 minutes, bitcoin miners can contribute to mitigating net load forecast errors, compensating for loss of generation capacity,

(Figure 40: Illustration of a duck curve.)

handling risk associated with net load ramps, or stepping in during limited capacity availability for Security-Constrained Economic Dispatch (SCED).

Ancillary Services, which help ensure the stability and reliability of the power grid, can be sourced from a variety of providers, including bitcoin miners. However, the cost of these services can vary significantly depending on the source. Bitcoin miners, with their flexible demand and capacity to quickly ramp up or down, can often provide these services at a relatively low cost.

If Ancillary Services are not procured from bitcoin miners, ERCOT must source these services from other, potentially more expensive providers. This is because the total quantity of Ancillary Services that ERCOT needs to ensure grid reliability has been increasing due to electrification and the growth in renewables. It's a fundamental requirement to guarantee the stable operation of the grid, matching supply and demand, and mitigating the risk of power outages.[223]

BITCOIN AS A TOOL FOR MODERN STATECRAFT

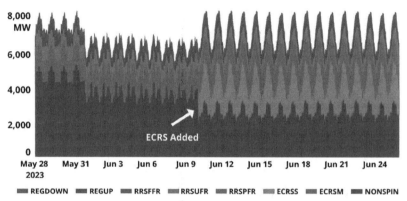

(Figure 41: ERCOT ancillary service procurement volumes. Source: GridStatus.)

If bitcoin miners are artificially limited or excluded from participating, the supply side of the Ancillary Services market becomes less competitive, which results in higher procurement costs for ERCOT. Integrating bitcoin miners into the Ancillary Services market provides ERCOT with a flexible, responsive resource, and promotes healthy competition and helps reduce overall system costs.

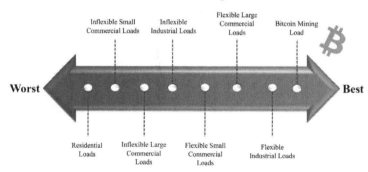

(Figure 42: Resources for grid operators.)

In summary, by participating in ERCOT's Ancillary Services products, bitcoin miners transform their energy-consuming operations into a dynamic demand response tool, enhancing ERCOT's ability to manage reliability in a variety of challenging scenarios.

Four Coincident Peaks

Another example of demand response from Texas is ERCOT's Four Coincident Peaks (4CP) program. This program focuses on periods of peak electricity demand, typically on hot summer days. By accurately predicting these peaks and reducing their energy consumption during these times, bitcoin miners with Interval Data Recorder meters can substantially decrease their electricity delivery costs. Various services provide notifications to help miners anticipate these peak periods, enabling them to minimize disruptions to their operations while contributing to overall grid stability.

Economic Curtailment

An alternative mode of demand response for bitcoin miners involves economic control based on the marginal economics of spot electricity prices and the marginal value of hashrate, often referred to as the hashprice. If a miner is not selling a control option to ERCOT, their decision making to turn their load on or off is driven by the real-time electricity market price.

When spot electricity prices rise above a breakeven electricity price, for example $100 per MW, it can become unprofitable for bitcoin miners to continue operating. The unit economics at these elevated prices turn negative, thus incentivizing the miners to voluntarily curtail their operations. In this instance, miners aren't controlled by the grid operator, but instead respond independently based on economic principles. This economic load shedding does still help the grid, as it makes electricity available for other consumers, and concurrently acts as a price stabilizing mechanism.

The breakeven price is largely a function of the spot BTC/USD exchange rate and the total number of miners currently competing for the reward, called the network hashrate or difficulty.

Mining Profitability Matrix - Bitcoin Price vs. Network Hashrate

S19 Pro Miner Profitability Matrix - Revenue per MWh

Network Hashrate (EH/s)	Bitcoin Price USD/BTC											
	$5,000	$10,000	$15,000	$20,000	$25,000	$30,000	$35,000	$40,000	$45,000	$50,000	$55,000	$60,000
150	$ 43	$ 86	$ 129	$ 172	$ 215	$ 258	$ 301	$ 344	$ 387	$ 430	$ 473	$ 516
160	$ 40	$ 81	$ 121	$ 161	$ 201	$ 242	$ 282	$ 322	$ 363	$ 403	$ 443	$ 484
170	$ 38	$ 76	$ 114	$ 152	$ 190	$ 228	$ 265	$ 303	$ 341	$ 379	$ 417	$ 455
180	$ 36	$ 72	$ 107	$ 143	$ 179	$ 215	$ 251	$ 287	$ 322	$ 358	$ 394	$ 430
190	$ 34	$ 68	$ 102	$ 136	$ 170	$ 204	$ 238	$ 271	$ 305	$ 339	$ 373	$ 407
200	$ 32	$ 64	$ 97	$ 129	$ 161	$ 193	$ 226	$ 258	$ 290	$ 322	$ 355	$ 387
210	$ 31	$ 61	$ 92	$ 123	$ 154	$ 184	$ 215	$ 246	$ 276	$ 307	$ 338	$ 368
220	$ 29	$ 59	$ 88	$ 117	$ 147	$ 176	$ 205	$ 234	$ 264	$ 293	$ 322	$ 352
230	$ 28	$ 56	$ 84	$ 112	$ 140	$ 168	$ 196	$ 224	$ 252	$ 280	$ 308	$ 336
240	$ 27	$ 54	$ 81	$ 107	$ 134	$ 161	$ 188	$ 215	$ 242	$ 269	$ 296	$ 322
250	$ 26	$ 52	$ 77	$ 103	$ 129	$ 155	$ 181	$ 206	$ 232	$ 258	$ 284	$ 309
260	$ 25	$ 50	$ 74	$ 99	$ 124	$ 149	$ 174	$ 198	$ 223	$ 248	$ 273	$ 298
270	$ 24	$ 48	$ 72	$ 96	$ 119	$ 143	$ 167	$ 191	$ 215	$ 239	$ 263	$ 287
280	$ 23	$ 46	$ 69	$ 92	$ 115	$ 138	$ 161	$ 184	$ 207	$ 230	$ 253	$ 276
290	$ 22	$ 44	$ 67	$ 89	$ 111	$ 133	$ 156	$ 178	$ 200	$ 222	$ 245	$ 267
300	$ 21	$ 43	$ 64	$ 86	$ 107	$ 129	$ 150	$ 172	$ 193	$ 215	$ 236	$ 258

◈ LANCIUM

(Figure 43: Mining profitability matrix - bitcoin price v. network hashrate. Source Lancium.)

Bitcoin operates on a deflationary model, where the rate of new bitcoin creation — part of the reward for miners validating transactions on the blockchain — undergoes a scheduled reduction. This process, known as halving, takes place every 210,000 blocks or approximately every four years.

During each halving event, the mining reward — specifically the part attributed to the addition of new BTC to the ledger — is slashed by 50%. This reduction has significant implications for the economics of mining. Assuming all other factors remain constant, this will effectively halve the breakeven electricity price for bitcoin miners.

As a result of this dynamic, miners who are unable to maintain profitability under these new conditions — typically those using outdated hardware or with access to more expensive electricity — are likely to exit the market. This market-driven mechanism constantly pressures the mining community to seek more energy-efficient operations and cheaper energy sources, driving the evolution and improvement of bitcoin mining technology.

Bitcoin mining efficiency, which essentially indicates how much computational power — hashrate — a rig can produce per unit of electricity consumed, has a significant impact on breakeven electricity prices. A higher efficiency rig can generate more hashrate for the same amount of energy, which means it can produce more bitcoin for the same electricity cost. Consequently, high-efficiency rigs can sustain profitability at higher electricity prices, leading to a higher breakeven electricity price.

On the other hand, lower efficiency rigs use more electricity to produce the same hashrate as their higher efficiency counterparts.[224] Therefore, their operational costs are higher, and they can only remain profitable when electricity prices are relatively low. This results in a lower breakeven electricity price for less efficient mining rigs.

Cooling technologies significantly affect the efficiency of a mining facility as well. Bitcoin mining generates a substantial amount of heat, and if not properly managed, this heat can lead to hardware damage or reduced performance. Different cooling methods can have varied impacts on the overall efficiency of the operation.

Water cooled and immersion cooled systems, for instance, can often be more efficient than traditional air-cooled facilities.[225] These systems use liquids (like water or specially engineered fluids) to absorb and dissipate heat. Because liquids can transport heat away more efficiently than air, these methods can maintain optimal operating temperatures more effectively.

(Figure 44: Air cooled bitcoin miners.)

Consequently, the mining hardware can run at higher performance levels for longer periods, improving the overall mining efficiency.

This variation in efficiency between different mining rigs and cooling systems creates a range of breakeven electricity prices among bitcoin miners. Some miners, with high-efficiency rigs and advanced cooling systems, can stay profitable even when electricity prices are relatively high. In contrast, others with lower efficiency equipment or less advanced cooling will need to cease operations when prices rise beyond their lower breakeven point.

Economic load curtailment also aids in managing the dispatch curve of power generation. As miners react to the electricity price above their breakeven by reducing their demand, the pace of power consumption through the grid's generation stack is decelerated, offering more time for supply to catch up and potentially averting critical grid situations.

(Figure 45: Immersion cooled bitcoin miners.)

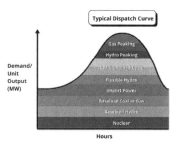

(Figure 46: Typical dispatch curve.)

Moreover, this form of demand response from bitcoin miners can also mitigate the probability of scarcity pricing events. The $5,000 per MW maximum price in ERCOT is a ceiling seen during periods of extreme scarcity on the grid. By curtailing their operations at prices far below this threshold, bitcoin miners help alleviate the likelihood of such drastic price spikes, thereby contributing to overall grid stability and cost efficiency. Researchers at Texas A&M found that bitcoin miners de-stress the grid when the rest of system demand is peaking.[226]

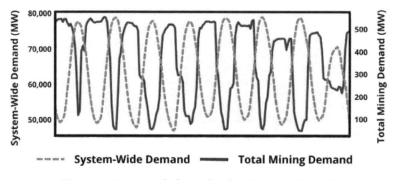

(Figure 47: System-wide demand and total mining demand.)

Transmission Costs

When bitcoin miners buy electricity from the grid, they pay for transmission costs and are contributing to the maintenance and development of the power grid. These payments can be significant, given that bitcoin mining facilities often require substantial amounts of electricity. Transmission costs, which are typically collected by grid operators, are used to cover the expenses associated with the operation, maintenance, and upgrading of power lines, substations, and other common grid infrastructure. As such, the revenues collected from bitcoin miners can be directly reinvested in enhancing grid reliability, capacity, and the integration of new technologies.

One area where these funds can be particularly beneficial is in the investment in smart grid technologies. Smart grids use digital communications technology to detect and react to local changes in usage, improving the reliability and efficiency of electricity distribution. By contributing to the financing of these technologies, bitcoin miners can help foster a more resilient, efficient, and sustainable power grid.

Therefore, the involvement of bitcoin miners in paying transmission costs not only ensures they bear a fair share of the infrastructure they use, but also presents an opportunity to facilitate more substantial investment in advancing the grid infrastructure. In this way, bitcoin mining can contribute positively to the broader energy sector and play a role in the transition towards more modern and efficient electricity systems.

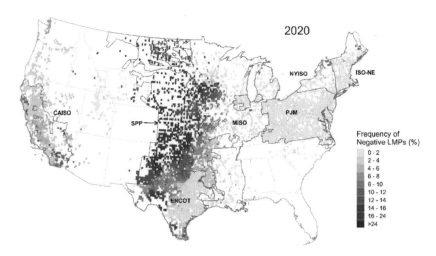

(Figure 48: Frequency of negative LMPs (%) 2020)

Power Purchase Agreements

Apart from utilizing Ancillary Services and self-determined economic curtailment, bitcoin miners can leverage Power Purchase Agreements (PPAs) with for-profit energy producers. These PPAs permit miners to acquire electricity at a predetermined rate for an extended duration, potentially spanning years or decades. The underlying energy assets can be located anywhere on the grid, subject to transmission limits, and do not necessitate miner co-location with the generation site.

This arrangement provides dual advantages. For miners, it mitigates the risk of energy price volatility, offering a financial hedge against future cost uncertainty. From the power companies' perspective, the PPAs, featuring substantial upfront payments from miners, secure committed future sales, thus fostering investment in additional capacity.

The negotiation of these agreements is competitive and intense, given the significant stakes for both parties. The result is a strategically crafted contract that, while allowing bitcoin miners to manage their operational energy risk, simultaneously catalyzes infrastructure growth for power producers.

Well-crafted PPAs provide for the flexibility to resell unused portions on the wholesale day-ahead and spot markets. This feature allows hedged miners to remain responsive to the same price signals that unhedged bitcoin miners purchasing on the spot market react to. The volatility of electricity prices can increase with the supply growth from intermittent renewables. However, bitcoin miners, through their ability to resell pre-purchased electricity during high-demand periods, can help to mitigate this volatility.

Moreover, bitcoin miners with PPAs can become highly competitive bidders in ERCOT's Ancillary Services auctions. Their participation drives down the cost of these essential services, which help maintain grid stability and are paid for by all electricity ratepayers. As bitcoin miners' share of total electricity load increases, they could potentially outbid and outcompete both traditional incumbents and new technology contenders, such as battery storage, in these auctions.

In summary, PPAs offer an economic hedge against electricity price volatility for bitcoin miners and contribute positively to grid stability and reliability. The strategic use of PPAs by bitcoin miners can help drive competition, lower costs, and spur innovation within the energy sector.

Risks of Economic Curtailment

Voluntary economic curtailment among bitcoin miners carries a risk related to the clustering of their breakeven price per MWh. If miners' breakeven prices are similar, a sudden shift in the electricity market could trigger large and rapid load shedding, leading to abrupt and potentially disruptive grid imbalances. In some circumstances this could also lead to market price oscillation as load shedding can push the spot electricity price back below the breakeven, a feedback loop emerges of bitcoin miners turning on and off between 5- or 15-minute settlement windows.

This dispersion of breakeven points due to efficiency differences contributes to the stabilization of the grid. Instead of a large group of miners coming on and off the grid at the same price point, miners' phase in and out over a range of prices, leading to smoother transitions and less strain on the grid infrastructure. This reduces the risk of sudden demand spikes or drops, which could potentially destabilize the grid.

The risk can be further mitigated by enabling bitcoin miners to participate in a dispatch schedule, akin to how power generators operate. By bidding into this schedule, miners' economic load shedding can be coordinated in an orderly manner through a transparent market mechanism, avoiding simultaneous and uncontrolled load drops.

Bitcoin miners' participation in Ancillary Services already assists in addressing this issue. These services, competitively auctioned by ERCOT, give the grid operator visibility and control over the mining load. ERCOT buys an option and strategically exercises it to maximize grid reliability. For example, the grid operator can keep a bitcoin mining load off even when electricity prices fall below the mining breakeven point, or to keep it on even when prices are above the breakeven. This management approach ensures that the timing of demand response from bitcoin miners is decided by the grid operator based on reliability considerations, and not by spot market economics.

Voltage Ride Through

The industrial-scale mining of bitcoin introduces unique challenges to maintaining grid stability, particularly concerning voltage ride-through configurations. Bitcoin mining rigs individually exhibit substantial resilience against voltage sags, compared to most other loads. However, protection schemes at the interconnection substation of an industrial-scale mining facility might be set to trip and disconnect the load before there's an actual risk to the equipment.

Voltage ride-through capability refers to a device's ability to continue functioning during short periods of reduced supply voltage. Tripping mechanisms, intended to safeguard the equipment, can sometimes be overly sensitive, disconnecting loads at the slightest dip in voltage. If this occurs unexpectedly at a large mining facility, it could cause sudden load reductions that destabilize the grid.

To mitigate the risk of unexpected and uncontrolled load disconnections, bitcoin miners should engage with transmission companies and the grid operator. This collaborative effort aims to fine-tune the protection scheme parameters, adjusting the sensitivity of tripping mechanisms, and establishing clearer thresholds for when loads should be disconnected. This approach ensures that mining facilities only disconnect when necessary, thereby supporting grid stability while also providing a reliable power supply for bitcoin mining operations.

Large Flexible Load Registration

Considering the unique collaboration required between bitcoin miners and grid operators, having a distinct registration category makes sense. In Texas, the legislature created the Large Flexible Load category to represent industrial-scale bitcoin mining facilities.[227] Such a category will help ensure a more streamlined approach to communication and coordination, enhancing the grid's ability to manage the unique load characteristics of bitcoin mining and optimizing the demand-response benefits it offers. For example, load ramping — the speed at which a power consumer like a bitcoin mining facility can increase or decrease its electricity consumption — plays a crucial role in the smooth operation of a power grid and in a miner's participation in Ancillary Services.

Rapid load ramping capabilities can provide valuable flexibility to the grid, allowing it to respond more effectively to sudden changes in supply or demand. For instance, if a power plant unexpectedly goes offline, a miner with the ability to quickly curtail its operations can help prevent an undersupply situation. Conversely, in times of excess power generation, a fast-ramping miner can quickly ramp up its operations to consume this excess power, preventing potential under-frequency conditions.

However, the ramping capability can vary significantly between different mining facilities. It may range from mere seconds to minutes or even hours, depending on the operator's processes. For example, a mining facility using advanced hardware and cooling systems may be able to change its load significantly faster than a facility using older equipment and less efficient cooling.

When bitcoin miners wish to participate in Ancillary Services, they must demonstrate to ERCOT their ramping capabilities align with the product's specifications. For example, in the Regulation Service, miners should be able to change their load every four seconds to help balance supply and demand between dispatch intervals.

Regulators, bitcoin miners, and academic researchers need to work together to identify the most appropriate ramping configurations that respect grid reliability requirements. This process should be based on robust, data-driven analysis to ensure it reflects the realities of both bitcoin mining operations and grid dynamics. Such an approach can help optimize the integration of bitcoin mining into the grid, enhancing both the efficiency of mining operations and the overall stability and reliability of the power grid.

ERCOT has shown leadership in this area. Before the legislature took action, ERCOT recognized the unique characteristics and potential of bitcoin mining as a load resource and established the Large Flexible Load Task Force. This task force brings together a variety of stakeholders, including bitcoin miners, power generators, grid operators, and other consumers of electricity. Their goal is to develop a practical framework that embraces the benefits of bitcoin mining's demand-response capabilities, while also effectively mitigating potential risks to the grid.

Through this task force, ERCOT aims to harness the potential of bitcoin mining to contribute to grid flexibility and stability, helping to shape the future of the grid in a way that balances innovation, reliability, and resilience. This task force model could serve as an example for other grid operators globally as they grapple with the complexities introduced by large-scale bitcoin mining.

Mining Behind the Meter and Off-Grid

Bitcoin mining's versatility in terms of its energy sourcing and operational setup marks it as a transformative energy technology. A particularly efficient method employed by miners is operating "behind the meter". This setup allows a mining operation to be directly attached to a generator that is connected to the grid. When the mining operation reduces its load, the surplus power from the co-located generator becomes available to the grid, transforming a load into a highly flexible generator. This configuration not only enhances the power generator and mining operation's efficiency but also boosts the grid's resilience by providing a supplementary power source during high demand periods.

Additionally, bitcoin miners can operate completely "off-grid", utilizing energy sources that would otherwise be wasted. For instance, they might be in remote regions where they can capitalize on stranded energy such as flared natural gas. By converting this wasted energy into an asset, bitcoin mining contributes to a more efficient and sustainable energy landscape.

There's also a diverse range of smaller-scale mining operations. Some home miners, for example, utilize the heat generated by their mining rigs for domestic purposes, such as warming their homes or heating their swimming pools. This recycling of energy underscores the creative ways in which bitcoin mining can contribute to energy efficiency. Small mining loads can aggregate to contribute to the same demand-response strategies as large mining operations.[228]

Given these diverse configurations — from large-scale, grid-connected operations to small, off-grid setups leveraging otherwise wasted energy — bitcoin mining is demonstrating its transformative potential in the energy sector. It's not only aiding grid stabilization and increasing energy efficiency, but also promoting the utilization of stranded resources, highlighting its capacity to serve as a revolutionary tool in the broader energy ecosystem.

Excise Taxes

Placing an excise tax on electricity for bitcoin miners as has recently been proposed is an arbitrary and selective financial burden. It results in deterring investment in bitcoin mining operations, consequently limiting the potential benefits these operations bring to the wider energy sector and the economy.

Large-scale bitcoin mining operations, like other substantial industrial consumers, contribute to overall demand in the energy market. Higher demand stimulates growth in the energy sector, incentivizing infrastructure development, technological innovation, and the exploration of efficient energy production methods.

The economies of scale generated through this growth result in lower electricity rates for all consumers. In essence, the increased demand encourages more significant investment in generation capacity and grid infrastructure, distributing fixed costs across a broader demand base and thereby reducing the cost per unit of electricity.

Conversely, selectively imposing higher tax burdens on bitcoin miners discourages their participation in the energy market. This reduced demand slows growth in the energy sector and curtails the benefits of economies of scale that could otherwise be achieved, leading to higher electricity rates for all consumers in the long run.

It is crucial to ensure a level playing field where all large consumers, including bitcoin miners, are treated equitably. Such fairness encourages competition, stimulates growth, and ultimately drives down electricity costs across the board, benefiting all consumers.

Mining and Renewable Energy

The energy requirements of bitcoin mining have stimulated investment in renewable energy infrastructure.[229] By providing a flexible demand for power, mining operations can improve the financial feasibility of renewable energy projects, which often face challenges in selling their intermittent power to traditional grids. This, in turn, can encourage more widespread deployment of renewable energy resources, enhancing the diversity of the energy mix and contributing to environmental sustainability. Indirectly, bitcoin mining may reduce electricity grids' greenhouse gas emissions by replacing natural gas and coal peaking power plants.[230]

Bitcoin mining can be conducted anywhere with access to electricity and an internet connection, making it uniquely suited for remote locations. This geographical flexibility allows bitcoin miners to utilize renewable power resources that are often located far from demand centers.

Renewable energy sources, such as wind, solar, and hydro, are often most abundant in remote areas that are not easily accessible or are too far from urban centers where electricity demand is high. The infrastructure to transport this electricity to high-demand areas is costly and can result in significant energy losses during transmission.

By placing their operations near these renewable power sources, bitcoin miners can ensure that the electricity generated is consumed on-site, eliminating the need for long-distance transmission and making full use of the power generated.

Furthermore, bitcoin mining can help to monetize stranded energy assets, which are energy sources that are economically unviable to utilize due to their remote location. By harnessing these otherwise wasted resources, bitcoin mining can increase the viability and attractiveness of renewable energy investments, potentially accelerating the transition towards a more sustainable energy system.

Grid Interconnections

Texas, with its independent energy grid that is market driven, stands out as an attractive destination for miners seeking affordable, abundant energy, and a technology-neutral regulatory environment.

The interconnection and integration of industrial-scale bitcoin mining facilities into the grid necessitates a structured, well-defined process. Encouraging bitcoin miners to initiate early registration, provided they meet the requisite financial and planning qualifications, can aid in better forecasting of grid requirements and planning.

Clear communication is vital throughout the integration process. Bitcoin miners should regularly update construction milestones and provide an anticipated energization schedule. Such transparency fosters coordination between all stakeholders, enabling the grid operator to plan and manage the capacity requirements accordingly.

Furthermore, bitcoin miners should consistently update the grid operator regarding the current and projected future load capacity of their facilities. In certain scenarios, real-time telemetry may be required to provide instantaneous updates on load conditions. Such information can be crucial in enabling grid operators to maintain balance and reliability within the network, even as new, substantial loads come online.

As the entities with expert knowledge and deep understanding of the complexities of grid management, system reliability operators are best positioned to make decisions about load shedding during an emergency. They must dynamically balance supply and demand while considering a variety of factors such as transmission constraints, grid stability, and frequency stabilization. Legislatively forcing grid operators to shed specific loads, such as bitcoin mining operations, could inadvertently exacerbate an emergency.

Proactive registration, open communication, and constant updates form the foundation of effective integration of industrial-scale bitcoin miners into the grid, promoting grid stability and cooperative growth between these new demand entities and traditional grid stakeholders.

Grid Resilience

Bitcoin mining, particularly in areas such as Texas, has a positive impact on electricity grid resilience. It does so in a number of ways, primarily by encouraging technological development and innovation in the energy sector. Given the intense energy demands and the focus on cost-effectiveness within the bitcoin mining process, there's a strong push for improvements in energy storage and distribution technologies. As such advancements occur, the overall resilience of the grid is enhanced, making it better prepared to handle various situations.

Furthermore, bitcoin mining promotes the shift towards a more distributed and robust energy system. With the creation of geographically diverse points of energy demand, this industry fosters the growth of microgrids and other localized energy solutions. Such a transition reduces dependency on large, centralized power plants, thus improving the energy system's resilience against disruptions.

The importance of resilience becomes evident when we consider the array of threats our energy systems face, both man-made and natural. On the one hand, weather conditions such as hurricanes, tornadoes, extreme heat, floods, ice storms, and events like Winter Storm Uri pose significant challenges. On the other hand, we have man-made threats, including cyber-attacks, war, intentional damage or sabotage, targeted attacks on electrical equipment that could trigger cascading failures, and resource shortages.

Another factor to note is the impact of population density, escalating energy demand, infrastructure wear and tear, and shifting climatic conditions. All these elements demand a resilient power grid that can withstand and quickly recover from such challenges.

The role of bitcoin miners in this context is crucial. They are not just beneficiaries of a resilient grid but also contributors to its strength. Post-disaster recovery is one aspect of this, with miners learning how to enhance their infrastructure to 'build back better.' This includes developing and implementing strategies to mitigate the risks that threaten grid resilience.

Finally, there's a strong link between energy efficiency and resilience. The more efficient our energy use, the less strain we place on the grid, reducing the chances of failures and improving its ability to bounce back from any disruptions. Therefore, any industry, including bitcoin mining, that drives energy efficiency indirectly contributes to enhancing grid resilience.

The disruptive influence of bitcoin mining on the energy sector and grid operations has presented a unique set of challenges. However, these challenges also open opportunities to explore innovative strategies for grid management, harness new energy sources, and improve grid resilience. By leveraging the unique characteristics of bitcoin mining, from its flexibility in energy sourcing to its large-scale demand for power, we can transform what initially appears as a burden into a valuable asset for the energy sector and the grid.

Collaborative efforts between bitcoin miners, grid operators, and regulatory bodies are essential in this transformation. By working together, these stakeholders can optimize protection schemes, define large flexible load categories, fine-tune ramping configurations, and ensure effective grid interconnections. Moreover, they can work towards making better use of renewable energy sources, capitalizing on stranded energy assets, and enhancing grid resilience.

It's important to keep in mind that regulation in this sector should be fair and beneficial for all. Levying excise taxes or enforcing undue restrictions on bitcoin miners could prove counterproductive, discouraging growth in the energy sector and potentially leading to higher electricity rates for all consumers. On the other hand, nurturing a supportive, technology-neutral regulatory environment can incentivize bitcoin miners to invest in the energy sector and contribute to its growth.

Bitcoin mining, thus, holds enormous potential in shaping the future of our energy ecosystem. By integrating this innovative industry into our energy strategy, we can tap into its transformative potential. Embracing this new paradigm, we can pave the way towards an energy landscape that's not only more efficient and resilient but also more equitable and sustainable. In this future, bitcoin mining will no longer be viewed merely as a consumer of energy but as a valuable participant and contributor to our energy economy.

QR Code to **Chapter 5** Endnote Links and Figures on the Bitcoin Today Coalition website:

211 Bitcoin: A Peer-to-Peer Electronic Cash System – Satoshi Nakamoto The Nakamoto Institute
212 How Bitcoin Mining Can Transform the Energy Industry – J. Mellerud and A. Helseth, Arcane Research
213 The Signal & the Nonce – K. Helmy, L. Nuzzi, A. Mead, and K. Waters, Coin Metrics
214 Bitcoin Net Zero – N. Carter and R. Stevens, NYDIG
215 Texas Work Group on Blockchain Matters Report – TX BCWG
216 How Bitcoin Mining Can Transform the Energy Industry – J. Mellerud and A. Helseth, K33 Research
217 High resolution modeling and analysis of cryptocurrency mining's impact on power grids: Carbon footprint, reliability, and electricity price – A. Menati, X. Zheng, K. Lee, R. Shi, P. Du, C. Singh, and L. Xie, Science Direct
218 Modeling and Analysis of Utilizing Cryptocurrency Mining for Demand Flexibility in Electric Energy Systems: A Synthetic Texas Grid Case Study – A. Menati, K. Lee, L. Xie, IEEE Xplore
219 December 2022 Cold Weather Operations: Preliminary Observations – Dan Woodfin, ERCOT Public
220 Optimization of Cryptocurrency Miners' Participation in Ancillary Service Markets – A. Menati, Y. Cai. R El Helou, C. Tian, and L. Xie, ARXIV
221 Physical and Economic Viability of Cryptocurrency Mining for Provision of Frequency Regulation: A Real-World Texas Case Study – R El Helou, A. Menati, and L. Xie, ARXIV
222 Webinar: ERCOT Contingency Reserve Service (ECRS) – P. Du, ESIG
223 Two Weeks of Firsts in Texas: ECRS and New Records – Grid Status
224 Efficiency of Bitcoin Mining Hardware – IEA
225 Economics of Immersion Cooling for Bitcoin Miners – Braiins
226 Optimization of Cryptocurrency Miners' Participation in Ancillary Service Markets – A. Menati, Y. Cai. R El Helou, C. Tian, and L. Xie, ARXIV
227 Texas Legislature Looks to Solidify State's Role as Bitcoin Mining Hub – Kyle Torpey, Yahoo Finance
228 Non-intrusive Monitoring of Edge-level Cryptocurrency Mining in Power Distribution Grids – R. Shi, A. Menati, and L. Xie, IEEE Xplore
229 Tesla, Block and Blockstream Team up to Mine Bitcoin off Solar Power in Texas – MacKenzie Sigalos, CNBC
230 Can Bitcoin Stop Climate Change? Proof of Work, Energy Consumption and Carbon Footprint (SoK) – J. Ibanez and A. Freier, ARXIV

CHAPTER 6

NUCLEAR POWER PLANTS AND BITCOIN MINING: SYNERGIES FOR A CLEAN ENERGY TRANSITION

By Lindsey Daley

Lindsey Daley *commissioned through Navy ROTC at the University of Rochester with a degree in Computer Science, going on to serve as a Submarine Officer just a few years after the Navy authorized women to serve aboard submarines in 2010. Following rigorous study of the nuclear engineering principles required to operate the nuclear reactors onboard, Lindsey completed multiple Strategic Deterrent deployments on ballistic missile submarines. Lindsey entered into the bitcoin mining industry directly after transitioning out of the Navy, working in multiple roles directing operations for large-scale energy infrastructure and bitcoin mining endeavors. She currently serves as Network Operations Center Manager for Marathon Digital Holdings, overseeing operations and analytics for Marathon's global bitcoin mining facilities.*

Nuclear Power Generation: Nuclear Reactor Plants

While nuclear power generation might appear intimidating due to its underlying physics, the core concepts are surprisingly comprehensible.

At its essence, nuclear power harnesses the energy released from nuclear fission, releasing energy in the form of heat and radiation. A basic pressurized water reactor plant utilizes radioactive fuel, most commonly Uranium or Plutonium, which undergoes controlled fission, generating a significant amount of energy. These reactions will induce further fission from the surrounding atoms, creating a chain reaction of heat generation that characterizes the self-sustaining nature of a nuclear reactor.[231] Coolant travels over the fuel area and captures the heat from this process exactly like the coolant in a car absorbs heat from the engine. Instead of transferring the heat to the air through a radiator, the coolant in a nuclear reactor travels to a boiler in a closed system where steam is produced to drive turbines and ultimately generate electricity. Reactors also have control rods comprised of a neutron-absorbing material which will prevent the chain reaction from continuing; lowering the rods cause the reactor to reduce output or shut down completely.[232]

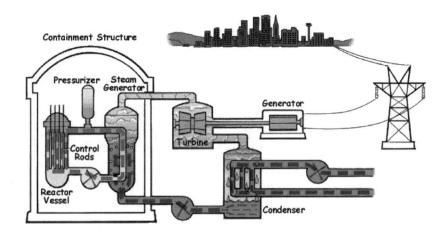

(Figure 49: The Pressurized Water Reactor (PWR) 2017).[233]

Nuclear Power Generation: Radiation

Prior to discussing radiation exposure and associated concerns in the following section, we will briefly cover a foundational understanding of radiation, its origins, and its relevance within the realm of energy generation. All atoms consist of a nucleus composed of protons and neutrons, surrounded by electrons. The positive and negative charges of the nucleus and electrons create a balanced system by releasing excess energy. For certain atoms, such as a Uranium isotope used in reactor fuel, a collision with a neutron disturbs this equilibrium, leading the atom to split and release that radiation and heat we use for electricity generation.[234] This phenomenon of an unstable atom releasing energy in the form of radiation is something that we encounter in everyday life and in a variety of forms.

Even if one is not actively getting an X-ray at the doctor, taking a ride on an airplane, or sitting out in the sun, radiation is encountered in the air we breathe and even the food we eat. While most of the radiation exposure from daily life carries no real risk to our health, it is essential to treat it with respect. Ionizing radiation, the type involved in nuclear power plants, can damage cells depending on the level and duration of exposure. However, the average person's exposure to radiation from living near a nuclear power plant is minimal and comparable to various routine activities like air travel or sun exposure.[235] The average person receives an estimated exposure level of 300 millirem per year from natural background sources; residing within 50 miles of a commercial nuclear power plant exposes a person to an average radiation dose of .01 millirem per year.[236]

In every aspect of the intensely regulated nuclear industry, radiation is monitored and controlled. In addition to strict limits to radiation releases, nuclear plants are held to standards of keeping radiation not just within these limits but "As Low As Reasonably Achievable" (ALARA). The Nuclear Regulatory Commission requires data, sampling, and system verification results to be released on a yearly basis and posts these annual reports online, available to the public.[237]

Just like any other employee working in the nuclear power or radiation industry, I was required to wear dosimetry onboard the submarine at every possible moment to measure the levels of radiation exposure. Despite the years I spent working, living, and sleeping within feet of an operating nuclear reactor for months at a time, I received negligible levels of radiation exposure.

Nuclear Power: Clean, Reliable, Safe

With significant pushback on the arguments surrounding Nuclear energy's clean claims, the summary in this chapter will assess a few common points of contention. This is not meant to be a comprehensive review of the full debate around nuclear, but to bring up useful points to capture a bit of perspective behind those who support the continued operation and development of nuclear energy as a clean, reliable, and safe energy generation source.

1. The mining, milling and enrichment of uranium into nuclear fuel are extremely energy-intensive and result in the emission of carbon dioxide into the atmosphere.

The fission process from a nuclear reactor is able to create energy without producing carbon dioxide (CO_2) or other greenhouse gasses (GHG) that contribute to climate change, similar to wind and solar energy production.[238] However, it also is true that the fuel fabrication process, the construction of materials used, and the decommissioning/dismantling processes in a power plant require energy — also true of solar and wind generation materials. It seems natural to support adoption of these carbon-free renewable energy sources despite the potential GHG emissions involved in the production of solar panels and wind turbines; in order to apply the same assessment to nuclear power, it is vital to assess the entire lifecycle of the power plant and all processes involved.

A 2022 study conducted by the United Nations Economic Commission for Europe assessed sources of energy generation with respect to their life cycle impacts in order to allow evaluation of energy technologies across a wide range of environmental indicators. For nuclear power, this included fuel element supply chain (from extraction to fuel fabrication), core processes (construction/decommissioning/operation of the plant), and back end processes (spent fuel management, storage, final repository). The study concludes that although there are a variety of factors to be considered, nuclear power's lifecycle emissions are estimated between 5.1 - 6.4 g CO_2 eq. /kWh on a global average, with wind and solar power averaging, respectively, 7.8 and 8.0 g CO_2 eq./kWh and above. In comparison, solar and wind technologies are also low in GHG emissions but not below nuclear due to its long lifecycle and large capacity generation. The study found solar and wind to vary by region, but not below 7.4 (solar) and 7.8 (wind) CO_2 eq/kWh.[239]

The study is an interesting read, diving into depth on other effects of the entire lifecycle of these generation sources including land use, overall human toxicity, etc. Although available data and research methods continue to evolve around these analyses being conducted, the scale at which nuclear power generation appears to scale similarly with other available research. A seemingly more critical study from 2014 assesses lifecycle emissions of nuclear much higher at 66 g CO_2 eq/kWh, but still lining up much closer to their assessment of solar power at 32 g CO_2 eq/kWh rather than the natural gas at 443 g eq/kWh.[240] A visualization from an additional 2014 analysis through the Intergovernmental Panel on Climate Change is included below.

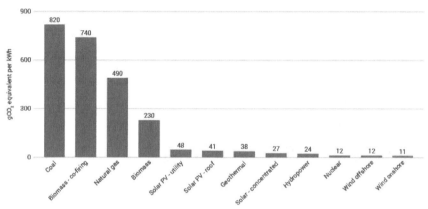

(Figure 50: Average life-cycle carbon dioxide-equivalent emissions for different electricity generators. Source: IPCC)

Although nuclear power plants require a significant amount of energy in their life cycle, a plant produces carbon-free energy at an impressive scale for a long lifetime. When assessed in the perspective of the plant's life cycle and resulting electricity output, nuclear falls in the same area as many favorable renewable resources.

2. Nuclear reactors generate a vast amount of nuclear waste, which remains dangerously radioactive for a long time.

Nuclear power is a valuable source of geographically flexible baseload power that holds great potential in the clean energy space. However, it faces criticism due to the generation of radioactive waste and its non-renewable nature. Although nuclear power plants have extended lifespans before needing to dispose of fuel and materials, concerns about the radioactivity and potential risks to human health persist.

Radioactive waste from nuclear power can vary in intensity, ranging from slightly higher than natural background levels to the higher radioactivity of used (spent) reactor fuel and parts that have undergone fission over the reactor's lifetime.[241] Despite these concerns, the benefits of nuclear power generation stem from its remarkably energy-dense nature, resulting in relatively small amounts of waste. For example, the waste produced from a reactor supplying a person's electricity needs for a year would only be about the size of a brick, with a mere 5 grams of it being high-level waste — equivalent to the weight of a sheet of paper.[242]

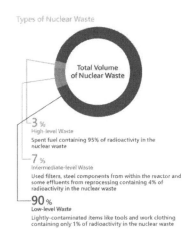

(Figure 51: World Nuclear Association)

To put the scale of radioactive waste into perspective, let's consider spent fuel. In the United States, approximately 2,000 metric tons of spent fuel are generated each year. While this might initially sound substantial, it is equivalent to about half the volume of an Olympic-sized swimming pool, while providing enough clean energy to power more than 70 million homes. Since the 1950s, U.S. commercial reactors have generated around 90,000 metric tons of spent fuel, which could fit on a single football field at a depth of less than 10 yards.[243]

While thought experiments may suggest that radioactive waste is a relatively small industry concern, the nuclear power industry remains committed to reducing these numbers to truly negligible levels. Efforts are underway to use spent nuclear fuel to power new advanced reactors, with fourth-generation reactors seeking to revolutionize waste management by utilizing fuel from existing reactors and stockpiles of depleted uranium, thereby reducing the significance of uranium mining efforts.[244] With continued research and commitment to responsible waste management, nuclear power can play a pivotal role in achieving a sustainable and cleaner energy future.

3. Nuclear reactors are too dangerous.

The safety aspect of nuclear power is a crucial consideration given the two historical catastrophes at nuclear power plants — Chernobyl and

Fukushima — and likely the most important piece involved in public perception around nuclear power. Although I aim to put into context the safety of the nuclear industry despite these incidents, the energy dense nature of nuclear power and the effects of these accidents is not meant to be downplayed in any sense. I can attest that my experience in the Nuclear Navy highlighted the importance of safety in our industry. In addition to learning nuclear reactor engineering principles, we studied and discussed the lessons learned from every possible failure or accident in the nuclear industry. Safety culture is ingrained within the nuclear power world, where engineering flaws and operator errors are openly discussed and used as lessons to enhance safety protocols.

Even with conservative death estimates from major disasters, the confirmed deaths remain relatively low. Chernobyl stands out in its severity and impact, with two worker deaths from the initial blast and 28 fatalities due to acute radiation syndrome in plant staff and emergency workers.[245] Confirmed deaths from longer term effects are more difficult to assess, with higher cases of thyroid cancer observed in those exposed to radiation, but anticipated to be anywhere from 100-400 additional deaths in the future. Reports indicate that the Fukushima disaster did not lead to a discernible increase in cancer rates. The United Nations Scientific Committee on the Effects of Atomic Radiation concluded in 2013 (and reaffirmed in 2015) that "no radiation-related deaths or acute diseases have been observed among the workers and general public exposed to radiation from the accident".[246] Instead, the death toll primarily resulted from the evacuation and long-term displacement caused by the accident.[247]

Overall, the commercial nuclear power industry has incurred over 18,500 cumulative reactor-years of operation in 36 countries, with the aforementioned incidents standing out as the outliers in these operations. In terms of deaths per terawatt-hour (TWh) of electricity, nuclear power ranks in the realm of hydro and wind power, solidifying its position as one of the safest energy sources. Figure 52 uses conservative

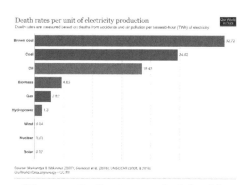

(Figure 52: Death rates per unit of electricity production. Source: Markandya & Wilkinson.)

death tolls from the Chernobyl and Fukushima accidents of 433 and 2314, respectively.

There's a stark disconnect between the safety record touted by proponents of the nuclear industry and the common public perception that nuclear plants are too dangerous to consider. My belief is that the way to reconcile the two is not by brushing aside the mistakes made by the nuclear industry, but instead to dive into it. The book "Atomic Accidents" by James Mahaffey provides a comprehensive and very readable history of nuclear meltdowns and disasters. Accidents are present in any industry, but their significance lies in the lessons they provide for growth and improvement. Embracing these experiences and actively learning from them becomes an essential aspect of progress and development.

Baseload Power and the Clean Energy Transition

The discussion of nuclear and its favorable position in terms of safety, GHG emissions, and environmental impact is not meant to provide an argument against renewable energy sources. On the contrary, many who argue for nuclear's place in the transition towards combating climate change tout its use alongside renewables.

As the world strives to transition towards renewable energy sources in the quest for a zero-carbon future, the focus on negating reliance on fossil fuels has been paramount. In the United States, the shift away from coal and the rapid rise in renewable generation mark significant progress. However, amidst this transition, maintaining grid stability and security emerges as a critical consideration. The role of baseload power generation still plays a crucial role in supporting grid demands consistently throughout the day.

The Pursuit of 100% Clean Energy

In the spring of 2022, California made historic progress in the quest for clean energy by producing enough renewable electricity to meet all of consumer demand for a brief period of time.[248] While the record marks our progress in the path toward a cleaner future, there are still fossil fuels burning throughout the state, and weaning off of them is no simple task. When the sun sets, dropping solar output without a resulting drop in electricity demand, California relies on natural gas power plants and imports from other states.[249]

Baseload electricity generation provides a constant and reliable supply of electricity, meeting the demand regardless of the time such as in the case of natural gas, coal, nuclear, hydropower, and geothermal plants. In contrast, renewable sources such as wind and solar are intermittent, producing energy only when the wind is blowing or the sun is shining. Although some assert that baseload power is not inherently necessary, it is essential to consider the long-term implications and the need for grid stability.

Senate Bill (SB) 100 lays out California's landmark policy establishing targets to reach the goal of 100 percent renewable and zero-carbon resources by 2045. The 2021 SB 100 Joint Agency Report by the California Energy Commission highlights the difficulties in divorcing baseload power generation, stating in its analysis that "natural gas capacity is largely economically retained in the SB 100 core scenario, but fleetwide utilization decreases by half compared to a 60 percent RPS future. The gas fleet is primarily retained because natural gas capacity is the most economic option to provide capacity for reliability needs with the current resource assumptions".[250]

Historically, the energy industry has valued a diverse mix of electricity sources to ensure grid stability and security, mitigating the risks of volatility. Maintaining this emphasis on energy diversification promotes economic growth and energy security, as well as protecting consumers from price spikes. Baseload generating units appear on the cheapest part of the hypothetical electricity market supply curve.

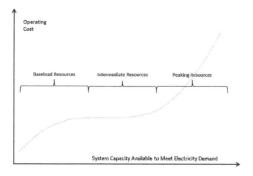

(Figure 53: System capacity available to meet electricity demand.)

Efficiently integrating renewable projects into the grid requires regional coordination, flexible loads, and energy storage to ensure resilient, reliable, and cost-effective power generation. While renewable energy plays a crucial role in reducing carbon emissions, the coexistence of baseload power, particularly nuclear power, remains essential to maintain grid stability and security during the transition to a cleaner energy future.

The journey towards a fully renewable energy-powered world is a noble goal. However, to achieve this vision while ensuring grid stability and security, baseload power generation, like nuclear power, is a necessary component. A diverse electricity mix that values both renewable energy and reliable baseload power sources is crucial for a resilient and sustainable energy grid. By striking the right balance, we can achieve a clean energy transition that safeguards our environment and guarantees a stable power supply for generations to come.

Nuclear Power as a Baseload Source

Nuclear power stands out for its exceptional reliability, boasting an impressive capacity factor of 92.7%. Unlike coal or natural gas, which operate at around 50% capacity factors, nuclear power plants maintain a consistent output. Nuclear plants had 8% share in US capacity in 2021, but produced 19% due to high capacity factor.[251]

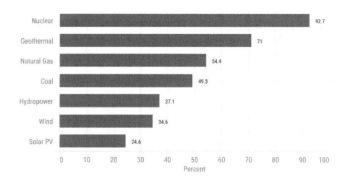

(Figure 54: U.S. capacity factor by energy source - 2021. Source: EIA)

Nuclear power plants require less maintenance and are designed to operate for longer stretches before refueling.[252] It is also the only large-scale power source that can be tapped in even the most extreme weather conditions. The scale of safety required at every nuclear power plant means that they are designed to withstand tornados, hurricanes, floods, and record-breaking winter snow and ice.

As baseload power sources continue to play an important role in supporting the transition efforts towards a cleaner energy technology spread, nuclear power presents a compelling method of providing that reliable power at scale. In addition to being one of the world's largest and most reliable sources of low-carbon electricity, nuclear power requires significantly less area to occupy in order to provide this power.[253] As the world continues to pursue more aggressive methods to reduce GHG emissions, nuclear power is an attractive partner in the quest for a zero-carbon future.

Bitcoin Mining — A New Player in Grid Reliability

Bitcoin's rising global popularity underscores its significance in promoting freedom and security by democratizing finance and empowering individuals with financial autonomy. Increasing institutional adoption of bitcoin further cements its promising outlook.

The energy-intensive process of mining bitcoin has been met with criticism throughout its history, as illustrated by a piece published by the New York Times in April of 2023. The article creates comparisons of electricity usage by bitcoin mines to household consumption and lays out the environment of miners operating smoothly while surrounding households go without power, insinuating that these flexible data centers are stealing residential electricity and causing consumers to go without power.[254]

Additionally, it provides unfounded claims on bitcoin miners' impact on electricity prices for consumers, and mischaracterizes the nature in which miners profit from their ability to curtail at opportune times. Riot Platforms, Inc, named in the article, discusses the distortions in a detailed response to address the misrepresentation of the relationship between their bitcoin mining operations and the Texas grid.[255]

Despite these misguided criticisms infiltrating the media streams, a shift in the narrative around bitcoin mining and its relationship to grid reliability and environmentalism is beginning to be observed. Many in the industry have long professed the beneficial relationship between bitcoin mining and energy consumption,[256] but demonstrating that potential to the mainstream has been a challenge. Contributing to this shift is the effort to improve data visibility in the research of bitcoin mining energy use, highlighting areas where bitcoin's carbon footprint and electricity consumption are being potentially overestimated and misrepresented.[257]

Bitcoin mining processes have many unique flexibilities. Unlike traditional energy consumers, bitcoin mines can be easily located in rural areas where stranded energy resources are abundant, making use of untapped energy that would otherwise go to waste. Demand response programs also highlight the mutually beneficial collaborations between energy providers and bitcoin mining, aiding in grid balancing by curtailing operations when electricity demand is high.[258] Bitcoin miners are already seeking partnerships with renewable generation projects, in a collaboration that prevents wind or solar farms from having to curtail generation when there is more wind or sun available than the electric demand requires for supplying the resulting power.[259,260] Along with the added benefit of providing jobs to rural communities and boosting their tax base, bitcoin mining presents a unique potential to contribute positively to grid stability and renewable energy projects.

Leveraging Nuclear Power and Bitcoin Mining for Clean Energy and Financial Gains

Marrying the objectives of nuclear power and bitcoin mining can create a symbiotic partnership that not only caters to business interests but also contributes significantly to achieving zero-carbon energy goals. This collaboration addresses the challenges faced by nuclear power plants in competing with cheap natural gas and presents a potential revenue stream for unused energy, making it economically attractive. Furthermore, bitcoin mining's demand for zero-carbon energy aligns with the global pursuit of clean energy solutions, and the partnership can foster grid stability and energy security while reducing carbon emissions.

For bitcoin mining companies, we have discussed how nuclear power plants offer a massive amount of zero-carbon energy. The industry faces mounting pressure to reduce its carbon footprint in order to align with goals against climate change. Such partnerships can contribute to bitcoin mining's compliance

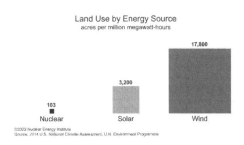

(Figure 55: Land use by energy source. Source: NEI.)

with these goals and enhance its public perception. Nuclear power is an attractive partnership due to its energy-dense and immensely reliable nature of electricity generation. The physical footprint of nuclear energy is small, generating power with 31 times less land than solar facilities and 173 times less land than wind farms.[261]

From the perspective of nuclear power, collaborating with bitcoin miners represents a transformative opportunity to overcome various challenges and advance towards a sustainable future. Despite nuclear power being an economic source of electricity generation when evaluated on a lifetime basis,[262] the financial viability of the industry is impacted by competition from cheap natural gas dominating electricity markets.[263] Through partnerships with bitcoin miners, nuclear power plants gain a stable and committed electricity customer, ensuring a reliable revenue stream for their operations. The steady revenue from these partnerships enhances the economic viability of nuclear projects, facilitating investments in new facilities and infrastructure upgrades.[264]

Secondly, the collaboration with bitcoin miners allows nuclear power plants to utilize their surplus energy. For a plant that typically operates at full capacity,[265] this allows a profitable demand for energy during times when solar and wind are able to provide for the needs of the grid. Nuclear reactors are traditionally designed to operate at their rated capacity rather than scale up and down in order to meet demand.[266] Although nuclear technologies are advancing towards flexible operation of nuclear power plants, as can be seen in France and Germany where load following is already practiced regularly,[267] bitcoin mining provides the opportunity to bridge this need without the development of a new plant. If we consider a grid system with both a nuclear power plant and a renewable source such as solar, energy can flow from the solar plant to consumers while the output is such that it can meet demand, while the nuclear plant powers the bitcoin mine. In times where solar generation falls and demand will exceed the supply, bitcoin miners can quickly curtail their consumption to allow the nuclear power plant to send power to the consumers. In this way, bitcoin mining presents a unique way to bridge the strengths of both energy sources in order to provide a stable and reliable energy grid.

The two industries are already beginning to recognize and embrace these synergies in their operations. Talen Energy announced a partnership with U.S. based bitcoin mining company TeraWulf Inc. to build a bitcoin mining facility adjacent to Talen's nuclear power generation station.[268] Similarly,

Energy Harbor Corp. is embarking on a partnership to couple the bitcoin mining operations of Standard Power to their nuclear facility in Ohio.[269]

Through these partnerships, nuclear power plants contribute to the wider adoption of clean energy technologies and foster public support for nuclear power, helping to dispel common misconceptions and improving its public perception. Both opportunities offer location flexibility and the added benefit of introducing well-paying jobs to communities. By leveraging the unique advantages of nuclear power and the demand for zero-carbon energy from the bitcoin industry, these partnerships hold the potential to drive meaningful progress towards a sustainable and environmentally responsible future.

Challenges in the Nuclear/Bitcoin Partnership

Despite the many synergies between the two industries, and their potential benefit as more nuclear energy providers and bitcoin mining companies seem to be realizing, there are also obstacles to the pursuit of these relationships. In relation to the nuclear industry, the first obstacle is cost. With the stringent safety standards and regulations surrounding nuclear power comes a higher cost involved in the capital expenditure involved with this mining infrastructure compared to pursuing cheaper sources of power. This can be a significant barrier to entry for bitcoin miners and the businesses they operate. However, with the global pressure on the bitcoin industry to reduce their carbon footprint, pursuing these partnerships can still result in ultimately low electricity costs[270] as well as attract investors with ESG concerns.

In order to realize the true benefits of these relationships in the context of a cleaner energy future, these agreements and partnerships must also be strategic in how the relationship will play out. If a bitcoin miner operates adjacent to a nuclear power plant (or a renewable energy source) in order to capitalize on the carbon-free energy and it results in competition with grid resources in a way that the consumer demand needs to be filled by a fossil fuel source, the mining process becomes another obstacle in the road to a zero-carbon future rather than a facilitator. Just as the synergistic integration into the world of renewable energy revolves around bitcoin miners pursuing the vast amount of energy around the world that is stranded or curtailed,[271] nuclear generation and bitcoin mining partnerships should be scrutinized in how they contribute to grid stability and emissions goals.

Despite these challenges, bitcoin mining provides the potential to increase the rate of return on investments and bring additional investors to the zero-carbon power generation industry. Their uniquely flexible and location agnostic nature allows them to be placed in areas where energy providers face issues balancing their grid or exporting power to places that need it. With the global pressure across all industries to decarbonize, the exploration and adoption of relationships with nuclear power providers allows for a potentially symbiotic relationship. The pursuit of these partnerships can aid the ability of nuclear power to compete with cheaper and less clean sources of power, and thus contribute to grid stability and energy diversity while supporting a clean, safe, and reliable energy source.

QR Code to **Chapter 6** Endnote Links and Figures on the Bitcoin Today Coalition website:

231 Nuclear fission and controlled chain reactions – HSC physics, Science Ready
232 Nuclear 101: How does a nuclear reactor work? – Office of Nuclear Energy
233 The Pressurized Water Reactor (PWR) – United States Nuclear Regulatory Commission
234 Radiation Basics – United States Nuclear Regulatory Commission
235 Nuclear Power Plants – United States Environmental Protection Agency
236 Frequently Asked Questions (FAQ) about Radiation Protection – United States Nuclear Regulatory Commission
237 Backgrounder on Environmental Monitoring at Nuclear Power Plants – United States Nuclear Regulatory Commission
238 Nuclear Energy – Anne White, MIT Climate Portal
239 Carbon Neutrality in the UNECE Region: Integrated Life-Cycle Assessment of Electricity Sources – T. Gibon, A. Menacho, and M. Guiton United Nations
240 Assessing the lifecycle greenhouse gas emissions from solar PV and wind energy: A critical meta-survey – D. Nugent, and B. Sovacool, Energy Policy 65, 229-244

241 Nuclear Explained: Nuclear Power and the Environment – U.S. Energy Information Administration
242 What Is Nuclear Waste, and What Do We Do with It? – World Nuclear Association
243 5 Fast Facts about Spent Nuclear Fuel – Office of Nuclear Energy
244 Recycling Gives New Purpose to Spent Nuclear Fuel – Kelsey Adkisson, Pacific Northwest National Laboratory
245 Sources and effects of ionizing radiation – United Nations Scientific Committee on the Effects of Atomic Radiation (UNSCEAR) Reports, II
246 Sources, Effects and Risks of Ionizing Radiation – United Nations Scientific Committee on the Effects of Atomic Radiation, UNSCEAR 2013 Report to the General Assembly with Scientific Annexes (2013) (Vol. I)
247 Fukushima Daiichi Accident FAQ – World Nuclear Association
248 California Just Ran on 100% Renewable Energy, but Fossil Fuels Aren't Fading Away Yet – Lauren Sommer, NPR
249 California State Energy Profile – U.S. Energy Information Administration
250 2021 SB 100 Joint Agency Report: Achieving 100 percent clean electricity in California: an initial assessment – L. Gill, A. Gutierrez, and T Weeks, California Energy Commission
251 What Is Generation Capacity? – Office of Nuclear Energy
252 Nuclear Power Is the Most Reliable Energy Source and It's Not Even Close – Office of Nuclear Energy
253 Comparison of the Performance, Advantages and Disadvantages of Nuclear Power Generation Compared to Other Clean Sources of Electricity – J. da Mata, R. Neto, and A. Mequita, 2017 International Nuclear Atlantic Conference
254 The Real-World Costs of the Digital Race for Bitcoin – Gabriel Dance, The New York Times
255 Riot Platforms, Inc. statement in response to The New York Times' Politically Driven Attack on Bitcoin Mining Is Full of Distortions & Outright Falsehoods – Riot Platforms, Inc.
256 How Bitcoin Mining Strengthens Electricity Grids – Mike Hobart, Bitcoin Magazine
257 Bitcoin Electricity Consumption: An Improved Assessment – Alexander Neumueller, University of Cambridge Judge Business School
258 Demand response provides a competitive edge through optimal crypto mining energy consumption – David Chernis, CPower
259 Why no one saw the success of demand response coming Jemma Green, Forbes
260 Bitcoin Mining Is Set to Turn Greener – Rohan Reddy, Global X
261 Nuclear Needs Small Amounts of Land to Deliver Big Amounts of Electricity – Emma Derr, Nuclear Energy Institute
262 Economics of Nuclear Power – World Nuclear Association
263 MIT: Cheap Gas, Not Renewables, Caused Nuclear Woes – Robert Walton, Utility Dive
264 Talen Energy Teaming up with TeraWulf Inc. To Build Bitcoin Mining Facility – Penn's Northeast
265 Keeping the Balance: How Flexible Nuclear Operation Can Help Add More Wind and Solar to the Grid – Ivy Pepin, MIT News
266 Nuclear-Renewable Hybrid Energy Systems – International Atomic Energy Agency
267 Load-Following with Nuclear Power Plants – A. Lokhov, Nuclear Energy Agency News
268 Talen Energy Corporation Announces Zero-Carbon Bitcoin Mining Joint Venture with TeraWulf Inc – Talen Energy, PR Nnewswire
269 Energy Harbor and Standard Power to Develop Nuclear Energy Data Infrastructure – Energy Harbor, PR Newswire Accessed 4 Oct. 2023
270 TeraWulf Starts Nuclear-Powered Bitcoin Mining with Nearly 8,000 Rigs at Nautilus Facility – Eliza Gkritsi, Coindesk
271 Can Crypto Miners Make the World Greener? – E. Gkritsi and S. Handagama, Coindesk

CHAPTER 7

CHINA'S CRYPTO BAN: HOW DECENTRALIZED NETWORKS REACT TO HOSTILE POLICY INTERVENTIONS

By Major Gabriel Royal, PhD

Major Gabriel Royal, PhD *is an Instructor of American Politics in the Department of Social Sciences at the United States Military Academy at West Point. His research focuses on American public finance and cryptocurrency/digital asset public policy. Gabe commissioned as an Army Aviation officer in 2012. He served as an attack aviation platoon leader in Afghanistan and as a company commander in Iraq. He holds a Ph.D. in Public Policy and Administration, an M.P.A. from The George Washington University, and a B.S. in U.S. History and American Politics from West Point. Gabe lives in New Windsor, NY with his wife, Michelle, and their son, Caleb.*

Introduction

The field of public policy lacks studies examining the impacts of exogenous policy shocks to organizations and/or assets which run on decentralized network consensus mechanisms (e.g., decentralized autonomous organizations, public blockchain-based cryptocurrencies). These organizations attempt to replace the hierarchical, centralized structure of traditional institutions with an open network. They use smart contracts embedded into code to govern the allocation of resources, assign roles and responsibilities, and automate processes. *This study asks, "How did the bitcoin network change after China's cryptocurrency mining ban?" to fill that gap.*[272]

After providing some background information, this chapter establishes, defines, and explains the significance of key metrics of cryptocurrency asset viability. On-chain data from the bitcoin blockchain, cryptocurrency exchange pricing data, and IP address-based geolocational data speak to network security and decentralization, perceptions of bitcoin's value as an asset, and its utility as a medium of exchange. I then use statistical analyses to compare those metrics before and after the policy intervention to describe the ex-ante and ex-post states of the bitcoin network and explore whether ex-post changes correlate with the timing of China's mining ban. The ban serves as an opportunity to see how the digital-automated aspects of bitcoin's core software compensate and/or adapt to a sudden loss of computational power. The actions of cryptocurrency miners displaced from China provide insights into the decision-making calculus of the network's human element relative to host nation-state cryptocurrency policy disposition.

Background

The cryptocurrency-state relationship is a complex one. Blockchains are fundamentally disintermediated, transnational, and resilient. They enable anonymous exchanges of value and data transfer, and they lack specific legal and policy frameworks for addressing them comprehensively.[273] Prasad echoes the concerns of many economists in imploring U.S. policymakers to consider whether the combination of stablecoins, cryptocurrencies, and CBDCs could threaten macroeconomic stability, U.S. monetary sovereignty, and existing national currencies.[274] Others believe this new technology can revolutionize financial transactions and create a new form of apolitical international economics.[275] Aside from the potential economic implications of cryptocurrency development, the physical nature of mining operations yields environmental policy concerns about energy use and greenhouse gas emissions.[276] Finally, the digital assets themselves can help facilitate illicit finance and present a host of questions about how they should be treated (i.e., regulated) as financial instruments when used legally.[277]

These policy implications led President Biden to call for a review of digital assets among all federal agencies dealing in financial regulation to develop a comprehensive, interagency approach to addressing DeFi.[278] The order comes at a time when the United States is now the world leader in energy-intensive bitcoin mining by global share of network hashrate and several DeFi products and cryptocurrency exchanges are the subjects of government-led litigation.[279] As for non-state cryptocurrencies on public blockchains (e.g., bitcoin), the order focuses on the energy, climate, and pollution impacts of cryptocurrency mining. The subsequent White House Office of Science and Technology Policy report on 'crypto-assets,' climate, and energy proposes no specific policy prescriptions but recommends Congress and the Biden administration "might consider legislation to limit or eliminate the use of high energy intensity consensus mechanisms for crypto-asset mining" should other methods of regulation (e.g., establishing environmental evidence and performance-based standards for mining) prove ineffective.[280]

A country-wide ban on cryptocurrency is not unique to China, but it is still an extreme approach to cryptocurrency policy relative to the rest of the world. According to a Thomson Reuters study, cryptocurrency use is highly restricted or completely illegal in just thirteen countries.[281] As more countries and territories establish laws, regulations, and policies specific to cryptocurrency, subsequent studies might analyze the relationship between regime type and cryptocurrency restrictions. So far, authoritarian regimes are more likely to restrict cryptocurrency use and legality. Of the 13 countries where cryptocurrency is illegal or heavily restricted by law, only one is considered "free".[282]

Despite similar environmental and regulatory concerns about cryptocurrency use, the United States' approach to cryptocurrency regulation stands in stark contrast to China's. Dion sees the U.S. following long-standing precedent of recognizing other legal currencies or mediums of exchange.[283] The dollar remains the country's legal tender, but the law does not require the exclusive use of dollars in the exchange of goods and services. The Federal Reserve has regulations designed to monitor and regulate banking and lending practices where the PBOC has a wider scope for issuing laws and regulations designed to maintain tight control on capital.[284] Xie argues the Chinese approach is designed to "maintain existing regulatory consistency and conserve institutional resources," and that the U.S. is more comfortable with folding technological ambiguity into existing legal frameworks wherever possible.[285] Another possibility is that China views blockchain technology as an opportunity to seize a geopolitical monetary advantage with their own CBDC and views other cryptocurrencies as competitors.

Measuring Cryptocurrency Asset Viability

Decentralized Autonomous Organizations (DAOs) and digital assets are broadly defined terms encompassing a wide range of network/organizational structures and financialization. The set of relevant public policy concerns necessarily differs for each type of asset. Even a focus on cryptocurrencies alone is too broad in scope for meaningful empirical or theoretical research. Several estimates suggest roughly 20,000 different cryptocurrencies existed as of 2022.[286]

This essay focuses on the impact of China's cryptocurrency ban on bitcoin specifically for several reasons. First, it has the highest market capitalization of any crypto-asset — over twice that of the next highest cryptocurrency by market cap, Ethereum — and it has maintained this dominance since its inception for over a decade.[287] This speaks to its current significance despite the emergence of other cryptocurrencies and its sustained popularity over time. Second, launched in 2009, bitcoin is the original and longest-tenured cryptocurrency.[288] Most importantly, from a research perspective it is the easiest to study due to its data availability. Transactions, wallet addresses, block timing, and other information are all fully transparent and available on the blockchain. Accurate market pricing data have been available since its inception as well.

Describing potential impacts of the Chinese ban on bitcoin requires objective metrics of its utility and viability as a digital asset. This necessitates some examination of both bitcoin's original, expressed purpose (i.e., *what was bitcoin meant to do?*) and its most popular use case currently (i.e., *how do people view/utilize cryptocurrencies today?*).

It is widely accepted that money serves three purposes: 1) a store of value; 2) a medium of exchange; and 3) a unit of account. The bitcoin white paper focuses overwhelmingly on the mechanics of functioning as a medium of exchange.[289] Nakamoto set out to establish "an electronic payment system based on cryptographic proof instead of trust, allowing any two willing parties to transact directly with each other without the need for a trusted third party".[290] The white paper briefly explains the intent of having an eventual hard cap on the number of coins in circulation to be "completely inflation free" but otherwise mentions value only in the context of transactions or as it pertains to incentivizing good behavior.[291]

Today, bitcoin is clearly used as both a medium of exchange and a long-term store of value. In 2022, the bitcoin network processed between 200,000 and

300,000 transactions/day for most of the year on its base layer.[292] However, hundreds of thousands of small payments between vendors and customers transacting in bitcoin now take place on the Lightning Network — a 'Layer 2' protocol designed to facilitate micropayments and free up traffic on bitcoin's base layer blockchain.[293]

But the majority of bitcoin in circulation remains in the hands of long-term holders, defined as users who have bought and held their bitcoin for at least six months. Since 2019, on-chain data shows 70% and 80% of all bitcoin supply has been held by long-term holders.[294] Despite several bear market periods in which the market price of bitcoin has dropped over 60% in a short period of time, long-term holders rarely divest their bitcoin holdings. Data shows the most committed holders typically acquire more bitcoin during periods of low prices.

Table 1 is a summary of key metrics of bitcoin's viability as a financial instrument: as a store of value and a medium of exchange. Blockchain-based cryptocurrencies with DAO governance are different than other commodities in that their value is so closely tied to the health of the network which processes transactions and runs core software.[295] If gold mining and bullion exchanges ceased to exist, gold would retain its intrinsic value and individuals could still find ways to trade it, if needed. But bitcoin miners effectively execute all base layer transactions. For this reason, several metrics in Table 1 have to do with the distribution and security of different aspects of the bitcoin network.

Metric	Units	Data Source	Description
Total Network Hashrate	TH/s	Blockchain Explorer	The amount of computing power dedicated to mining across the entire Bitcoin network
Country Share of Hashrate	% per country/month	CBECI	The amount of computing power dedicated to mining by country
Mining Pool Hashrate Distribution	% blocks/day	blockchain.com	% of blocks mined by each pool
Market Price	$USD	Yahoo! Finance	daily closing price of 1 BTC denominated in USD
Transactions per second	transactions/sec (7-day moving avg.)	Coin Metrics	average number of Bitcoin transactions processed per second per day
Block Time	minutes	BitInfo Charts	daily average of time between blocks added to the blockchain
Nodes Online*	# nodes	bitnodes.io	number of reachable nodes verifying transactions
Nodes by Country*	%	bitnodes.io	% distribution of nodes by country

(Figure 56: Measures of bitcoin network security, health, and distribution.)

Design of the Natural Experiment

The nature of the treatment in this natural experiment — the Chinese cryptocurrency ban — is multifaceted and requires clarification regarding the kind of knowledge that can be gleaned from pre/post statistical analyses. The first aspect of China's ban was announced on May 18, 2021, targeting financial institutions participating in "business related to virtual currency."[296] Three days later, a forthcoming ban on cryptocurrency mining was announced, but not formally instituted across all of China until June. The final aspect of the ban barring any form of cryptocurrency exchange took effect in September.

The timing of the three different aspects of the ban, and gaps between announcements and formal implementation complicates claims of causality and the identification of causal mechanisms therein. For example, the first aspect of the ban was the third of three such crackdowns (2013, 2017, 2021) specific to financial institutions. Following the 2013 and 2017 announcements, the price of bitcoin dropped over 30% within the next 10 days. Price action following the announcement of the forthcoming mining ban was likely impacted by the financial institution aspect of the ban and a host of other potential contributing factors which are difficult to control for. Bitcoin's price tumbled 13% from $56,700 to $49,100/BTC in one day after electric-vehicle maker Tesla announced it would no longer accept bitcoin as a form of payment on May 12. When the PBOC's expanded ban on financial institutions was announced six days later, the price of bitcoin was already down almost 15% from the previous day, closing at roughly $37,000/BTC. For some metrics (e.g., total network hashrate, country share of network hashrate), drawing a causal relationship between the ban and changes to that metric are clearer than others (e.g., market price), but most of the analysis in this study is necessarily descriptive and correlational.

This study focuses on the mining aspect of the ban and relies on statistical analyses of several bitcoin metrics to paint a picture of the bitcoin network before and after miners in China were ordered to shut down their operations. The mining aspect of the ban represents the greatest departure from previous Chinese policy positions. Mining is also critical to bitcoin's use as a medium of exchange. The crackdown specific to crypto-related financial services is not insignificant, but bitcoin was designed to facilitate value exchange without the involvement of third-party intermediaries (i.e., financial services industry).

Furthermore, the financial services ban did not constitute a stark change in China's cryptocurrency policy disposition. The third and final aspect of the ban clearly states all "virtual currency-related activities are illegal financial activities" which represents some departure from previous policies which allowed private Chinese citizens to continue trading cryptocurrencies.[297] But China had already prohibited the exchange of fiat currency for cryptocurrency and barred Chinese financial services industries from facilitating such cryptocurrency trading in China four years prior.[298] The only new specified "virtual currency-related [activity]" in the order which had not been barred prior to September 2021 was the "[exchange] of one virtual currency for another."[299]

The policy intervention is also designated as a period (May '21 through June '21) rather than a single point in time. As previously mentioned, evidence suggests some miners in certain provinces began shuttering operations as early as April 2021, but news reports of the forthcoming ban broke in May before the formal ban was implemented in June. Starting with the one-year period (May '20 through April '21) before PBOC's crypto ban allows us to build an ex-ante profile of the overall condition of the bitcoin network by each metric before the policy intervention. The period for ex-post analysis of network conditions is designated as the one-year period (July '21 through June '22) when dislocated miners found new hosting sites outside of China. Data for all metrics in Table 1 is available from May 2020 through June 2022 except for *country share of hashrate* since locational mining data from the Cambridge Bitcoin Electricity Consumption Index (CBECI) has only been published through January 2022.

Summary of Quantitative Analysis

During the 12-month *ex-ante* period before China's cryptocurrency ban, hashrate generally increased by 154,000 TH/s per day.[300] After approaching a new all-time high on May 13, 2021, China's massive share of global hashrate came offline in the span of just two months. Network hashrate crashed from 186 million TH/s to just 58 million TH/s on June 27. But bitcoin's mining difficulty — which adjusts every 2016 blocks — dropped on July 3 making it easier for miners based elsewhere.[301] Older, less efficient mining equipment suddenly became profitable.[302] No evidence exists that a serious 51% attack was attempted during the intervention period, despite half the network hashrate coming offline. Hashrate recovered at a rate of 281,000 TH/s per day during the *ex-post* period, surpassing the previous all-time high by early December 2021. Average daily block time actually decreased during the *ex-post* period.

Table 2. Statistical Analyses of Key Metrics (before/after the ban)

Metric	Descriptive/OLS Statistic	ex-ante	ex-post	Paired two-sample t-test results	
Total Network Hashrate (TH/s)	mean (TH/s)	134.648	172.058	t-statistic	-24.6614
	variance	445.272	1621.460	P(T<=t) two-tail	1.1815E-79
	observations	365	365		
	slope (standard error)	0.1541 (.0067)	0.3473 (.0083)		
	R-squared	0.5936	0.8281		
Non Top-4 Mining Pool Hashrate (%)	mean	50.13%	44.30%	t-statistic	14.1805
	variance	0.0022	0.0037	P(T<=t) two-tail	1.19925E-36
	observations	365	365		
Market Price ($/BTC)	mean ($/BTC)	24369.43	42954.46	t-statistic	-13.6103
	variance	326612577.57	107511232.74	P(T<=t) two-tail	2.1794E-34
	observations	365	365		
	slope (standard error)	153.61 (3.98)	-47.46 (4.52)		
	R-squared	0.8043	0.2333		
Transactions per second	mean	3.570	2.943	t-statistic	29.2410139
	variance	0.147	0.128	P(T<=t) two-tail	1.45542E-97
	observations	365	365		
	slope (standard error)	-0.00034 (.00019)	0.00053 (.00018)		
	R-squared	0.0086	0.0248		
Average Daily Block Time (minutes)	mean	10.054	9.858	t-statistic	2.4675
	variance	1.456	1.012	P(T<=t) two-tail	0.0141
	observations	365	365		

(Figure 57: Statistical analyses of key metrics before/after the ban.)

Table 2 compares only the one-year *ex-ante* and *ex-post* periods using a paired two-sample t-test of means and the ordinary least squares method of a linear best fit for total network hashrate, market price, and transactions per second.[303] A low p-value provides some support for claims that the treatment effect had a significant impact on mean hashrate between the two periods. In fact, mean hashrate increased during the year following the intervention period. Hashrate increased at a faster rate after the ban, and OLS statistics indicate the regression model provides a better explanation for the higher variance seen in the *ex-post* year than the year prior.

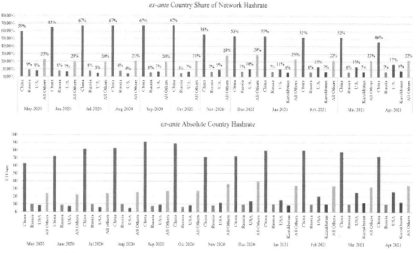

(Figure 58.1 Ex-ante country share of network hashrate (top))[304]
(Figure 58.2 Ex-ante absolute levels of country network hashrate (bottom))

Both CBECI data (Figures 58.1 and 58.2) and news reports indicate a disproportionately large share of bitcoin's network hashrate was based in China prior to instituting a complete ban on cryptocurrency mining. Quantitative evidence supports claims that the mining ban played a significant role in the unprecedented drop in network hashrate between May and July 2021 as China-based miners shut down operations and began to relocate. However, the drop in network hashrate cannot be entirely explained by the loss of China-based hashrate. Monthly network hashrate grew in absolute terms through May 2021 while China's absolute hashrate began its decline in March. Total network hashrate dropped by 41.1 EH/sec from May to June, while China's absolute hashrate decreased only 29.9 EH/sec over the same period (Table 3).

Table 3. China and Total Network Hashrate Around the Policy Intervention					
	March	April	May	June	July
Total Network Hashrate (monthly avg., EH/sec)	159.6	157.2	161.2	120.1	100.4
Change from previous month (EH/sec)		-2.4	4.0	-41.1	-19.7
% Change from previous month		-1%	3%	-26%	-16%
China monthly absolute hashrate	78.3	72.4	71.0	41.1	0
Change from previous month (EH/sec)		-5.9	-1.4	-29.9	-41.1
% Change from previous month		-8%	-2%	-42%	-100%

(Figure 59: China and total network hashrate around the policy intervention.)

Bitcoin's sudden decline in market value during this period likely contributed to network hashrate losses. While hashrate does not typically correlate with bitcoin's market price, studies suggest there may be some unidirectional causal relationship from bitcoin price to hashrate, just as oil and gas revenues/losses drive the purchase/shut down of rigs.[305]

Miner revenues are tied to bitcoin's market value, so miners with less efficient ASICs can often afford to keep their machines on when the price of bitcoin is high. These miners will keep less efficient ASICs running so long as the price of energy is below the breakeven price at which they know their machines will be profitable.[306] All else being equal, more efficient mining machines effectively raise this breakeven price of energy. As bitcoin prices drop, the rational, but less efficient miners will be forced to turn off their machines while more efficient miners continue to be profitable.[307]

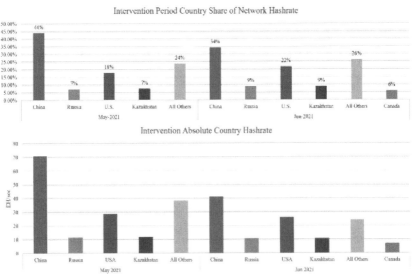

(Figure 60.1 Intervention country share of network hashrate (top)[308]
(Figure 60.2 Intervention absolute levels of country network hashrate (bottom)

Absolute hashrate CBECI data suggests China-based mining was virtually non-existent in July and August 2021 and then 30 EH/sec suddenly came back online in September 2021. The amount of power and physical infrastructure required to support mining that much hashrate means the likelihood that those operations shut down, moved, and subsequently returned is highly improbable.[309] The more likely explanation is that CBECI's data collection methods lead to useful estimations of geolocational mining distribution but fall short of meeting a reliable enough standard to justify robust empirical support for causal analysis.

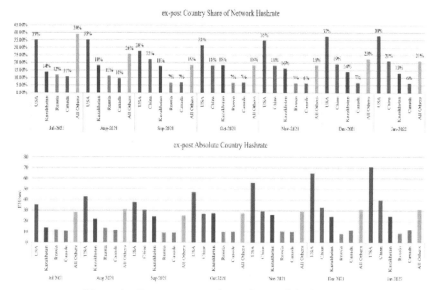

(Figure 61.1 Ex-post country share of network hashrate (top)
(Figure 61.2 Ex-post country share of network hashrate (bottom)

Still, the Cambridge Center for Alternative Finance (CCAF) maintains IP address tracking limitations usually "only moderately impact" the validity of CBECI estimates unless "sudden shocks" occur which alter miner risk tolerance and expectations.310 They argue China's ban represents such a shock which prompted "a non-trivial share of Chinese miners" to operate covertly with foreign proxies (high in network latency) until determining local proxy services (relatively lower in network latency) offered sufficient protection from Chinese state enforcement.311 This theory is supported by anecdotal evidence from several news reports.312 Regardless of how exactly miners obfuscate their locations, quantitative and qualitative evidence show large-scale mining operations still exist in China, calling the ban's efficacy and/or China's enforcement mechanisms into question.

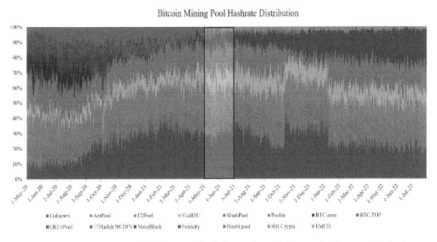

(Figure 62: Percentage of blocks won daily by major mining pools. Source: Author)[313]

Figure 62 shows the percentage of blocks won daily by major mining pools from May 2020 through July 2022.[314] While the share of blocks won by specific pools certainly changes, the overall distribution remains consistent throughout the time around China's ban, with no single pool amassing more than 31.5% of network hashrate at any time.[315]

Table 2 includes a comparison of the means of the daily percentage of blocks won by all miners outside the top four most dominant pools during the *ex-ante* and *ex-post* periods. Though no single mining pool approached the 50% threshold, the top four mining pools became more dominant after the ban. Prior to the mining ban, miners outside the top four mining pools were responsible for half the blocks won compared to 44% after the ban. If this trend continues, independent miners and smaller mining pools are less likely to win block rewards and pressure to join a dominant mining pool will increase. However, there is no reason to suspect China's mining ban is responsible for this trend. Three of the top four dominant mining pools during both the *ex-ante* (AntPool, F2Pool, and Poolin) and *ex-post* (AntPool, F2Pool, ViaBTC) periods are based in China. AntPool and F2Pool remained in the top four during the *ex-post* period and Poolin continued to win a significant number of daily blocks.[316] ViaBTC, headquartered in Shenzhen, China, was a top-four miner during the *ex-post* period as well.[317]

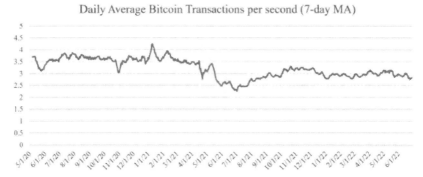

(Figure 63: Average daily bitcoin transactions per second, 7-day moving average. Source: Author)[318]

Figure 63 shows the 7-day moving average of the daily average of bitcoin transactions per second to present a smoother depiction of the metric over time, but the t-test and OLS trend statistics in Table 2 use the daily averages only. OLS modeling accounts for little variation in daily averages (r-squared) when removing the moving average component. However, the t-test of the means indicates a significant difference between transactions per second before and after the ban. Before the ban, an average of 3.57 bitcoin transactions were processed every second compared to just 2.94 during the *ex-post* period.

The use of bitcoin as a payment system on the base layer is still a long way away from all-time highs in December 2017, but it may have something to do with the advent of bitcoin's 'Layer 2' protocol, better known as the 'Lightning Network.' The "Blockchain Trilemma" is the idea that the design of any decentralized network involves tradeoffs between security, decentralization, and scalability. The Lightning Network was invented to solve bitcoin's scalability problem and break the Blockchain Trilemma by establishing a series of peer-to-peer micropayment channels between users to facilitate payments and unburden the main blockchain.[319] Because these transactions occur off-chain, reliable data on exactly how many transactions occur is hard to approximate. One study estimates over 120,000 payment channels opened between January 2018 and July 2019,[320] which would help explain the drop in average daily bitcoin transactions (Figure 5).

Key Findings and Implications for Policymakers

Current approaches to cryptocurrency regulation across countries and jurisdictions vary based on existing and precedent-setting regulatory frameworks, the domestic cryptocurrency activity within each country, and each government's general disposition towards strict or flexible financial regulation.[321] Historically, the United States and China have adopted different approaches towards currency and the role of the state in regulating new forms of value exchange. We should not expect the United States to mirror China's approach to cryptocurrency regulation, but policy analysts should objectively consider the merits of their aggressive approach. The specific research questions of this study are aimed at determining what impacts China's mining ban had on bitcoin. But the macro implications of this essay speak to whether the policies of a single government can influence the behavior, actions, value of a highly decentralized autonomous organization. These findings include both analysis specific to bitcoin as it relates to the China ban and what it might mean for cryptocurrency policy more broadly.

1. Nation-state policies may impact cryptocurrency values over the short-term, but evidence suggests bitcoin recovers from price drops and retains its value over time.

First, there is little to no evidence to suggest the ban impacted bitcoin as a store of value over the long term. Other studies suggest the announcement of adverse state policies in the past negatively impacted bitcoin's market price over the short-term.[322] While the price of bitcoin dropped after the ban was announced, it recovered to new all-time highs within four months. Perhaps China's 2021 mining ban had the same effect as other past announcements of adverse state policy. But major news specific to institutional adoption of bitcoin (i.e., Tesla's announcement), broader macroeconomic dynamics, and bitcoin's history of sudden downside price volatility make determining causal mechanisms difficult in this case.

Nakamoto touted bitcoin as an innovation in monetary policy which could offer people a hedge against "the arbitrary inflation risk of centrally managed currencies".[323] But the volatility in bitcoin's price action has made it so that only long-term holders willing to endure massive unrealized gains and losses could possibly view it that way. Bitcoin has suffered price drops of 40% or more in a four-month span seven times since 2011.[324] Still, policymakers should not expect wild price swings to threaten the long-term appeal of bitcoin. Even if bitcoin performs more like a speculative stock than a true inflation hedge, its risk-adjusted rate of return over time has been strong enough to keep long-term holders from selling their holdings.[325] Bitcoiners clearly see strong enough fundamentals to endure over 70% losses, so *market price* cannot be the only metric of asset value, although it is the most obvious place to start.

Hashrate is a key metric of network security in bitcoin. Much of the asset's value is tied to whether bitcoin works as intended. Aggregate network hashrate establishes a threshold for the mining control bad actors would need to add invalid blocks to the chain or alter transactions. The distribution of both where that hashrate is based geographically and how much individual mining pools control are matters of decentralization also critical to network security. While multiple sources of quantitative and qualitative evidence point to miners using proxy services to obfuscate their locations, China-based miners were responsible for the majority of network hashrate throughout the pre-ban period and the ban resulted in most of that hashrate coming offline for some time. Drops in aggregate network hashrate occur during the intervention through some combination of the loss of China's hashrate (Table 3) and less efficient miners being forced offline due to tightened profit margins as bitcoin's market value dropped. Top mining pools became somewhat more powerful after the ban, but no single pool came close to controlling 51% of total hashrate.

The rapid recovery of overall network hashrate during the ex-post period is the most significant policy takeaway for consideration from this study. Increases in hashrate based outside of China before the ban resumed during the ex-post period. Both CBECI geolocational data and aggregate hashrate data show a robust and sustained recovery to previous highs in just four months. Through some combination of rapid miner relocation and increases in absolute hashrate already underway at the time of the ban, the broader mining network supporting bitcoin proved quite resilient.

This calls the limits of unilateral state action into question when it comes to affecting geographically distributed DAOs. Bitcoin is far from immune to broader negative economic market sentiments and further still from serving as a hedge against inflation under a three-year time horizon. Macroeconomic trends, news regarding institutional adoption, and/or nation-state policy still has a significant ability to damage perceptions of bitcoin's value (i.e., *market price*), even as network fundamentals and measures of its intrinsic value (i.e., *network hashrate*) remain solid. Again, because aggregate hashrate is critical to the network's ability to defend against attacks in proof-of-work based systems, it serves as a proxy for the network's intrinsic value. It speaks to how much energy the network is dedicating to the asset's security. Impacting network fundamentals like total hashrate would likely require coordinated action by nation-states since the ability to locate nodes and mining operations which drive network success anywhere help make DAOs resilient to geographically-isolated policy.

Federalism presents special challenges to such coordinated action within the United States. Policymaker attitudes towards cryptocurrency mining vary across states and local governments. We can expect states with deregulated energy markets, relatively low energy prices, and crypto-friendly policy dispositions (e.g., Texas) to continue attracting cryptocurrency mining companies. Resilience in the market value of bitcoin makes it economically rational for miners to operate at maximum capacity most of the time.[326] Absent some intervention, miners will continue to operate their equipment so long as bitcoin's market value continues to facilitate high breakeven energy prices. In such deregulated environments, economic incentives become the only real governor of mining activity. Miners' demonstrated willingness to relocate to crypto-friendly regions means the current state-by-state, piecemeal approach to cryptocurrency mining regulation in the United States may do little to affect country-wide mining behavior over the long term.

2. Bitcoin's difficulty adjustment embedded in its core software makes it more resilient to adverse events (e.g., sudden loss of network hashrate).

Hashrate also plays a role in facilitating bitcoin's use as a medium of exchange. Bitcoin's ability to adapt to sudden, massive losses in hashrate is governed by the algorithms in its core software. Difficulty adjustments occur every 2016 blocks, based on the previous 2015 blocks, and difficulty "cannot be altered above [+300% change] or below [-75% change] four times the current difficulty level."[327] In theory, a policy intended to devastate bitcoin's ability to add new blocks and complete new transactions would have to remove a tremendous amount of hashrate early in a 2016-block cycle with near immediacy across several regions where bitcoin operates. Given the robustness of bitcoin's network at this point, this seems almost impossible to do.

China's mining ban — while not designed to destroy bitcoin completely — called for an "orderly phasing out" of cryptocurrency mining in the country.[328] Even with roughly half of bitcoin's hashrate coming offline, it took almost seven weeks to do so, and enough hashrate existed outside of China to keep adding blocks to the chain during the intervention period, albeit slower. Transaction volume decreased somewhat following the ban, indicating reduced use of bitcoin's Layer 1 blockchain for final settlement, but block time returned to normal less than a month after the cryptocurrency mining portion of the ban formally took effect. In total, the ban appears to have no discernible long-term effects on bitcoin's functionality as a medium of exchange.

Researchers and policy analysts at the Federal Reserve, Department of the Treasury, and the Office of the Comptroller of the Currency should consider why people continue to choose decentralized blockchain protocols as a method of value exchange. The technology underlying cryptocurrencies like bitcoin may facilitate efficiencies in final settlement and cross-border payments.[329] This same technology can be leveraged for fiat currencies in the form of CBDCs (e.g., China's eCNY) and/or stablecoins and policymakers must consider the advantages and disadvantages of each. CBDCs already face opposition in the United States primarily due to financial privacy concerns.[330] Both CBDCs and stablecoins may also threaten the stability of the fractional reserve banking system.[331] Rapid, widespread adoption of either CBDCs or stablecoins could impact banknote deposit levels, reserve requirements, and lending costs.[332] But failure to provide a more efficient settlement system for fiat currencies could lead to further adoption of decentralized methods of value exchange outside the purview of state control.

3. The use of proxies and other technologies to obfuscate the locations of various cryptocurrency network-related activities complicates geolocational data analysis and presents a policy enforcement challenge.

CBECI's data collection process suffers from some methodological limitations and this study lacks fidelity on the sources of node activity reporting, but available data indicates the bitcoin network became more evenly geographically distributed in terms of node and mining control (i.e., hashrate) after the ban. If this data is accurate, it indicates the bitcoin network is even less susceptible to the policies of individual nation-states today. But there are several reasons to suspect geolocational data is unreliable, or incomplete at the very least.

This study illuminates several potential cryptocurrency policy enforceability problems caused by widespread use of privacy-enhancing technologies (i.e., VPNs and TOR). CCAF protects miner anonymity at the CBECI application programming interface, recognizes VPN activity in their data — and adjusts estimates accordingly — and relies on the network latency associated with VPN use to discourage IP address spoofing.

But the sudden re-emergence of 30+ EH/sec China-based hashrate in September 2021 points to the limits of these measures in accurately accounting for VPN use. CCAF should provide more details about these limitations and a sensitivity analysis of the parameters involved in determining their estimation if CBECI data is to be empirically useful to policymakers. Policymakers should consider the use of VPNs and TOR to protect the locations of miners and node operators when crafting rules and regulations.[333] Any policy designed to limit or restrict mining and/or cryptocurrency operations would require some degree of non-IP address-based tracking enforcement to be effective.

Policymakers might also consider how to encourage honest and transparent mining practices and data sharing. Use of TOR and VPNs increased during the ex-post period, though this study lacks evidence to support claims of a causal relationship between the ban and increased privacy measures.[334] The privacy of network participants was a chief concern for Nakamoto and early cypherpunks working on bitcoin.[335] It is possible that adverse public policy measures only further incentivize trends towards anonymity and discourage data sharing transparency while putting bitcoin proponents on the defensive. This is counter-productive and disadvantageous to governments looking to implement bitcoin mining policies.

4. Despite the ability to obfuscate their locations, network participants still factor the anticipated local regulatory environment into their decision-making calculus.

Though the results of this study suggest there is little correlation between China's cryptomining ban and long-lasting changes to the bitcoin network, policy environment clearly matters to many cryptominers. Evidence suggests some miners based in China remained there after the ban; either shutting down operations temporarily and restarting or using proxy services to obfuscate their locations until they deemed it safe to return to business as usual.[336] But both quantitative and qualitative evidence shows several major mining operations were dislocated by the ban and specifically sought a more favorable regulatory environment. The United States saw an influx of displaced miners from China and a migration within the country away from states with unfavorable cryptocurrency policy dispositions, simultaneously.[337] Despite the ability to obfuscate their locations, local regulations and policies still factor into bitcoin miner decision-making.[338] Policymakers should consider the merits of more accommodative bitcoin policies, including deregulated energy markets and low barriers of market entry for bitcoin businesses (e.g., Texas). Bitcoin companies can provide jobs, stimulate regional economic growth, and expand the corporate tax base. But these benefits must be weighed against the potential negative impacts of bitcoin mining.

Understanding how digital assets and DAOs function and how they differ from traditional financial instruments and institutions is key to the development of effective policy. The results of this study point to the challenges even large, influential nation-states face when unilaterally implementing policies designed to affect digital assets governed by well-distributed networks. But this study examines policy impacts from the perspective of bitcoin network participants. While the bitcoin network survived and may have even grown more resilient as a result of China's ban, it is entirely possible that the ban served its purposes in the eyes of the PBOC and Chinese Communist Party.

Another study might consider the ban's effectiveness from that perspective, including an analysis of the kind of capital outflows and renminbi circulation China sought to control two years earlier with its State Administration of Foreign Exchange policy without a ban in place.

Finally, this study is mostly quantitative and limited to statistical analyses of newly developed metrics for understanding how these new organizations work. The human element of DAOs (e.g., bitcoin miners) requires a closer qualitative look (e.g., deliberate, semi-structured interviews) than the one included in this essay to unpack the relationship between anticipated regulatory environment and decision-making considerations.

QR Code to **Chapter 7** Endnote Links and Figures on the Bitcoin Today Coalition website:

272   In May 2021, the People's Bank of China (PBOC) prohibited financial institutions from conducting cryptocurrency transactions. The PBOC then banned the mining of cryptocurrency specifically in June. Finally, all forms of cryptocurrency exchange were banned in September 2021 (PBOC 2021). This chapter focuses on the cryptocurrency mining aspect of the ban, specifically.

273   Blockchain and the Law: The Rule of Code – P. DeFilippi and A. Wright

274   The Future of Money: How the Digital Revolution Is Transforming Currencies and Finance – Eswar Prasad; Bitcoin: Economics, Technology, and Governance –R. Bohme, N. Cristin, B. Edelman, and T. Moore, American Economic Association

275   Economics of Blockchain – S. Davidson, P. De Filippe, and J. Potts, SSRN; Crypto-economic Design: A Proposed Agent-Based Modelling Effort – D. Babitt and J. Dietz, Swarm Economics; Zamfi; Blockchain Technology: Principles and Applications – Marc Pilkington, SSRN

276   When Cryptomining Comes to Town: High Electricity-Use Spillovers to the Local Economy – M. Benetton, G. Compiani, and A. Morse, SSRN; Life cycle assessment of behind-the-meter Bitcoin mining at US power plant – M. Roeck and T. Drennen, Semantic Scholar

277   Reports show scammers cashing in on crypto craze – Emma Fletcher, FTC; Statement on Cryptocurrencies and Initial Coin Offerings – Jay Clayton, SEC; Crypto-Securities Regulation: ICOs, Token Sales and Cryptocurrencies under EU Financial Law – P. Hacker and C Thomale, SSRN

278   Exec. Order No. 14067 Ensuring Responsible Development of Digital Assets – Federal Register

279   Cambridge Bitcoin Electricity Consumption Index – CBECI; The U.S. Securities and Exchange Commission (SEC) announced litigation against Ripple Labs Inc. in 2020, Chicago Crypto Capital LLC in 2022, and the former CEO of FTX Trading Ltd., Samuel Bankman-Fried in 2022 to name just a few.

280   Climate And Energy Implications Of Crypto-Assets In The United States – White House Office of Science and Technology Policy

281 Cryptocurrency regulations by country – Thomson Reuters: Private cryptocurrencies only, excludes CBDCs and state-sponsored digital assets. Turkey is the only country to institute a cryptocurrency ban around the same time as China (Turkey's ban was announced in April 2021); Cambridge Bitcoin Electricity Consumption Index – CBECI: However, there is no evidence of a significant bitcoin mining presence in Turkey prior to the ban.

282 Cryptocurrency regulations by country – Thomson-Reuters; Freedom In The World 2022 – Freedom House; Russia, China, India, Iran, Mexico, Colombia, Bolivia, Bangladesh, Turkey, Egypt, Algeria, Morocco are all considered "not free" or "partly free" according to Freedom House's Freedom in the World weighted-scale methodology. Ecuador is the only nation with a "free" designation and somewhat restrictive cryptocurrency regulations according to the Reuters study.

283 I'll Gladly Trade You Two Bits On Tuesday For A Byte Today: Bitcoin, Regulating Fraud In The Economy Of Hacker Cash – Derek Dion, University of Illinois

284 In 2014, Federal Reserve Chairwoman Janet Yellen said, "The Federal Reserve simply does not have authority to supervise or regulate Bitcoin in any way. This is a payment innovation that is taking place entirely outside the banking industry" – Ryan Tracy, WSJ

285 Why China had to "Ban" Cryptocurrency but the U.S. did not: A Comparative Analysis of Regulations on Crypto-Markets Between the U.S. and China – Rain Xie, Global Studies Law Review, page 491

286 Crypto firms say thousands of digital currencies will collapse, compare market to early dotcom days – Arjun Kharpal, CNBC; Are there too many cryptocurrencies? – Chris Jones, Cointelegraph; Because cryptocurrencies are relatively simple to create, require no official approval, and are not all listed for trading on exchanges, it is impossible to know precisely how many different cryptocurrencies exist.

287 Coinmarketcap

288 Ethereum launched in 2015. Vitalik Buterin, Ethereum's lead designer and creator, was a Bitcoin enthusiast who co-founded Bitcoin Magazine in 2011.

289 Bitcoin: A Peer-to-Peer Electronic Cash System – Satoshi Nakamoto

290 Ibid.

291 Ibid. It does not mention unit of account, either. Most likely because any brand new, unadopted currency would obviously not serve as anyone's unit of account.

292 Coin Metrics' State of the Network: Issue 186 – Coin Metrics

293 One study, The State of Lightning - Volume 2 – Arcane, estimated the Lightning Network processed over 800,000 transactions in February 2022. See Essay 1 of this dissertation series, The State of Lightning, for a more in-depth explanation of the Lightning Network.

294 Research: Miners sent 57K Bitcoin to exchanges in 2022; selling pressure decreasing – A. Radmilac and J. Van Straten, Cointelegraph

295 Cryptocurrency ownership also differs from equities ownership. Equities or stocks serve as shares or portions of a company. Bitcoin "possession" is nothing more than ownership of ledger entry numbers.

296 关于进一步防范和处置虚拟货币交易炒作风险的通知 – People's Bank of China

297 Ibid.

298 Why China had to "Ban" Cryptocurrency but the U.S. did not: A Comparative Analysis of Regulations on Crypto-Markets Between the U.S. and China – Rain Xie, Washington University in St. Louis Global Studies Law Review: In 2013, the PBOC specifically prohibited the use of bitcoin as a payment instrument for goods and services as well.

299 In the "Notice on Further Preventing and Resolving the Risks of Virtual Currency Trading and Speculation" – PBOC: Section 1.2 lists illegal "virtual currency-related activities." Nearly all the listed activities were already prohibited between 2013-2017.

300 Each Antminer S19 Pro miner has a maximum hashrate of 110Th/s. So, this is roughly the equivalent of adding 1400 new ASICs-worth of mining power across the network each day

301 2016 blocks occur roughly every two weeks.

302 Bitcoin mining is now easier and more profitable as algorithm adjusts after China crackdown – MacKenzie Sigalos, CNBC

303 The two-month intervention period is excluded because it is likely to be driven by many idiosyncratic factors that are of little interest to policymakers.
304 Cambridge Bitcoin Electricity Consumption Index – CBECI: Raw data from 2023.
305 Does the Hashrate Affect the Bitcoin Price? – D. Fantazzini and N. Kolodin, SSRN; A time–frequency comovement and causality relationship between Bitcoin hashrate and energy commodity markets – M. Rehman and S. Kang, Science Direct
306 The decision for whether bitcoin miners will turn their machines on or off is mostly dependent on four things: the price of bitcoin, the price of energy, the efficiency/performance level of the mining equipment, and network hashrate. Though ASIC efficiency erodes over time, their lifecycle is relatively predictable. Based on the known hashing efficiency of their ASICs, miners can generate a profitability matrix based on the two more volatile variables in this equation, bitcoin price and the overall hashrate of the network, to determine how much revenue they can generate per unit of energy. This results in a breakeven price for energy, below which miners know their machines will be profitable, and above which it is effectively counterproductive and economically unfeasible to mine.
307 Bitcoin mining is now easier and more profitable as algorithm adjusts after China crackdown – MacKenzie Sigalos, CNBC: This assumes a constant overall network hashrate. If network hashrate and mining difficulty drops low enough, it can make older equipment more profitable again. As mentioned earlier, this occurred once network hashrate bottomed out in July, but less efficient miners were likely priced out by drops in market value in June.
308 Cambridge Bitcoin Electricity Consumption Index – CBECI: Raw data from 2023.
309 China Can't Seem to Stop Bitcoin Mining – George Kaloudis, CoinDesk
310 Bitcoin mining – an (un)surprising resurgence? – CCAF, University of Cambridge Judge Business School
311 Ibid.
312 China Can't Seem to Stop Bitcoin Mining – George Kaloudis, CoinDesk; China's cryptocurrency market still among world's strongest despite Beijing's crackdown on trading, mining of digital assets – Coco Feng, SCMP; Bitcoin production roars back in China despite Beijing's ban on crypto mining – Ryan Browne, CNBC
313 Aggregated by Blockchain.com (2023), pulled from the on-chain explorer and data from known mining pools. Intervention period highlighted in yellow. Blockchain.com did not have data for daily blocks won for Foundry USA during this time period. I pulled Foundry USA's daily blocks won and added it to the data set shown in these figures; Multiple Mining Pools Are Facing Connectivity Issues – Eliza Gkritsi, CoinDesk: Several mining pools, particularly those with a history of being based in China, reported connectivity issues towards the end of 2021. This may explain the sudden drop off of reported blocks won by Poolin between October 2021 and January 2022.
314 Known pools with a low capacity to win blocks (<2 blocks per day on average) were excluded from these Figures and analysis.
315 F2Pool hit the high mark for the time period in December 2020.
316 AntPool is owned by Bitmain Technologies, a privately owned company with its headquarters still located in Beijing. F2Pool officially lists their location as "decentralized," but its headquarters was originally established in Beijing. Poolin is also headquartered in Beijing.
317 Foundry USA, based in Rochester, NY, won the second-highest amount of blocks during the ex-post period.
318 Raw data from Coin Metrics in 2023. Intervention period highlighted in yellow.
319 The Bitcoin Lightning Network: Scalable Off-Chain Instant Payments – J. Poon and T. Dryja; A full explanation of the Lightning Network is outside the scope of this essay, but users effectively transfer bitcoin locked up on the base layer to Lightning wallets and conduct peer to peer transactions on layer 2. They can close these two-way micropayment contracts and transfer their funds back to the base layer whenever they choose. Since lightning network transactions occur between two known parties on their own private channel, they are not broadcast to the entire network and settle nearly instantaneously without the need for energy-intensive PoW protocol.
320 Lightning network: a second path towards centralisation of the Bitcoin economy – J. Lin, K. Primicerio, T. Squartini, C. Decker and C. Tessone, New Journal of Physics

321. Global Crypto Asset Regulatory Landscape Study – A. Blandin, A. Cloots, H. Hussain, M. Rauchs, R. Saleuddin, J. Allen, B. Zhang, and K. Cloud, University of Cambridge Judge Business School
322. Regulation spillovers across cryptocurrency markets – N. Borri and K. Shakhnov, Science Direct; Why China had to "Ban" Cryptocurrency but the U.S. did not: A Comparative Analysis of Regulations on Crypto-Markets Between the U.S. and China – Rain Xie, Global Studies Law Review
323. The Book Of Satoshi: The Collected Writings of Bitcoin Creator Satoshi Nakamoto – Phil Champagne
324. 88%, 54%, 44%, 60%, 46%, 41%, 55% drops in 2011, 2014, 2015, 2018, 2021, and 2022 (twice).
325. Research: Miners sent 57K Bitcoin to exchanges in 2022; selling pressure decreasing – A. Radmilac and J. Van Straten, CryptoSlate: Since 2014, bitcoin has never lost value (in $USD terms) over a three-year span. It is possible that long-term holders also see bitcoin's liquidity as an advantage within their portfolio, rather than its other functional use as a money for those who need to save their value day-to-day.
326. The higher the price of bitcoin, the higher the breakeven price of energy (all else equal). Absent a policy intervention (e.g., various demand response programs) it is economically rational (i.e., profitable) to mine whenever energy prices are below the breakeven price of energy.
327. This can be seen in the Bitcoin Core software (and viewed in Python) which can be found on the GitHub website. For ease of communication, I reference a plain English translation: Bitcoin Mining Difficulty: Everything You Need to Know – Andrey Sergeenkov, CoinDesk
328. China: National Development and Reform Commission Issues Notice Restricting Cryptocurrency Mining – Laney Zhang, Library of Congress
329. Blockchain and Money – Gary Gensler, MIT; Geneva 21: The Impact of Blockchain Technology on Finance: A Catalyst for Change – edited by M. Casey, J. Crane, G. Gensler, S. Johnson, and N. Narula, CEPR; Liquidity Management in a Multi-Currency Corridor Network – Onyx, JP Morgan
330. Senators Mike Lee (R-UT), Ted Cruz (R-TX) and Representative Tom Emmer (R-MN) introduced three pending legislative proposals designed to restrict or prohibit the establishment of a CBDC in the United States during the 118th Congress.
331. Digital Innovation, Data Revolution and Central Bank Digital Currency – N. Yanagawa and H. Yamaoka, Ideas REPEC
332. Report on Stablecoins – President's Working Group on Financial Markets, FDIC - OCC
333. Governance of Blockchain and Distributed Ledger Technology Projects – B. Howell, P. Potgieter, and B. Sadowski, SSRN
334. Ibid.
335. The Book Of Satoshi: The Collected Writings of Bitcoin Creator Satoshi Nakamoto – Phil Champagne
336. A deep dive into Bitcoin's environmental impact – Alexander Neumueller, University of Cambridge Judge Business School; China Can't Seem to Stop Bitcoin Mining – George Kaloudis, CoinDesk; China's cryptocurrency market still among world's strongest despite Beijing's crackdown on trading, mining of digital assets – Coco Feng, SCMP; Bitcoin production roars back in China despite Beijing's ban on crypto mining – Ryan Browne, CNBC
337. Bitcoin miners: China's cryptocurrency crackdown pushes companies overseas – C. Fengin, C. Panin, and M. Borak, SCMP; How the U.S. became the world's new bitcoin mining hub – MacKenzie Sigalos, CNBC; How the U.S. benefits when China turns its back on Bitcoin – J. Rutwich and E. Feng, NPR; Bitcoin mines come to rural Georgia communities. They're bringing opportunities — and tensions – Lars Lonnroth, NPR; America's Bitcoin Miners See Georgia as the New U.S. Hot Spot – Josh Saul, Bloomberg; New York passes first crypto-mining ban in US – Christopher Hutton, Washington Examiner
338. Spatial analysis of global Bitcoin mining – W. Sun, H. Jin, F. Jin, L. Kong, Y. Peng, Z. Dai, Scientific Reports

CHAPTER 8

THE IMPLICATIONS OF BITCOIN ON GLOBAL ILLICIT FINANCE

By Thomas Wood, DBA

Thomas Wood, DBA *is a Director on the Board of CleanSpark, Inc., a top tier publicly traded American bitcoin miner. A retired Naval Officer, he has also worked as a defense contractor and as a Civil Service employee in both the excepted and competitive service. His national security career has spanned nearly four decades in a broad range of operational areas including conventional ground force operations; humanitarian assistance; peacekeeping; disaster response; and interagency counterterrorism and counter-narcotics operations, including counter-threat finance. Tom holds a Master's Degree in Geotechnical Engineering and a Doctorate of Business*  *Administration, and is a licensed professional engineer. He was a contributing author to "The New Face of Transnational Crime Organizations (TCOs): A Geopolitical Perspective and Implications to U.S. National Security" published by the Office of the Secretary of Defense and Joint Staff, March 2013. He is also a co-inventor on U.S. Patent Number 11,402,525 B2.*

Introduction

I retired from the U.S. Navy as a Commander in 2006, and immediately went to work for a defense contractor supporting the Joint Interagency

Coordination Group for Counter Terrorism (JIACG-CT) at U.S. Pacific Command, Camp H.M. Smith, Hawaii.[339]

Our mandate was less focused on direct, or kinetic, action and more on the achievement of indirect effects; disrupting support networks and enablers that gave terrorists operational reach. Federal Law Enforcement and Regulatory Agencies participated in the group by providing some of their best and brightest people to work with us. One of ours was a sanctions investigator from the U.S. Department of the Treasury, and we also had other representatives such as FBI and State. Several years later, I joined Joint Interagency Task Force West (JIATF-W), PACOM's counterdrug task force, as their Deputy Operations Officer. This same, now former, Treasury employee worked for me as the task force's Counter Threat Finance Specialist.

Over the course of nearly thirteen years working with her and many others, I learned a great deal about illicit finance in the context of nation-states, terrorists, and transnational criminal organizations.

My own introduction to bitcoin came through this work as bitcoin was considered another means of moving resources to fund terrorists. Because of that, for many years I viewed it mostly through the lens of the threats that it posed rather than its potential.

I now see it as a technology that has great potential for goodness, but like most things, it can also be used for evil. The legal and regulatory policies that are ultimately developed should reflect this duality; with a balanced approach towards facilitating legal uses where bitcoin provides substantial benefit, while addressing the risks posed by the technology in a pragmatic way. Some suggestions are provided throughout this chapter.

Illicit Finance: What is "Illicit Finance"?

The International Monetary Fund uses the following definition to describe illicit financial flows:[340]

> "Illicit financial flows refer to the movement of money across borders that is illegal in its source (e.g. corruption, smuggling), its transfer (e.g. tax evasion), or its use (e.g. terrorist financing)."

From this definition, we see that there are really three types of illicit money: 1) the "proceeds of crime", or funds that result from an activity that is itself a crime; 2) funds where the act of transferring the funds is the crime and the source of the funds, legal or otherwise does not matter; and 3) funds being transferred to conduct or facilitate a crime. Funds may also meet more than one of these criteria, such as drug proceeds used to finance terrorist activities as we saw extensively in Afghanistan throughout the U.S. military's involvement there.[341]

Connection to National Security Interests

From a national security perspective, illicit finance is simply an enabler. It gives threat actors the capability to do the things that they want to do — which are activities that threaten national security. The same activities that governments seek to prevent.

The Department of Defense (DoD) recognizes that: "…the links among threat networks, engaged in illicit drug trafficking, transnational organized crime, criminal finance, and terrorist activities have multiplied and strengthened. Furthermore, we see collaboration between these networks and state actors who threaten U.S. national security."[342]

Because these activities often "transcend law enforcement, intelligence community, and other U.S. Government (USG) spheres of action"[343] a whole of government or interagency approach has become the norm in dealing with these threats. Over the last twenty plus years we have learned that it is much more effective to bring experience and authorities from a wide variety of disciplines and agencies together to address this problem set. We have developed a multitude of interagency constructs to bring agencies together to combat these increasingly complex threats.

That threshold between crime and national security is not always clear and well defined. The direct financing of activities that are threats to national security (e.g. terrorism, WMD proliferation) is an obvious national security threat. But it is not always clear when other things we normally associate with "criminal activity" rise to that level. Examples where it does meet the threshold might include a cyber-ransom attack that affects critical infrastructure or destabilizes a financial market, or large-scale counterfeiting operations that undermine the U.S. dollar, such as operations allegedly carried out by DPRK:

> *"For the United States the allegedly large-scale counterfeiting of U.S. currency by the DPRK is a direct challenge to U.S. interests. Any counterfeiting, whether done by North Korea or not, could undermine confidence in the U.S. dollar and, if done extensively enough, potentially damage the U.S. economy. It also is a direct attack on a protected asset of the United States and a violation of U.S. and other laws."*[344]

As another example, drug trafficking is a crime. Most nation-states define it as such, and there are international treaties that do the same. As complex and difficult as the international drug trafficking problem is, it is generally law enforcement cooperation amongst jurisdictions that addresses it. However, at some level,[345] it can rise from the level of crime to an actual direct threat to national security.

The catastrophe that is Afghanistan today is one example. The trafficking across the U.S. southern border as this chapter is being written is another. The sheer volume moving into the U.S. now poses a threat to the American people and the Nation *as a whole*, and therefore logically crosses a threshold. Thus, the problem, and the solution, may now transcend law enforcement, just as it did in Afghanistan two decades ago. *Scale* matters.

Trafficking in other "commodities" such as humans, arms, etc. are likewise criminal acts, but because of a "convergence of threat networks", are considered by the DoD to represent "a growing, multilayered, and asymmetric challenge to U.S. national security".[346]

Because the lines between criminal activity and legitimate national security threats are blurry at best, we tend to view the threats as existing on a spectrum. On the one end are localized threats that affect one, or a few people: retail drug trafficking, homicide, even "mass" shootings. On the other end is regional military conflict, up through nuclear war. In between is a messy mix of large-scale crime, terrorism, proliferation of weapons of mass destruction, etc. Crime is defined by statute at some level of government, state, local, Federal, etc. So, the lower end of the spectrum is clear. War is defined by an act of Congress, making the upper end also clearly defined. Everything in between those two extremes is situationally dependent. Few would argue that the recent conflicts in Afghanistan or Iraq were not legitimate national security threats, but they did not meet the formal definition of a war.

There is no real practical benefit to attempting to bin the threat actors neatly into one or the other. Today's opium farmer can be tomorrow's IED maker, the fraudulent document specialist does not care whether his "client" is a terrorist or a criminal, and the professional money laundering organization earns their fee on the value of money laundered, not the source or purpose of the funds.

Magnitude of Illicit Trade

Estimating the amount of money involved in illicit trade within any given market or globally is necessarily inexact. Rand Corporation estimates that the criminal revenue in European markets alone ranges from approximately $100-200 billion.[347]

Authoritative sources generally put the value of worldwide illicit trade between 2-5% of Global GDP.[348,349] A further breakdown of this number into some "market segments" looks like this:[350]

Transnational Crime	Estimated Annual Value (US$)
Drug Trafficking	$426 billion to $652 billion
Small Arms & Light Weapons Trafficking	$1.7 billion to $3.5 billion
Human Trafficking	$150.2 billion
Organ Trafficking	$840 million to $1.7 billion
Trafficking in Cultural Property	$1.2 billion to $1.6 billion
Counterfeiting	$923 billion to $1.13 trillion
Illegal Wildlife Trade	$5 billion to $23 billion
IUU Fishing	$15.5 billion to $36.4 billion
Illegal Logging	$52 billion to $157 billion
Illegal Mining	$12 billion to $48 billion
Crude Oil Theft	$5.2 billion to $11.9 billion
Total	**$1.6 trillion to $2.2 trillion**

Source: Global Financial Integrity

(Figure 64: Estimated annual value of transnational crime. Source: Global Financial Integrity.)

Law enforcement worldwide spends tremendous effort on the international drug trade, at least partly because of the direct and immediate impact on human life. However, as shown above, drugs make up between a quarter and a third of the worldwide illicit trade and are not the largest category by a significant margin.

The scale of global illicit trade is *massive*.

Profits are high and risks are generally low. While most of the "market segments" above do not have a direct impact on U.S. national security, they do affect U.S. political, economic, and social interests around the world. For example:

- Global oil theft, which includes the "crude oil theft" subcategory listed in the table above, is estimated to account for between five and seven percent of all crude oil and refined fuels produced worldwide.[351] The problem is so large that it measurably increases prices in the global energy market, negatively affecting consumers and economies worldwide.

- Fish do not recognize nation-state boundaries, so Illegal, Unreported, and Unregulated (IUU) fishing affects fisheries well beyond the geographic area where the crime occurs. Fish are a major source of dietary protein for about half of the world's population, so failure to sustainably manage international fisheries poses a significant risk to food security.[352]

- Both illegal logging and illegal mining exploit under-governed regions by stealing natural resources from the citizens of that region. In the process, the local environment is usually heavily damaged and local people are often displaced, exploited, or killed.

- Human trafficking in all its forms is a scourge on humanity. The United States, along with most other nations, has long been committed to efforts to eliminate this crime and the destruction of lives that comes with it.

In addition, the funds generated by these types of criminal activities can fund terrorist organizations and nation-states that are targeting U.S. national security interests. For example:

- Hezbollah operates as a transnational criminal organization to fund its operations, with operations centered primarily in Europe, Africa, and Latin America. Operations are believed to include drug trafficking, weapons trafficking, and professional money laundering operations.[353]

- Mostly due to longstanding international sanctions, the Kim regime in DPRK is desperate for hard currency of any kind. A UN Panel of Experts report from March 2023 estimated that DPRK cyber actors stole between $630 million and $1 billion worth of virtual currencies in 2022. This is a major source of funding for the regime and supports weapons of mass destruction and ballistic missile development programs.[354]

Categorizing these sorts of activities simply as "crimes" belies both the scale and the overall global risk.

Bitcoin Concepts

In simplest terms, bitcoin is a way of transferring value between parties on a peer-to-peer basis with no "trusted third party" involvement.[355] The direct peer-to-peer nature of the transaction is fundamental to bitcoin and is what provides an inherent level of privacy between the parties.[356]

The underlying technology of bitcoin was developed to create a decentralized authority system that could manage peer to peer transactions. It solves two longstanding and specific problems with decentralized systems. The first is the "double-spending problem", or how do you maintain scarcity and prevent the same "token" being used twice without a central trust authority. The second is the "Byzantine General's problem", or how to achieve group consensus without a centralized trusted adjudication authority to verify the authenticity of information sent by other members of the group. Bitcoin is the first practical solution to these two problems simultaneously.

In a traditional centralized financial transaction as shown below, there are multiple third-party centralized points where Bank Secrecy Act controls are applied and can be used to monitor — or control — transactions. That "third-party" trust authority is a single point of control.

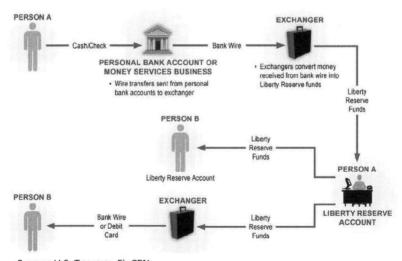

Source: U.S. Treasury, FinCEN

(Figure 65: Traditional centralized financial transaction. Source: FinCEN)

Since there is no trusted third party in the bitcoin network, there is also no central control, or registration of wallet addresses to a person or entity. Because of this, there is essentially no ability to apply "know your customer" (KYC) rulesets on the bitcoin network. While the blockchain indelibly records the fact that a transaction between two "wallet" addresses occurred, it does not record the identity of the person or entity that controls the wallet. In this way, bitcoin represents an "in-between" state between the complete anonymity of cash and the complete traceability of a check or credit card. This is called "pseudonymity" — that is, anonymous, up to a point.

However, the indelible record of the blockchain means that every transaction is ultimately traceable between addresses. The FBI has demonstrated that they are capable of tracing transactions through multiple addresses and ultimately seizing assets.[357]

This contrasts with cash, which, as a bearer instrument, provides full anonymity. Criminals prefer cash because there is often no way to determine the source, and in many jurisdictions seizure of the cash requires connecting the cash to the underlying crime.[358]

Pseudonymity remains true while transactions occur inside the bitcoin ecosystem, but at the point where any party exits that ecosystem, they must re-enter the traditional, centralized financial system. That almost always happens through a centralized point that is subject to traditional financial system rulesets such as the BSA and associated KYC, as imposed by the Financial Crimes Enforcement Network (FinCEN).

Policy Opportunity

The interface point between the bitcoin network and the traditional financial system is the best opportunity to apply traditional financial system rulesets.

Current policy requires bitcoin exchanges to register as MSBs and apply BSA requirements.

Facilitating the chartering, development, and continued operation of "bitcoin friendly" banks can provide another robust interface point. At the same time, being able to access these services through a more traditional format enhances the experience for bitcoin users.

Regulators, the bitcoin network, and users all benefit if consumers have unfettered access to the bitcoin network through traditional, familiar mechanisms.

(Figure 66: Policy Opportunity.)

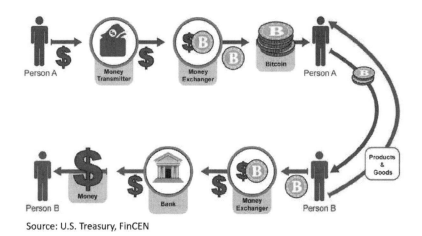

Source: U.S. Treasury, FinCEN

(Figure 67: Financial transaction. Source: FinCEN)

Enhancing Privacy on the Bitcoin Network

One of the reasons that people come to the bitcoin network is to regain some of the privacy that they have lost in the traditional financial system. Not everyone is satisfied with sharing all their financial transaction data across the internet. At present there are a couple of common options for increasing the privacy of transactions on the bitcoin network.

"Coinjoin" transactions use software to take multiple transactions and essentially blend them together to obfuscate which funds came and went from which wallet address. The wallet addresses are still visible on the public ledger, but what transactions occurred between which addresses is no longer distinctly clear. This technique provides a useful level of privacy for the average user but would be difficult to implement for numerous large-scale transactions. Its utility for threat actors is probably somewhat limited.

The Lightning Network is an application, not a part of the bitcoin protocol. While its purpose is to address several issues including speed, and scalability, it also creates additional privacy by removing the wallet addresses for the parties to the transaction from the public ledger. Instead of the wallet addresses of the parties, a two-party, multi-signature "channel" bitcoin address is entered on the public ledger. The actual transaction occurs within the channel address. Lightning allows immediate settlement of even very small amounts at low transaction costs, with high levels of anonymity.

In these respects, it is comparable to cash. However, because two-party consensus is required to finalize a transaction, it does not impose the risks of a "bearer instrument" on any user's bitcoin.

Bitcoin and Illicit Finance

What characteristics of bitcoin make it useful and desirable to the various threat actors? First and foremost is the increased level of privacy that it offers, but as we saw previously, that is not as robust as many people think.

FinCEN has outlined several additional reasons that bitcoin might be preferred over other value transfer mechanisms for illicit transactions, including low transaction fees; easy cross-border transfer; no transaction limits; and secure and irrevocable transactions.[359] Since, for the foreseeable future, the bitcoin ecosystem and the traditional financial system will coexist, managing the interface between the two in a positive way contributes to transparency and accountability and can help mitigate against criminal use.

Under current regulations, exchanges are considered "money transmitters" and therefore are subject to all the FinCEN requirements for a "money service business" (MSB). Since exchanges function as the primary interface point between the BTC ecosystem and the traditional financial system, in today's regulatory environment there are already controls in place to address many of the concerns regarding the use of bitcoin for illicit purposes.

In contrast, a "miner" is not considered to be an MSB and is not subject to the registration, reporting, and recordkeeping requirements imposed on an MSB:

> *"FinCEN understands that Bitcoin mining imposes no obligations on a Bitcoin user to send mined Bitcoin to any other person or place for the benefit of another. Instead, the user is free to use the mined virtual currency or its equivalent for the user's own purposes, such as to purchase real or virtual goods and services for the user's own use. To the extent that a user mines Bitcoin and uses the Bitcoin solely for the user's own purposes and not for the benefit of another, the user is not an MSB under FinCEN's regulations, because these activities involve neither "acceptance" nor "transmission" of the convertible virtual currency and are not the transmission of funds within the meaning of the Rule."*[360]

How Can Threat Actors Use Bitcoin?

There are two basic ways that threat actors can employ bitcoin to facilitate their activities. First, it can be used to conduct value transfers that can be less visible to law enforcement than other, more traditional methods, such as bulk cash smuggling or Trade-Based Money Laundering (TBML). The other advantages noted by FinCEN above also make bitcoin appear an attractive choice. Second, it can be used for direct purchases of goods and services with another party that is willing to conduct an illicit transaction in bitcoin. Arms dealers, drug suppliers, etc. may be willing to conduct business in bitcoin, in which case the transaction remains within the ecosystem and the pseudonymity remains intact.

In either case, all threat actors and all facilitators and suppliers are ultimately still faced with the very same issues that they face in traditional money laundering schemes. The entry and exit points — known as the "placement" phase and the "integration" phase in money laundering parlance — are still visible and vulnerable points.[361] Bitcoin exchanges are already monitored as MSBs and are responsible for reporting suspicious transactions in the same way that traditional finance institutions are. There is no free lunch.

The Dangers of Illicit Finance: Threat Actors, the "Who"

Looking through the broad lens of U.S. National Security interests, we can summarize the threat actors as follows:[362]

- Nation States
- Terrorist Organizations
- Transnational Criminal Organizations (TCO)
- Other criminal activity, not on a transnational scale

These threat actors generally describe the "who" that we need to be concerned with, but we should be aware that the line between these different actors is not always clear.

For example, Iran, a nation-state, often crosses into international terrorism. North Korea is also a nation-state, but acts in certain respects like a Transnational Criminal Organization (TCO).

TCOs are the powerful successors to the narcotics cartels of the '70s, '80s, and '90s. Forged in the evolutionary fire of a decades-long international "war on drugs", they are often the largest, most efficient, and most brutal players in the illicit trades.

Globalization and technology trends have expanded both the reach and efficiency of these organizations.[363] Today, most of these organizations are commodity agnostic and business opportunities are viewed primarily through the profit lens rather than through any preference for drugs over weapons, or people.[364] Many will have a particular expertise, such as drug smuggling, but are quick to exploit any business opportunities where they can leverage their expertise and support networks to increase profits.

As noted earlier, criminal activity that does not rise to the transnational level may not rise to the level of a threat to national security. But that is not a hard, well-defined boundary, so we cannot remove these threat actors from consideration completely.

The Venn diagram below illustrates how the U.S. DoD views the interconnections between these various actors and their activities.

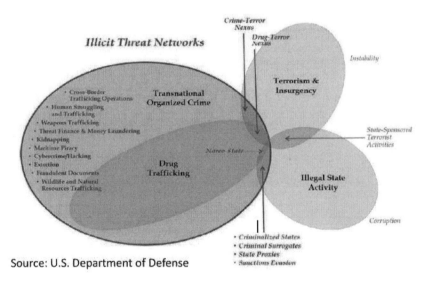

(Figure 68: Interconnections between parties. Source: US DoD.)

The people within these organizations may be motivated by greed, by power, or by ideology.[365] They may have multiple motivations at the same time or even change them over time. The common thread is this: all of them are willing, to a greater or lesser degree, to operate outside of reasonable civilized norms to succeed. Who suffers, gets hurt or killed, what businesses or economies are destroyed, how much of the world burns, matters not if they get what they want. All these actors pose different threats, and they operate within rulesets of their own making. They may cooperate or compete depending on circumstances. Ultimately, they are motivated only by their objectives, and are generally agnostic regarding how, or who they work with.

Admiral Harry Harris, USN, former commander of USPACOM and one of my former bosses, used to refer to a "Global Operating System" to describe the basic international norms that have maintained relative peace and stability for the world since the end of World War II. These threat actors have established their own operating system, and it is a very dangerous place.

On the opposite side of these threat actors are law enforcement, intelligence, and militaries that are necessarily constrained by rules and must operate within duly granted legal authorities. They are faced with extremely complex problems and adversaries that are unconstrained. The asymmetry between those two approaches increases the challenge of maintaining the current system.

Criminal Activities and National Security Threats: The "What" and The "How"

The U.S. Treasury Department defines illicit finance "threats" and "vulnerabilities".[366,367] Threats are the "what", i.e., the activity that is being conducted. Note that all the threats listed would also be themselves crimes, so regardless of the original source of the funds used to support these activities; these threats would fall within the IMF's definition of illicit finance.

THREATS
- Fraud
- Drug Trafficking
- Cybercrime
- Professional Money Laundering
- Corruption
- Human Trafficking and Human Smuggling
- Foreign and Domestic Terrorist Financing
- WMD Proliferation Financing

(Figure 69: Source: Author.)

In contrast, Treasury's listed vulnerabilities are the "how", i.e., what is the method by which money is being illicitly moved in order to facilitate the criminal or terrorist activity.

VULNERABILITIES
- Misuse of Legal Entities
- Real Estate
- Virtual Assets
- Cash
- Correspondent Banking
- Complicit Merchants
- Uneven AML Obligations on Financial Intermediaries and High Value Goods Dealers
- Compliance Deficiencies — Banks, MSB's, Securities Broker/Dealers, Casinos

(Figure 70: Source: Author.)

The above mechanisms are used to mask the source, owner, and ultimate destination of funds as part of money laundering schemes and to facilitate the transfer of funds amongst threat actors. In contrast to the threats, many of these vulnerabilities are not, by themselves, illegal. It is the context in which they are used that defines their criminality, or national security impact.

The Connection Between Crime and Terror

The more the USG has explored the role of illicit finance in terrorism, the more similarities and connections have been found to various forms of criminal illicit activity.[368] Drugs, guns, etc. all moved in similar ways, and often using the same facilitators. Facilitators that handle fraudulent documents, launder money, facilitate illegal border crossings, and so on are necessary for both criminals and terrorists to carry out their missions.

For any of these activities to be successfully executed, money must move between parties, usually multiple parties. Money is both the connective tissue and the fuel that enables both crime and terrorism.

Identifying and attacking the illicit flows of money is a way of accomplishing two distinct and important indirect attacks on threat actors: 1) tracking money illuminates the actors in a threat network and sets up potential targeting; and 2) seizing or freezing assets, or similar actions as allowed by law and regulation, can take away resources from threat actors, minimizing their capabilities. Finance is critical to all threat networks so attacking the finances is an extremely effective tool for degrading those networks. It has the advantage of being non-kinetic and can achieve effects at a distance, meaning we don't have to be geographically close to a target to cause an effect.

On the other side, threat actors are fully aware that governments focus on "following the money". They are also well aware of the long-term risks of having a permanent public record of their transactions. One hardware wallet or laptop picked up during a raid or arrest, even years later, could suddenly unravel hundreds or even thousands of transactions, exposing entire networks.

Would you leave a permanent, open record of your financing of a terrorist attack, knowing that if any single player's security is compromised through poor practice or even mischance, your entire operation would be exposed — even years or decades after the fact?

Attacking Threat Financial Networks
History of Counter Threat Finance

Between 2002 and 2004, the 9/11 Commission explored the question "How much does it cost to be Al Qaeda?" The answer, it turns out, was not that much, especially when weighed against the damage done. Estimates are that the entire 9/11 attack was carried out for less than $500,000.[369]

That simple question gave rise to a whole new approach to counterterrorism through the lens of what became known as "counter-threat finance" or CTF. "Follow the money" became a powerful new mantra. We used these techniques to attack the networks that enabled the 9/11 attacks and worldwide terrorism in general. And also, to develop actionable intelligence on the identities and relationships among the terrorists and their facilitators. As one FBI Supervisory Special Agent (SSA) once told me, "No one randomly sends money to an unknown person. If money moved between two people, there is a relationship, a connection, between those two people. We can build out the networks by understanding the relationships between the people."

Ultimately, attacking the networks that provide logistical support became as important as attacking the individual fighters. Because without their support networks, the fighters become combat ineffective. They can plan, but they cannot execute. Logistics is what makes them dangerous and capable of carrying out global attacks. As the old saying goes, "logistics is the difference between a bang and a click". Logistics always requires some transfer of value, and that almost always means money. For criminals and terrorists, using money within the world's financial systems usually requires that money to be laundered. When we dig into the mechanics of money laundering later in the chapter, we will see that — perhaps surprisingly to some people — bitcoin does not make money laundering easier.

Money Laundering

Criminal organizations are generally in the business of making money. Because the source of their wealth is criminal activity, their ability to enjoy the fruits of their labor is highly constrained.[370] Using the funds directly within the legal financial system risks arrest and prosecution.

Terrorists are generally in the business of terror, making money is not a primary goal of their fundraising efforts. However, their fundraising presents a vulnerability if funds are used directly for terrorist acts. Known fundraising sources can be monitored, and tracing the movement of funds exposes the networks and can lead to prosecution or interdiction before a terrorist act can be carried out.

Nation-states that have a desire to conceal their activities, or their identity regarding visible activities, also need to break the traceable connection between the source of funds for a covert or clandestine act, and the act itself. Using legal financial networks risks exposing their involvement.

For each of these threat actors, the common thread is that money must be disguised — its source, its destination, and its purpose. Money laundering provides the ability to mask all these characteristics.

The Importance of Cash

Cash, such as U.S. dollars, are bearer instruments. The bearer has beneficial ownership of the instrument and can use it to transfer value to another party. There is no requirement for a record of the transaction between two parties. The central issuance authority, such as the Federal Reserve, records that the cash exists, and local banks will record deposit and withdrawal information, but there is no central authority that records what amount of cash was spent for what purpose or who the parties to a particular transaction were. So, cash, and cash equivalents, like gift cards for example, provide an extreme level of anonymity between users.

Alternatively, Central Bank Digital Currencies (CBDC) which are discussed as an "official" alternative to bitcoin, are not bearer instruments. There will be no financial anonymity or privacy using a CBDC.

Cash is heavily monitored at the point where it re-enters the traditional financial system. As noted earlier regarding bitcoin transactions, the BSA requires banks and other MSBs to look for, among other things, transactions of cash. Large amounts of cash, typically any amounts more than $10,000, that are withdrawn or deposited can result in a bank filing a Suspicious Activity Report (SAR) or Suspicious Transaction Report (STR) with FinCEN.

The difference between those being whether the "activity" or the "transaction" is what triggered the suspicion. In addition, large purchases such as expensive merchandise or real estate purchases in cash can trigger scrutiny. Real estate has the potential to easily launder large sums. One report estimates that over $2.3 billion was laundered through the U.S. real estate market between 2017 and 2021.[371] Cash is used to either purchase a property outright or provide the necessary funds to close the transaction via down payment, etc. Once the escrow has closed, the title to the property is in the hands of the money launderer, giving them a legitimate asset. They can now either 1) lease the property through legitimate means and generate an ongoing cash flow; or 2) resell the property and take the proceeds as legitimate funds inside the banking system.

The money launderer may not even need to make a profit on the sale, since all money laundering efforts generally involve losses to the original value of the funds. This method has become so prevalent that FinCEN has created geographic targeting orders for high-value real estate markets that require Title Companies to identify the natural persons behind cash real estate transactions.[372]

Money Laundering Processes

By its very nature as a bearer instrument, cash is a vital part of most money laundering processes. In fact, EuroPol states that even today "…it remains the criminals' instrument of choice to facilitate money laundering."[373] While the U.S. DEA cites that drug cartels and money launderers are "increasingly incorporating virtual currency" into their activities,[374] the reality is that most of that activity is occurring at the retail level, largely through online digital marketplaces targeting consumers.[375] Consumers flock to the dark web for the ease and (assumed) anonymity, and digital currencies are readily available and accepted at dark web marketplaces. The weak point for the consumer trying to use bitcoin or crypto on the dark web is the original purchase of the currency. That typically happens through an exchange which is a regulated MSB. That single legal transaction can be the one piece of evidence that law enforcement needs to ultimately trace a whole series of illicit transactions across the blockchain. For bitcoin, the full transparency and accountability of the blockchain means that even when the transaction happens anonymously on the dark web, the financial record is still visible.

At the scale needed for wholesale (distributor/dealer) drug purchasing, buying drug precursors for manufacturing synthetic drugs — which can be industrial-scale transactions — could easily run in the millions of dollars. As shown below, the median transaction value on the bitcoin network is relatively low,[376] in the range of hundreds of dollars, not hundreds of thousands. Larger transactions are relatively few and easily stand out on the blockchain.

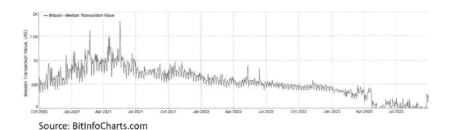

Source: BitInfoCharts.com

(Figure 71: Bitcoin median transaction value. Source: BitInfoCharts.com.)

In addition, reintegrating the digital currencies into the financial system would likely require a transition into cash to completely break the funds trail.[377] So despite the many concerns raised about digital currency as a major mechanism for transnational level money laundering, the evidence to date does not show extensive use, and for good reason. For true anonymity, cash is still — and likely always will be — King.

Money laundering is a multi-step process[378] that disguises funds that would meet any of the three IMF definitions of "illicit". It ultimately allows those funds to be used within the legal financial system without exposing their illicit origin. The process is usually described using three steps, as shown:

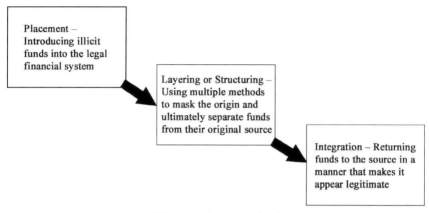

(Figure 72: Source: Author.)

In a traditional money-laundering scenario, the original funds are often cash. It could be cash from criminal activity like drug sales. Or it could be fundraising activity for a terrorist organization. Or it could be the withdrawal of cash from a "mule account" that was used in a cyber-ransom scheme (as noted earlier, digital currencies need to be converted to cash to break the trail before money laundering can begin).

In any case, regardless of source or ultimate destination, bulk cash presents a significant risk for any threat actor, and it must be disposed of. Placement is the entry point of this illicit cash into the legal financial system and is a significant vulnerability.[379]

Following the initial placement, any combination of techniques, listed above as the Treasury vulnerabilities, can be used to layer, or structure, the funds.

The entire purpose of this phase is to obscure the trail of the funds. Shell corporations, multiple funds transfers — preferably across borders into less restrictive regulatory regimes — specialized techniques like trade-based money laundering, black market peso exchanges, gift card smuggling, real estate holdings, high-end commodity purchases (art, jewelry etc.) are used to ultimately sever the connection between the original source of funds and the current holdings.

Once the trail has been completely broken, through whatever techniques, it is necessary to return control of the funds to the threat actor so they can use them. This is the integration phase, and it is the last step in the money laundering process.

> **Policy Opportunity**
>
> The interface point between the bitcoin network and the traditional financial system is the best opportunity to apply traditional financial system rulesets.
>
> Current policy requires bitcoin exchanges to register as MSBs and apply BSA requirements.
>
> Facilitating the chartering, development, and continued operation of "bitcoin friendly" banks can provide another robust interface point. At the same time, being able to access these services through a more traditional format enhances the experience for bitcoin users.
>
> Regulators, the bitcoin network, and users all benefit if consumers have unfettered access to the bitcoin network through traditional, familiar mechanisms.

(Figure 73: Policy Opportunity.)

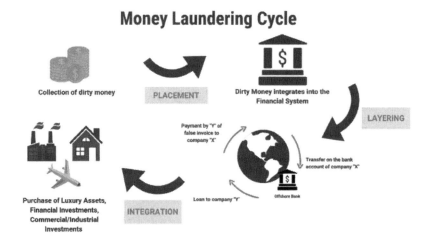

(Figure 74: Money laundering cycle. Source: UN Office of Drugs and Crime.)

Illicit Online Digital Marketplaces

The dark web is the colloquial name for an area of the internet that can only be accessed through an anonymous browser called "Tor" (short for "The onion router"). Using Tor is not illegal, it is simply a way to browse the internet anonymously. This can be a very positive thing for privacy, and for protecting people who live in regimes where the internet is heavily monitored or censored. Unfortunately, as with most things, including bitcoin, the browser can also be used for nefarious purposes, and there are websites available through Tor that market a wide variety of illicit goods.

(Figure 75: Silk Road website notification.)

One of the original and most highly recognized names was a website called "Silk Road" which operated for years on servers located primarily in Iceland. Silk Road was taken down in 2013 by an interagency operation that included FBI, IRS,HSI, DEA and others. Following the shutdown, this is what visitors the website saw:

Since the demise of Silk Road, other illicit marketplaces have arisen, and several have been taken down by law enforcement action; including AlphaBay, Hansa market, Wall Street Market, and Valhalla. However, there are still dozens of active sites that will, for example, ship drugs directly to your mailbox.[380]

The point of this section is that the tools being used, the Tor browser and bitcoin, are not the problem. The problem is that criminals will always exploit the system to their advantage by taking tools that are valuable and useful to the law-abiding citizen and using them for illicit purposes.

Why Bitcoin?

Put simply, bitcoin adds value to the world.

For the unbanked and underbanked population around the world, bitcoin provides a near frictionless way to transfer value across the street or around the world. For other people it restores a sense of control and privacy over their finances that they feel they have lost within the traditional financial system. Regardless of why, millions of users around the world have voted with their wallets and chosen to incorporate bitcoin into their financial world.

Many use it on an everyday basis. In the process, whole industries have been created — thriving businesses with well-paying jobs — often in rural communities. Those same rural communities often benefit from an increase in their tax base, allowing them to improve the quality of life for their residents.

Renewable power facilities are usually built in rural areas with little demand because renewables need a great deal of physical space per megawatt generated. Utilities can now sell that power to a flexible user and generate the revenue to support developing the grid transmission needed to deliver that power where it is ultimately needed. Nearly instantaneous demand response from miners provides a spinning reserve to the grid that can effectively shave peaks and greatly reduce brownouts and blackouts.

So, the question is no longer why bitcoin, it is how bitcoin.

How do we develop and implement policies that foster the thriving innovation and growth of the bitcoin industry while lowering risk to the traditional financial system and mitigating against threat actors who would exploit these same features to threaten our national security?

QR Code to **Chapter 8** Endnote Links and Figures on the Bitcoin Today Coalition website:

339 USPACOM is now known as U.S. Indo-Pacific Command, often abbreviated as "IPC" –PACOM
340 The IMF and the Fight Against Illicit Financial Flows – IMF
341 Seeds of terror: How heroin is bankrolling the Taliban and al Qaeda – Gretchen Peters
342 Framework to Counter Drug Trafficking and Other Illicit Threat Networks – U.S. Department of Defense
343 Framework to Counter Drug Trafficking and Other Illicit Threat Networks – U.S. Department of Defense, page 3
344 North Korean Counterfeiting of U.S. Currency – Congressional Research Service, page 1
345 What Is National Security? – Kim Holmes, Heritage Foundation 2015 Index of Military Strength, 17-26
346 Framework to Counter Drug Trafficking and Other Illicit Threat Networks – U.S. Department of Defense, page 1
347 Understanding the revenues earned on criminal markets and their reinvestment in the EU legal economy – Rand Europe, Retrieved August 3, 2023

348	Money Laundering – United Nations Office on Drugs and Crime. Retrieved July 4, 2023
349	Ibid.
350	Transnational Crime and the Developing World – Channing Mavrellis, Global Financial Integrity
351	Countering global oil theft: responses and solutions – Etienne Romsom, UNU-WIDER
352	2023 Report to Congress Improving International Fisheries Management – NOAA Fisheries
353	Lebanese Hezbollah – Congressional Research Service
354	Treasury Targets DPRK Malicious Cyber and Illicit IT Worker Activities – U.S. Department of the Treasury
355	Bitcoin: A Peer-to-Peer Electronic Cash System – Satoshi Nakamoto
356	Privacy vs Transparency – J. Purcell and I. Rossi, Finance & Development, 56(3), 18-21
357	Did the FBI Hack Bitcoin? Deconstructing the Colonial Pipeline Ransom – Tuan Phan, ISACA
358	Why is Cash Still King? – EuroPol, page 11
359	Statement of Jennifer Shasky Calvery, Director Financial Crimes Enforcement Network, United States Department of the Treasury Before the United States Senate Committee on Banking, Housing, and Urban Affairs Subcommittee on National Security and International Trade and Finance Subcommittee on Economic Policy
360	Application of FinCEN's Regulations to Virtual Currency Mining Operations – FIN-2014-R001
361	Why is Cash Still King? – EuroPol, page 42
362	Framework to Counter Drug Trafficking and Other Illicit Threat Networks – U.S. Department of Defense, page 1
363	Crime, Illicit Markets, and Money Laundering – Phil Williams, pg 109
364	Crime, Illicit Markets, and Money Laundering – Phil Williams, pg 108
365	In his "History of the Peloponnesian War" the Greek General Thucydides ascribed similar motives to nation-states when going to war. "War's nature is unchanging and is based on the contest for power. "Fear, honour, and interest" are human characteristics immutable through time and have generally been the cause of wars throughout history.
366	National Strategy for Combating Terrorist and Other Illicit Financing – U.S. Department of the Treasury, page 5
367	Crime, Illicit Markets, and Money Laundering – Phil Williams, pg 111
368	Framework to Counter Drug Trafficking and Other Illicit Threat Networks – U.S. Department of Defense, page 3
369	9/11 Commission Report, page 169
370	Why is Cash Still King? – EuroPol, page 9
371	Acres of Money Laundering: Why U.S. Real Estate is a Kleptocrat's Dream – L. Kumar and K. de Bel, Global Financial Integrity
372	FinCEN Renews and Expands Real Estate Geographic Targeting Orders – FinCEN
373	Why is Cash Still King? – EuroPol, page 7
374	The Crypto Question: Bitcoin, Digital Dollars, and the Future of Money – A. Siripurapu and N. Berman, Council on Foreign Relations, Retrieved July 4, 2023
375	Countering the Evolving Drug Trade and the Digitalization of Illicit Networks in the Americas – Celina Realuyo, pages 11-13
376	Bitcoin (BTC) price stats and information – BitInfoCharts, Retrieved September 30, 2023
377	Why is Cash Still King? – EuroPol, page 43
378	Why is Cash Still King? – EuroPol, page 9
379	Ibid.
380	Countering the Evolving Drug Trade and the Digitalization of Illicit Networks in the Americas – Celina Realuyo, pages 11-13

CHAPTER 9

BITCOIN AND ECONOMIC EMPOWERMENT

By Ian Gaines

Ian Gaines serves as the Assistant Director of Government Relations at COSSA and is an Advisor at the Bitcoin Policy Institute. Previously, he acted as a Communication Director at Black Bitcoin Billionaires, a bitcoin-centric financial literacy organization. Ian's work delves into the societal implications of emerging monetary networks, offering incisive policy insights to Capitol Hill. He champions socio-economic growth through enhanced financial accessibility, community-focused lightning network applications, and researching behavioral economic shifts in a digital era. His position has led to policy advisory contributions to the New York State  legislature, the Department of Justice, and an array of state and federal agencies. Of particular note, he's played an educational role in shaping Fintech task force policy knowledge in DC, mapping global competition, and consumer protection guidelines as well as direct policy recommendations setting the stage for a robust framework in digital assets on both a local and national level. He continues to advocate economic policies that empower all Americans, by way of public speaking engagements, federal advisement, and written agency guidance. Ian is an alumnus of the University of Chicago, where he pursued a Bachelor's degree in Political Science.

Introduction

From Wall Street investors to rural community organizers, a financial awakening is stirring. While many of the wealthiest in society still negotiate their investments in marble-lined boardrooms, a silent but seismic shift is germinating from the grassroots. Today, a fact that may seem counterintuitive to the casual observer is that 44% of US cryptocurrency holders are people of color. Furthermore, 30% of Black American and 27% of Hispanic investors possess cryptocurrency, compared to 18% of White investors.[381] This disparity reveals an often-overlooked reality: Black and Latino Americans are leading the nation in cryptocurrency adoption by over double digits. But what sparks this trend? Perhaps the more illuminating question would be: Which groups in society would most benefit from adopting systems that cannot arbitrarily exclude them?

This emergence is by no means an accident but rather the outcome of rational human action responding to systemic suppression driven by traditional, centralized frameworks. In contrast, as a fully decentralized monetary network, bitcoin is the tangible, real-world manifestation of incorruptible fairness. By paving the way for financial autonomy and limitless accessibility, bitcoin swings open the gates of economic participation to every untapped community that has never been afforded the privilege. This digital awakening carries the potential to unlock the dormant force of the American domestic economy, restore U.S. moral authority, and fortify our national strength on the global stage, and poetically so, our nation's most unlikely candidates are leading the way.

> *"Those who are most vulnerable are showing us the way forward; they are a test of our own development."*
> ~ Vandana Shiva

Fool Me Once: When Trust Crumbles in Centralized Systems

The growing affinity for censorship-resistant, fully decentralized digital property stems from a particular locus. **Why would a population enduring relentless economic disparities risk placing their limited, hard-earned wealth into a novel, unproven, and frequently volatile monetary system?** Is this disproportionate involvement merely the desperate reaction of the financially unsophisticated, maliciously tricked into a get–rich–quick Ponzi scheme, or could these communities possess unique insights into the flaws of a system that has repeatedly failed them?

The answer may lie within the concept of TRUST and the practical actions taken when there's been a complete erosion of it. At the core of the

American unseen lies the persistent reminder of how unchecked centralized control routinely weaponizes its authority against marginalized populations.

The first rupture in trust toward traditional financial institutions, specifically in Black American culture, dates back to the dawn of their independence. Established in 1865, the Freedmen's Savings Bank was the first and only federally created savings institution mandated to safeguard and manage the wealth of newly emancipated Black Americans. For ten years, the bank processed over $75 million in savings from former slaves, estimated to be worth $5 billion today.

In this era, under the leadership of a white-controlled board, the bank gradually morphed from a prudent long-term savings institution to a vehicle for reckless, high-risk speculation.[382] This places a spotlight — as we'll continue to find — on the recurrent ethical fragility of despotic power. By 1873, over half of all wealth held by Black Americans was overleveraged and mismanaged. Following continuous high-risk losses in real estate, railroad speculation, and blatant exploitation, the Freedmen's Bank shut down indefinitely, leaving no recourse for freed slaves to reclaim the millions they had lost. Institutional trust at this point was officially broken, and the painstaking journey towards unrestrained self-sovereignty began.

Sixty years later, the wealth-crippling effects of US federally funded programs only persisted. In 1933, the Home Owners' Loan Corporation (HOLC) introduced color-coded maps, marking areas with red lines — mainly composed of Black and immigrant communities — as "hazardous." This tactic, known today as "redlining," aimed to dissuade financial institutions from lending to these areas. This practice systematically redirected public funds away from Black and immigrant households, setting off a self-perpetuating cycle of adverse effects. Redlining significantly impeded minorities from securing mortgages and, consequently, homeownership.

The denial rate for Black applicants was 2.4 times higher than for White applicants with similar credit history and economic background, denying 36.2% of Black vs. only 15.2% of White Americans. Residents couldn't obtain loans to purchase or upgrade properties so housing conditions declined precipitously. Businesses often relocated, leading to diminished employment opportunities and community resources. Lower property values in redlined areas meant reduced local property tax revenue and underfunded schools. An unsavory collection of self-reinforcing elements that breed the hopeless conditions witnessed in modern urban America.

Arriving to the present day, systemic disenfranchisement carries the same embedded traditions, wisely evolving the tactics from its unacceptable past into a more elusive, irreproachable machination. These invisible chains that once overtly restrained social mobility have transmuted into subtler forms through credit inaccessibility, predatory lending, and prohibitive banking requirements. Compounding the problem, institutions today can further absolve themselves of responsibility by autonomously deploying AI systems. These modern inner workings generate near indistinguishable outcomes from the original prejudiced ideals of our nation's early central planners.

"Credit Invisibility" is a stark embodiment of these newly forged, invisible economic chains. This term denotes the predicament wherein an individual lacks a credit history with national credit reporting agencies, often due to never having borrowed or held any form of credit. Without this history, securing credit becomes a formidable challenge, as lenders lack the necessary information to assess creditworthiness. The absence of credit history often leads to outright loan rejection or the imposition of higher interest rates, further compounding financial adversity. In a 2015 Consumer Financial Protection Bureau report, approximately one in ten adults, or 26 million Americans, were "credit invisible." This issue disproportionately plagues low-income neighborhoods, where a staggering 45% of the population falls in this category, as opposed to a mere 9% in upper-income communities.[383]

The predicament of the unbanked and underbanked in America adds another layer of complexity. Nearly 19% of Americans, according to Federal Reserve research, are insufficiently served by mainstream banking services. This percentage climbs sharply among low-income, less educated, and Black and Hispanic adults. A combination of high minimum balance requirements, exorbitant bank fees, and a deep-seated mistrust of banking institutions have pushed this demographic towards suboptimal local financial services, frequently at a higher cost, such as payday loans and check cashing services. Unbanked Americans shell out an astonishing $189 billion a year solely in fees and interest on financial products, unnecessarily draining the modest resources of Americans without any recourse for better options.[384]

Predatory lending compounds these systemic economic disparities. African American communities often find themselves the target of high-cost subprime mortgages, most insidiously showcased during the build-up to the 2008 financial crisis. A Center for Responsible Lending report revealed that African Americans were 105% more likely than their white counterparts to hold high-cost mortgages, even after adjusting for income and loan comparability. These subprime loans resulted in foreclosures, decimating home equity and exacerbating the racial wealth gap.

The narrative of distrust is further exemplified by the capricious actions of centralized banking institutions in determining loan approvals. During the 2021 Mortgage Refinancing Boom, Wells Fargo rejected an alarming 47% of Black applicants, a rate starkly higher than other lenders. These rejections extended even to high-achieving, underrepresented professionals. Some denials reached almost satirical proportions: as an example, a Black Microsoft engineer married to a doctor with an 800 credit score was declined.[385] This happened, without any executive-level punishment.

A 2007 lawsuit against H&R Block again proves unfortunate differences in treatment between Black and White borrowers. One case highlighted a Black borrower with a credit score of 523 being charged $10,635 to refinance a $167,000 loan. In contrast, a White borrower with a slightly lower 520 credit score was only charged $2,275 to refinance a larger loan of $200,000.[386] And possibly the most egregious display of how prejudiced beliefs unavoidably matriculate into institutional decision-making was revealed by Wells Fargo in 2012. The lawsuit unveiled internal emails among corporate employees who derogatorily referred to Black customers as "mud people." Later, Wells Fargo launched a subprime loan campaign that specifically targeted black churches, which they disparagingly labeled as "ghetto loans".[387]

> This is not an ideal way to engender trust amongst an already skeptical consumer base.

> After this experience, *would you trust them?*

Understanding this context of historical economic suppression allows us to more deeply examine the premise introduced at the beginning of the section. Throughout American banking history, centralized legacy finance has systematically perpetrated modes of exploitation against vulnerable populations, leaving a lasting impact. This long-standing mistreatment not only diminished hope but also ingrained a deep-seated psychological mistrust in the system, even when at times it becomes detrimental to one's own self-interest.

An example of ingrained mistrust influencing a lack of participation is evident in a study by the National Bureau of Economic Research. It reveals that Black business owners, even those with credit scores in the

75th percentile, are more than twice as likely to avoid applying for a loan out of fear of unfair rejection, compared to their white counterparts with similar credit profiles.[388] Showcasing a level of psychological conditioning that would satisfy even Sun Tzu's most ideal method of victory.

> "The supreme art of war
> is to subdue the enemy without fighting."

Further evidence of this mistrust is found in banking preferences: Black communities express higher trust in community credit unions, with a preference rate of 17%, compared to 12.8% for traditional banks.[389] Additionally, the increased use of mobile banking services among Black communities suggests a perception that digital platforms, which don't "see" users in the traditional sense, are less likely to discriminate.

Through this exhaustive experience, over time these communities have extracted a painful yet enlightened lesson: **The only system that can reliably guarantee trust is one COMPLETELY removed from personal subjectivity.** Anything less allows one's self-interest to naturally permeate into institutional determinations. In fact, this hard-learned lesson has become a beacon of wisdom illuminating the path for a greater majority toward equitable, impartial, decentralized alternatives. Fundamentally, the question arises: who oversees the overseers?

In bitcoin, eliminating individual subjectivity from system governance ensures that even your worst adversary cannot undermine your role as a network participant. Their involvement, in any capacity, only reinforces greater accessibility for you. Creating a model where individuals acting in their own self-interest only further strengthens the security and accessibility for all other individuals within the network. Like in judo, where a player uses his opponent's own momentum to advance past a compromising position, **bitcoin uses humanity's inescapable narrow self-interest as the very means to transcend it.**

Consequently, the apparent overrepresentation of historically disenfranchised groups' involvement in bitcoin does not indicate financial naivety. On the contrary, it reflects a profound understanding of the deep-seated flaws within centralized financial intermediaries and the desire to peacefully pursue fairer, more inclusive options. These communities are not merely reacting to their circumstances; they are proactively securing their future where monetary networks, at base level design, are inherently unbiased, untampered, and trustless. Bitcoin is the purest form of immutable moral authority materialized into tangible form and this chapter pedestals the ones keenly adept to recognize it.

Exploring Beyond Bitcoin: CBDCs and PoS Protocols

Having established the need for an alternative system in some capacity, let's broaden our perspective beyond just bitcoin. Our focus will be on evaluating alternatives based on principles like accessibility, fairness, and individual autonomy — values that are becoming increasingly paramount for Americans. While an exhaustive review of every available option is beyond our scope, we'll concentrate on two significant players in the crypto ecosystem: decentralized finance (DeFi) proof-of-stake protocols and Central Bank Digital Currencies (CBDCs). We aim to discern their potential to rectify the inefficiencies inherent in traditional banking and gauge their promise to enhance domestic economic empowerment in a manner comparable to bitcoin.

A CBDC in Search of a Problem

CBDC stands for "Central Bank Digital Currency," a digital fiat currency issued, controlled, and regulated by a central bank. Unlike any other cryptocurrency, CBDCs are direct liabilities of central banks and carry no liquidity, credit, or market risks. CBDCs are touted to enhance financial inclusion, promote transparency, and reduce transaction costs between banking intermediaries. While CBDCs offer a unique utility by combining the advantages of digital currencies with the stability and regulatory oversight of central banks, integrating nationwide centralized monetary control into the expansive programmability of blockchain technology poses significant risks. Such monopolistic integration raises concerns of privacy invasion by the state, which could undermine individual economic liberty and the preservation of democratic values.

CBDCs' autocratic design enables a level of statewide surveillance and transactional control unimaginable in prior history. Its scope is far-reaching. In authoritative hands, this system can flag, block, or reverse transactions at will and expose the identities of transacting parties. It is not just the ability to block or censor transactions that is worrying; the opposite also holds true — it's the ability to require or incentivize transactions. For example, with a central design, a CBDC could be programmed to be spendable only at certain retailers or service providers, by certain people, at certain times. Federal arbiters could maintain lists of "state-favored company providers" that they encourage Americans to spend with versus "discouraged providers" that would deter transactions among less cooperative companies. Yesterday's Orwellian fantasies become today's programmable code. With CBDCs, cash effectively transforms into a state-issued token, like a food stamp, that can only be spent under predefined conditions. This system has the potential to curtail financial freedom and unfairly penalize dissenting Americans at a scale larger and more efficient than banking discrimination today.

In addition to surveillance and control, Federal actors can impose monetary policy directly into every citizen's digital wallet, such as negative interest rates or private cash holdings. These policies create an environment where every CBDC transaction, however trivial, is liable for taxation and can be extracted automatically without permission. The thought of being taxed for transactions as simple as giving your neighbor $20 or your child an allowance is not only egregiously undemocratic and invasive but a clear obstruction to wealth accumulation for economically disadvantaged households.

Banks could also disincentivize saving by capping cash balances (an approach already adopted by the Bahamas through their CBDC[390]) or imposing "penalties" — negative interest rates on balances — over a certain amount. Once CBDCs are implemented, no technical or legal barriers will prevent Central Banks from imposing direct haircuts or repossessions on anyone's cash holdings, regardless of their global location. In this theoretic digital panopticon, trust in banks would be further eroded if not entirely eliminated and would actively discourage the incentive to save responsibly — further condensing the time horizon for those already living paycheck to paycheck.

Implementing CBDCs also increases cybersecurity risks that could uniformly compromise the base layer of economic transactions in the United States. For instance, the Eastern Caribbean Central Bank's CBDC, DCash, went offline for nearly two months in early 2022 due to an expired certificate that caused a system-wide shutdown.[391] Most CBDCs worldwide are implemented on closed government databases like in this example, which is inherently prone to outages, crashes, and various security threats, due to vulnerabilities in centralized infrastructure design.

Despite their regular efforts to enhance technical capabilities, government IT infrastructures remain susceptible to sophisticated cyberattacks from well-resourced adversaries. Imagine the level of difficulty for a thief to pick the lock of one house (centralized security) versus trying to pick the lock of 100,000 homes all simultaneously without alarming any one of the hundred thousand homeowners (decentralized security). Humanly impossible. In the event of a breach in the United States' centralized blockchain database, malicious actors would gain immediate access to every American citizen's transactions, stored permanently on the CBDC ledger. This data is a potential honeypot for hackers, mainly as private blockchains often encode personal transaction data directly on-chain, assuming only "trusted" good-faith users can access the network.

Amid the heightened security and privacy risks, CBDCs offer a suboptimal remedy to a problem already solved. Bitcoin provides a superior protection design, enabling instant, low-cost, and borderless payments for users without compromising American democratic values, such as individual liberty, separation of power, and respect for private property.

Proof-Of-Never-Ending-Stake

On the other hand, Proof of Stake (PoS) protocols have garnered considerable attention as an alternative to bitcoin's Proof of Work (PoW) protocols. Unlike CBDCs, PoS maintains open-source democratic accessibility. While PoS is lauded for its presumed energy efficiency and scalability, a closer examination of its consensus model reveals that it may not be as economically empowering and inclusive as often advertised.

One of the critical issues with PoS protocols is their tendency to grant prominent stakeholders substantial influence over who can transact in the system. In PoS, the chances for a node to be selected and earn rewards are determined by one's stake size in the network. This cycle makes participants with higher stake amounts more likely to become chosen validators. Chosen validators are thus more likely to receive block rewards, which, in turn, further increase their abundant stake holdings. A structure commonly reflected in the current system, where the wealthy can more easily earn "interest" on their savings, while fair access participation from the poor increasingly extends beyond their fiscal means.

> Proof of Stake is a system that deceptively perpetuates the "Golden Rule."

Those who have the Gold make the rules

The design of this consensus structure enables the compounding of wealth and control over time, exacerbating wealth inequality within the network. While some PoS protocols attempt to address potential economic disparities through mechanisms like "Randomized Block Selection" and "Coin Age Selection," these systems still prioritize wealthy coin users receiving block rewards over less resourced users.

Even worse, PoS protocols often involve a significant pre-mine of the token supply, which grants undue decision-making power to elite insiders. Launching a new cryptocurrency usually necessitates the involvement of founders, developers, and venture capital funders. Frequently, these players reserve a large portion of the token's supply for themselves before internally coordinating the eventual sale of the remaining tokens on the open market. Messari 2021 research shows that many crypto projects took a significant portion of their issuance prelaunch. For instance, Solana's company members and VC stakeholders retained 48% of the token's issuance supply. Similarly, projects such as Avalanche, Celo, Blockstack, and Binance all retained 40% of the public market supply.[392]

This authority grants inside users tremendous voting leverage, including disproportionate voting rights to block, reverse, or redistribute transactions, a power made glaringly evident in the 2016 DAO hack. For context, the DAO was an Ethereum-based smart contract that aimed to operate as a decentralized venture capital fund. However, a vulnerability in the smart contract allowed an attacker to siphon off a significant amount of funds. Afterward, the Ethereum community faced a critical decision: to reverse the unauthorized transactions and return the stolen funds to their rightful owners or let them stand. This decision ultimately required a hard fork of the Ethereum blockchain.[393] During this process, influential stakeholders within the Ethereum ecosystem played a significant role in shaping the decision. The power to decide the fate of the stolen funds was not distributed evenly among all participants but rather concentrated in the hands of a few. The choice was made to hard fork the network and restore the stolen funds to their rightful owners. While some may see this decision as benevolent, it unveiled a disconcerting realization for many: "If a small group of node operators can vote for the return of my funds, **they possess an equal capacity to seize them.**"

Another claim made by PoS advocates is that the protocol is more accessible for most users since it does not require access to specialized hardware or cheap electricity, which are often required for PoW mining. While it is true that PoS does not rely on specialized hardware, it does impose staking requirements that act as a high barrier to entry for the typical user. For instance, Ethereum's PoS implementation, known as Ethereum 2.0, requires a minimum staking amount of 32 ETH to participate, which at the time of writing is over $55,000. Since 57% of Americans can not cover a $1,000 emergency with savings, meeting a $55,000 staking requirement is beyond the pale for most. Which, as a consequence, exclusively reserves participation rights for those with considerable disposable income.

The barrier to entry for PoW (Proof of Work) consensus is notably lower than PoS. Unlike systems that require significant initial investments, with PoW, there's no strict minimum to get started with bitcoin mining. Even amateur miners, who might earn a modest $60/month, can become part of a mining pool, reaping dividends proportional to their hash rate contribution.[394]

One intriguing ancillary effect of PoW is the broad applications of its resulting heat generation — such as bitcoin miners used as a heater for households. These devices serve a dual purpose: they not only heat rooms but also mine bitcoin in the process. Thus, homeowners can enjoy the warmth while simultaneously offsetting some of their electricity costs. This innovative approach exemplifies how PoW not only democratizes blockchain to all interested participants but, in doing so, can find practical applications in everyday life.

Bitcoin's fully decentralized proof-of-work protocol eliminates human bias and the "Golden Rule" from operations. It remains indifferent to a user's identity, beliefs, or locale. What fascinates and perplexes many is its capability to encode pure democracy into its design: one voice, one vote, ensuring a balanced distribution of influence. Unlike PoS, the amount of bitcoin an operator might hoard is inconsequential to their decision-making power on the network. This distinctive characteristic is what separates the path between autonomy and tyranny. While PoS might seem alluring on the surface, it only offers a mirage of equality, reflecting the same power imbalances found in age-old systems that marginalized voices seek to abandon.

Central planners ought to be on notice: in this digital age of boundless information, what was once considered privileged asymmetric knowledge for a limited few is now available to all. Bitcoin stands as the first and only monetary asset in existence, where all information is equally accessible to every market participant. This results in the globally trusted universality of bitcoin's price. And no matter how skeptics might artfully market to the contrary, a greater portion of society is beginning to discern the difference.

Lightning Network: How P2P Payments Preserve Domestic Wealth

One saving grace argument is that bitcoin critics consider CBDCs and PoS superior when comparing transaction costs, scalability, and payment processing speed. The following section examines this claim and how bitcoin uniquely dispels such concerns with its Layer 2 solution, the Lightning Network. The Lightning Network allows instant, scalable transactions through off-chain payment channels at a fee of a penny or less. Transactions can be dispatched instantaneously across the globe and are cryptographically secure. This new application layer utilization would be a significant step toward achieving widespread financial access for all. Payments through the Lightning Network can save billions of dollars annually for minority-owned small businesses and remittance payments. With instant transaction speeds at nearly zero cost, the Lightning Network has the payment rail — the infrastructure that allows money transfers between a payer and a payee — to provide peer-to-peer financial solutions that outcompete traditional and alternative money transfer platforms.

NOTE: The Lightning Network can operate purely as a payment rail, rendering the speculative volatility of bitcoin — which might be a deterrent for some — negligible.

Saving Small Businesses Billions

Now, let's consider the complexity of the typical credit card payment process when purchasing a $5 cup of coffee at Starbucks. This seemingly simple transaction undergoes a convoluted journey involving multiple banking intermediaries, each deducting a fee, often unbeknownst to most consumers. Consider the following scenario: caramel macchiato in hand, you swipe your card at the Starbucks register.

This triggers a digital chain reaction beneath the surface:

Step 1. The swipe activates the point-of-sale system at Starbucks to contact its acquiring bank (say, Bank of America), which subsequently gets your card's network (Visa) to process the transaction.

Step 2. Visa then reaches out to your issuing bank (Chase) to validate the transaction based on your creditworthiness, geographical background, education information, criminal history, etc.

Step 3. After validation, Chase makes the final transactional authorization, permitting Starbucks to receive your money, which you're reassured of as the terminal reads "Card Approved."

In stark contrast, the Lightning Network eliminates these intermediaries completely. By functioning as a digital bearer asset, the assurance of payment is embedded within the transaction itself. Your $5 tab for coffee bypasses all banks and traditional payment processors, removing extra fees, and sends payment directly to the recipient's account. This is financial democratization in its purest form, granting unprecedented control and financial autonomy to individuals and small businesses rather than seceding wealth to ineffectual middlemen.

The Lightning Network furthers this democratization with its global accessibility, transaction speed, and cost efficiency, unlocking the immense potential for financial inclusion. For instance, creditworthiness checks, a common roadblock in traditional banking systems, are not a requirement in the Lightning Network. Thus, individuals and businesses have permission to transact based solely on their bitcoin holdings rather than any indelible characteristics such as their identity. This functions much like cash: if you have it on hand, you can buy it. It is especially advantageous for small businesses, which often bear the brunt of interchange fees and delayed settlements in conventional systems. By eliminating these barriers, bitcoin and the Lightning Network can significantly enhance the profitability of US small businesses, who now are taking note.

To underscore this point, a Skynova survey found that nearly one-third of business owners and top executives now accept cryptocurrency payments, predominantly driven by the belief that cryptocurrency is the "currency of the future" (49%). 44% regard it as a "strategic marketing tactic to appeal to younger generations and attract new customers." Of all programmable money types, bitcoin is the top choice, favored by 58% of respondents.[395]

Interestingly, one in four small businesses that currently do not accept cryptocurrencies "would like to but lack the necessary knowledge" to do so.

Burdensome interchange fees from payment processors are a principal contributor to why small businesses seek better payment alternatives. These fees, which small businesses and minority owners often face, can severely hinder wealth accumulation and preservation. Interchange fees are charges incurred each time a credit or debit card is swiped for payment and have long been a taxing overhead for businesses. According to a 2023 study by the Nilson Report, these fees, primarily paid to major card companies like Mastercard and Visa, represented a colossal $160 billion in costs for US retailers.[396]

The disproportionate impact of interchange fees on small businesses is especially concerning. While large corporations managed to negotiate an average interchange fee of 1.5% in 2023, small companies, often lacking such bargaining power, were slapped with an average fee of 2.22%.[397] Every percentage point counts for such companies, and onerous fees can significantly inhibit business growth and profitability.

When we examine minority-owned businesses, which constitute approximately 16% of all US businesses, the scale of the burden becomes starkly evident. Given the $160 Billion in merchant fees paid nationally, minority business owners would pay roughly **$25.6 billion annually in interchange fees** to payment processing companies.

Bitcoin's Lightning Network offers an intriguing alternative. Even compared to the lower 1.5% fee that large businesses can negotiate, the Lightning Network can still provide unmatched savings for owners. For simplicity, let's imagine that each Lightning Network transaction incurs an average fee of 2 cents, although this may vary based on network traffic. To accurately compute the total cost of Lightning Network fees that minority-owned businesses would accrue annually, we need to know the annual number of transactions, a figure not provided here. Therefore, we'll make some assumptions to illustrate the scenario.

Assuming that the average transaction value for each sale is $50, the **$25.6 billion in interchange fees** paid by minority-owned businesses equate to roughly 512 million transactions (i.e., $25.6 billion / $50 per transaction).

If each transaction incurs a fee of $0.02, the Lightning Network as a payment option would cost minority businesses roughly **$10,240,000** annually in total transaction fees:

512,000,000 transactions * $0.02 per transaction = $10,240,000

By switching to the bitcoin Lightning Network, minority-owned businesses could lower their transaction fees from the estimated $25.6 billion they currently pay to Mastercard and Visa, down to $10.2 million. This indicates a staggering potential saving of virtually the full $25.6 billion annually, minus a few million.

Consider the profound impact that allocating an additional $25.6 billion as disposable income could have on addressing societal challenges in minority neighborhoods. Local businesses can reinvest these savings directly into their own operations instead of letting their wealth be reabsorbed back into heavily financed conglomerates. This means enhancing community infrastructures, supporting educational initiatives, and promoting long-term financial empowerment, all using funds sourced from within the community. In a time when inclusive growth is the key to national prosperity, leveraging innovative economic systems like the bitcoin Lightning Network signifies a step toward creating a more equitable and resilient economy. As minority-owned businesses become a significant bulwark against systemic disparities, the potential for nationwide transformation becomes palpable. It's an investment in the future, where community upliftment and national progress go hand in hand.

Remittance Family Savings

Much like interchange costs, expensive remittance fees also serve as a hidden economic burden, disproportionately affecting underrepresented Americans. In the United States, remittances play a crucial role in the domestic economy, with total remittance payments reaching $148 billion in 2017. The primary recipient countries of these remittances were Mexico ($30 Billion) and China ($16 Billion).[398]

Traditionally, entities like Western Union have held the reins, charging substantial fees to facilitate international money transmissions. Imagine sending money to a dear Aunt in Mexico or China and seeing a whopping 6.9% or 9.9% of your cash evaporate as a remittance fee. Price gouging customers on international transfers has long been a lucrative standard.

Corner the market, snuff out alternatives, and voila — unchecked exploitation without recourse. However, times have changed, and customers no longer need to settle for less. By tapping into Lightning's peer-to-peer money transfer network, Americans can send the total amount of their digital payment directly to their family members without intermediary meddling — at near zero cost.

Harnessing this swift and borderless payment method, the US Latino community sending money to Mexico alone could reclaim an impressive $2 billion of their hard-earned wealth yearly. In the same breath, Asian Americans could see an additional $1.6 billion remain in their accounts yearly just from the money they save from sending to China.

Imagine the ripple effect of such vast savings if this method expanded to the rest of the 194 countries Americans send to yearly — from bolstering education and health to seeding billions into new enterprises. These aren't just numbers; they're opportunities. Opportunities to reshape communities, invest in dreams, and drive a robust national economic surge.

Championing permissionless peer-to-peer global transfer systems, like the Lightning Network, ensures that the fruits of prosperity benefit our nation's core economic producers while preventing undue wealth siphoning by idle rent-seekers. But for small businesses and minority families, embracing this shift means more than just a switch in payment systems. It's an embrace of a socio-economic revolution that restores financial independence.

As outdated business models thriving on parasitic interchange and remittance fees grow harder to justify, one has to wonder: Why route payments through Visa or Western Union when direct, instant, fee-less transactions are a button push away? The modern customer demands more, and only businesses embracing a customer-centric tech approach will successfully adapt to the shaping digital landscape, leaving behind the relics of superfluous toll-collecting systems.

Stakeholders' Role in Bitcoin's Success

For bitcoin to succeed in America, it calls for the collective, well-intentioned efforts of all stakeholders. It demands innovation from legacy institutions — both public and private — to remain competitive in the digital age. Regardless of their political leanings, policymakers must engage in honest acknowledgment and constructive discussions.

Community leaders must spearhead grassroots initiatives to enhance financial literacy and accessibility to ensure widespread adoption and understanding. Through unimpeded collaboration and concerted efforts, communities in critical need of economic opportunity can stand a fighting chance to participate in a newfound digital awakening while the opportunity is still ripe, rather than again be sidelined by gatekeepers who reap the early spoils.

Policy Stakeholders

As an open-access, fully permissionless, transparent monetary network, bitcoin is fundamentally democratized and nonpartisan, which should attract interest across both left and right political spectrums. Government policymakers across party lines must recognize the natural bipartisan nature of this innovative technology. With strategic use, bitcoin can become a cease-fire common ground policy area, ushering political wins for Democrats and Republicans alike.

Democrats

The Democratic party has consistently championed fair access to financial services and inclusion. With its inherent pseudonymity, inclusivity, and consensus properties, bitcoin holds significant potential to alleviate challenges rooted deep in systemic economic inequality.

Central to the ethos of bitcoin is its challenge to hegemonic power structures. Its decentralized nature ensures that banking and lending aren't overseen by singular entities with potential biases or discriminatory tendencies. This translates to a democratized financial ecosystem where the traditional pitfalls of bank lending discrimination — such as inflated interest rates, biased loan denials, or subprime offerings based on race, gender, or geographic location — become obsolete.

When we consider the entrenched disparities — like the troubling lending biases against Black-owned businesses who on average pay 1.4% more in interest compared to White borrowers despite comparable creditworthiness[399] — bitcoin's decentralized architecture becomes a beacon of financial justice.

Further amplifying its progressive credentials, bitcoin is a champion of radical inclusivity. It's more than just a cryptocurrency; it's a movement for financial liberation. Every individual, regardless of their socio-economic status, ethnicity, or geographical constraints, is invited to participate in this economic revolution. Bitcoin tears down the oppressive walls of traditional finance, democratizing access and programmatically ensuring that every voice is heard.

For Progressives, embracing bitcoin transcends mere policy. It's an affirmation of the party's unwavering commitment to intersectionality, equity, and a bold vision of a more inclusive financial future. It represents a tangible stride towards dismantling systemic barriers and building a financial infrastructure rooted in justice, fairness, and collective empowerment. For those who envision a world where economic systems uplift rather than oppress, bitcoin is not just an ally — it's the way forward.

Republicans

From a global national security vantage, bitcoin emerges not just as a new technological marvel, but as a steward of American democratic principles. Nations are eagerly investing in blockchain, striving to redefine their stature in this tech-driven era.

Look at China's Belt and Road Initiative. This strategic maneuver grants infrastructure loans to developing nations that are structured in a way that entrenches Chinese dependence and grants greater global economic leverage. What's more concerning is the digital yuan, steeped in surveillance potential. Should it become a dominant trading currency, not only could the U.S. dollar's preeminence be at risk, but the very ideals of privacy and autonomy, cornerstones of American conservatism, could be under threat as authoritarian digital blueprints spread.

Yet, the landscape is mired in regulatory ambiguity. Our once-proud claim of being the frontrunner in innovation development is waning, losing 2% of our blockchain developer workforce to foreign nations annually due to our stifling regulatory barriers and uncertainty. Countries like the EU and Singapore, with their clear and welcoming crypto regulations, are beckoning more of our homegrown talent to their shores. If Republican policymakers value American leadership and the spirit of free enterprise, championing clear guidelines for bitcoin becomes unquestioned.

On a structural front, data security and protection from illicit finance is also a political priority. Bitcoin's robust encryption technology, a hallmark of privacy and security, ensures transactional sanctity, aligning with the conservative ethos of individual rights and privacy protections. And, as Tom Wood chronicled in the previous chapter, contrary to the myth of its 'dark-web' associations, bitcoin's infinite traceability makes illicit activities a poor choice for criminal actors, which over the years many have learned and largely been deterred. Chainalysis 2022 crime report confirmed this notion in a study, which found that only 0.24% of all blockchain transactions were flagged for even possibly being nefarious.

Lastly, any conservative recognizes the sanctity of hard-earned money. The alarming fact that nearly 80% of all U.S. dollars were printed between January 2020 and October 2021, leading to inflation rates soaring to 8% the following year, is a testament to the need for stable, value-preserving alternatives. The dollar's dramatic loss in value since its birth underscores this urgency. Bitcoin's limited supply and decentralized nature, offer a solution that aligns with conservative ideals of financial prudence, self-reliance, and stability. In championing bitcoin, Republican policymakers would be endorsing a system that safeguards American wealth, fortifies our domestic security, and reinforces the nation's core values.

Institutional Stakeholders

As bitcoin gains popularity, legacy financial stakeholders must reconsider their long-standing business models and innovate to remain competitive. Embracing consumer demands on their terms and ensuring unobstructed accessibility only bolsters America's economic strength rather than exposing any perceived instability. Far from a liability, this radical shift empowers the United States to unlock the full breadth of its untapped domestic economic potential.

Premier capital allocators already align with this tectonic shift, refusing to simply observe from the sidelines. Case in point: BlackRock, the world's largest asset manager presiding over $9.5 trillion, has registered a bitcoin exchange-traded fund (ETF) with the United States Securities and Exchange Commission (SEC). This move underlines the firm's acceptance of bitcoin as a legitimate asset class. It unveils a new pathway for cautious-minded investors to engage with bitcoin without needing to buy, hold, or secure the cryptocurrency themselves. Goldman Sachs' 2021 launch of its cryptocurrency trading desk as a part of the Global Currencies and Emerging Markets (GCEM) Division is another indication of the growing demand among its client base.[400]

Meanwhile, JPMorgan Chase unveiled Onyx in 2020, the world's first bank-led blockchain platform to expedite digital asset trading and settlements. The firm's pioneering venture bolsters bitcoin's credibility as a legitimate asset class. It underscores the importance of digital assets in ensuring that the United States remains at the vanguard of innovation for decades.[401]

These three institutions, which collectively manage over $12 trillion, are compelling evidence of bitcoin's journey from a fringe asset to a recognized player among established financial juggernauts. Bitcoin is increasingly recognized as a symbol for the economic ethos of our time — adaptation, innovation, and prosperity. As more institutions join this journey — through incidental altruism or otherwise — bitcoin acceptability spreads, further unlocking the economic potential of this nation.

Community Stakeholders

Community stakeholders play a pivotal role in utilizing novel technologies to bridge the economic divide. An initiative like BTC Impact, a Black-owned, female-led organization, is one such example of a community stakeholder harnessing the transformative power of bitcoin to address wealth inequality. Through their "S9S8" project, BTC Impact is partnering with local officials to integrate bitcoin miners into Section 8 housing units. This innovative approach generates revenue for housing departments and residents alike. The proceeds accumulated over a resident's stay can be channeled towards down payments for their first home, turning a perennial struggle into an achievable goal.[402]

Influential figures like artist Jay-Z and Block CEO Jack Dorsey are contributing to this burgeoning grassroots-led digital ecosystem. Together, they established the "Bitcoin Academy" in Bedford-Stuyvesant, Brooklyn, a community with approximately 2,300 residents living in Marcy project housing. This free, 2 ½ month intensive program provides in-depth education on bitcoin. It explores the network's utility, highlights responsible investing principles, and aims to close information gaps in the realm of cryptocurrency. An initiative that prioritizes early, in-depth education to ensure residents are equipped with the specialized financial knowledge that will likely influence their economic futures.[403]

The impact of these community-based initiatives extends far beyond bitcoin; they serve as a launchpad for broader financial literacy, exposing participants to vital concepts: responsible budgeting, asset-building, savings management, etc., all tools necessary to navigate the financial landscape confidently.

Community stakeholders are urged to use their grassroots credibility to penetrate the hearts and minds of neighbors more effectively than any top-down approach conceived. In this context, organizers have the chance to spearhead the dissemination of financial knowledge suited for our evolving times to the communities that stand most to benefit.

Final Thoughts

In the lexicon of national security, bitcoin presents itself as a strategic asset, not only due to its decentralized and transparent nature but also due to the profound accessibility it offers to all Americans. Ensuring that every citizen, irrespective of socio-economic background, has access to robust financial tools is a force multiplier in the context of national security. Historically, robust domestic economies have been the bedrock upon which national defense capabilities can be built. A universally accessible financial system, free from traditional barriers and gatekeepers, can significantly amplify this strength.

When segments of our society, particularly those traditionally suppressed, can transcend predatory systems through using tools of self-sovereignty like bitcoin, we're not merely observing an economic shift, but proactively reinforcing a critical pillar of our domestic infrastructure. This diversification of financial mechanisms, combined with its inherent inclusivity, strengthens our resilience against both internal economic inequalities and external financial threats.

By fostering economic participation and equity for all Americans, we're not just enhancing our national economy but also fortifying our polity against external adversities. As with any security strategy, diversity, adaptability, and inclusivity are key; bitcoin offers all three.

QR Code to **Chapter 9** Endnote Links and Figures
on the Bitcoin Today Coalition website:

381 More Than One in Ten Americans Surveyed Invest in Cryptocurrency – Norris Research Corporation at the University of Chicago
382 The Color of Money: Black Banks and the Racial Wealth Gap – Mehrsa Baradaran, pages 17-26
383 CFPB Report Finds 26 Million Consumers Are Credit Invisible – Consumer Financial Protection Bureau
384 Bitcoin Policy Institute Submits Report to US Department of Commerce on Digital Asset Competitiveness – Bitcoin Policy Institute
385 Wells Fargo Rejected Half Its Black Applicants in Mortgage Refinancing Boom – Bloomberg
386 From Redlining to Predatory Lending: The History of Housing Discrimination and Its Impact on the American Dream – Creditslips
387 The Color of Money: Black Banks and the Racial Wealth Gap – Mehrsa Baradaran, pages 17-26
388 Black and White: Access to Capital Among Minority-Owned Startups – Robert Fairlie, National Bureau of Economic Research
389 Diversity Counts for Credit Unions – Jim DuPlessis, Credit Union Times
390 Individual – Sand Dollar
391 Eastern Caribbean DCash Outage Is Test for Central Bank Digital Currencies – Jim Wyss, Bloomberg
392 Power and Wealth in Cryptoeconomies – Ryan Watkins, Messari
393 CoinDesk Turns 10: 2016 - How The DAO Hack Changed Ethereum and Crypto – David Morris, Coindesk
394 Bitcoin Miner: I Haven't Paid for Heat in Three Years – Yahoo Finance
395 Report: Nearly a Third of Small Businesses in the U.S. Currently Accept Payments in Crypto – Ana Grabundzija, CryptoSlate
396 US Merchant Processing Fees Top $160 Billion – The Nilson Report, Globe Newswire
397 New Jersey Enacts Law Capping Surcharges Lynne Marek, Payments Dive
398 Immigrants in the U.S. Sent Over $148 Billion to Their Home Countries in 2017 [Infographic] – Niall McCarthy, Forbes
399   Black Americans Feel Disproportionate Pain From High-Interest Rates – C. Daniels and S. Lane, The Hill
400 Goldman Sachs Unveils New Cryptocurrency Trading Team, H. Son and N. Turak, CNBC
401 Onyx – J.P.Morgan, Accessed August 29, 2023
402 Bringing Bitcoin Sovereignty to the People – BTC Impact Accessed August 29, 2023
403 The Bitcoin Academy Accessed August 29, 2023

CHAPTER 10

DEFECTION 2.0: WINNING HEARTS AND MINDS WITH BITCOIN

By Kyle Schneps

Kyle Schneps *is the co-founder of BTC VETS and an Advisor to the Bitcoin Today Coalition's Board of Directors. He has held a variety of Federal and State Government positions, most recently working as Special Advisor for State Operations in the New York State Executive Chamber. Prior to his role in NY State government, Kyle spent most of his career serving as a US Intelligence Officer, which was preceded by a diplomatic post as Advisor to the Special Envoy for Guantanamo Bay Closure at the US Department of State. He is a former White House Fellow, during which time he worked across different national security and federal budgeting roles. Kyle is now Vice President of Public Policy at Foundry, a Digital Currency Group Company. He holds two Masters degrees in International Affairs and Public Health from Columbia University.*

Introduction

Bitcoin is a permissionless and transparent ledger that is accessible to everyone no matter their race, religion, nationality, wealth, or political beliefs. The decentralized global network of computers that composes the bitcoin network is the largest and most secure digital network in the world, having never been hacked or corrupted. The intrinsic characteristics of the bitcoin network as mentioned above — namely its permissionless freedom to transact, systemic transparency, equal access, personal privacy, decentralized checked power, and real-world security

— are all similarly present in the founding democratic principles of the United States of America.

It is therefore fitting for the United States Government to adopt and promote this technology, if not yet as a currency and unit of account, then surely as a common onramp to American values for those who have not been born into the luxury of a democratic ideal.

By supporting the bitcoin network and promoting global access to it, the United States Government can renew itself as a beacon of democracy, guiding the hearts and minds of people across the world toward the American principles of freedom, equality, privacy, and private property. And away from tyrannical and oppressive regimes who oppose such pluralistic ideals in favor of socialized ownership, surveillance of citizenry, and centralized omniscience of personal finances.

In this chapter, I first outline why people living under tyrannical or corrupt regimes gravitate toward bitcoin adoption. Second, I demonstrate how the United States can win hearts and minds around the world by amplifying bitcoin's core values — which are also those of the United States. Finally, I argue that Cold War-era principles of promoting defection from US foreign adversaries can be done on a much larger scale with bitcoin — to the great advantage of United States world-leadership.

We start where I first encountered bitcoin: in Africa.

Real-World Causes of Bitcoin Adoption

My first encounter with bitcoin was in West Africa. I was sick with malaria in a small clinic and a nurse told me in conversation that she sometimes saves her money in bitcoin. Having only seen the occasional sensational headline about the subject, I inquired rather incredulously as to why she would do such a thing. Her answer took me aback: she did not trust her country's president. He was corrupt, she said, and she recounted how her family some generations earlier had had much of their savings plundered by a previous leader who subsequently fled the country. Bitcoin, she continued, allowed her to save privately and safely without using the country's banking system, which she believed served as a de facto slush fund for those in power. This is a common theme I've encountered during my time living outside the United States: people adopt bitcoin not to get rich, but to maintain their wealth in the face of corrupt governments and failed institutions.

Near a war-torn region in East Africa, I encountered similar stories. There were many migrants and internally displaced persons moving through or living in the area. It was common to see families or individuals struggling to carry what they could of their most precious belongings. Some would hide wads of their home currency upon their person, only to watch it become devalued and mostly worthless by the time they crossed the border.

Luckier families carried jewelry they hoped to trade. Some had US dollars, but these were increasingly hard — if not impossible — to obtain. All lived in constant fear that their valuables could be seized at checkpoints, ransacked by unpaid soldiers, or simply stolen by fellow migrants. One man I met and later befriended revealed to me that he traveled more securely storing his money in bitcoin. He wisely sent most of it digitally to a family member in Europe for safekeeping, and kept some of it accessible in a nondescript password written on a piece of paper. By doing this, he felt much more confident that nobody would steal his wealth — an advantage impossible with the various physical bearer instruments that other families carried.

This is another key reason why many people around the world rely on bitcoin: it allows unbanked people to store their wealth, send their wealth, and even carry it with them safely in the all-too-common events of natural or manmade disasters. Try doing that with gold bars!

While the above examples are merely anecdotal, they hint at larger trends that have developed in Africa over the past decade that can be backed up with data. Nigeria, for example, home to Africa's largest economy and population, has placed third in year-over-year growth of bitcoin and other cryptocurrency usage globally.[404] Countries like Kenya, Ghana, and South Africa are not far behind. As the Brookings Institute recently articulated: "Because cryptocurrency platforms bypass traditional banking services by introducing decentralized peer-to-peer lending services, they can help level the economic playing field and expand finance options to underserved customer markets." Nowhere is this truer than in sub-Saharan Africa.

Rapid bitcoin and digital asset adoption in Africa can be narrowed down to two fundamental causes: youth and functionality. According to the United Nations,[405] sub-Saharan Africa is home to the world's youngest population, with 70% of its people under 30 years of age. Such youthful populations are much more comfortable using new technologies and digital assets than their parents and grandparents. In fact, some of the most innovative drivers of bitcoin adoption, such as the ability to send bitcoin via text message without an internet connection,[406] have been developed in Africa. Consequently, there are now multiple bitcoin conferences on the continent that are highly attended by people from all over the world.

Regarding functionality, bitcoin serves key roles within the economies of African States and, more importantly, in the lives of everyday citizens. Many in sub-Saharan Africa — and across the world generally — rely on remittances from family and friends who earn money in other countries. The World Bank estimates that sub-Saharan African nations received $53 billion in remittance payments in 2022.[407] Due to the high fees and cumbersome cash wiring processes of companies like Moneygram and Western Union, many Africans are shifting to sending remittances with bitcoin or stablecoins because they settle instantly and have extremely low fees relative to traditional remittance service providers. This results in the cutting-out of unnecessary middlemen and larger payments being received by those in need.

Bitcoin's fixed monetary supply is also attractive to sub-Saharan Africans and across the world, as it results in a store of value for people's wealth, which is especially important for people living in nations with high inflation rates. Nigeria, for example, has an inflation rate of 24%, Ghana is at 43%, and Zimbabwe's is at over 100%.[408] Many across the continent do not even feel that they, or even their governments, have control over their own monetary policies, with many currencies on the continent controlled by former colonial powers, like France,[409] or beholden to the neo-colonial lending practices of massive international banks.[410]

Therefore, people living in these nations are turning to bitcoin, whose fixed issuance and supply offers refuge to those seeking easy access to a store of value over time, providing an economic life-raft despite the volatility resulting from the asset's nascency and supply inelasticity.

Remember, most people around the world — and even in the United States — do not have access to Wall Street investors and automated 401k retirement accounts. Instead, it's bitcoin that is increasingly seen by the unbanked as a long-term solution to many of the monetary disadvantages faced in the Global South. Many, if not all, of the above considerations can be applied to people living on every continent across the world. From Ukrainians in Europe wishing to safeguard their wealth in a time of war, to Argentines adopting bitcoin to protect against skyrocketing inflation.

We've discussed how many people around the world — who do not benefit from living under flags with strong democratic and financial institutions — are gravitating to bitcoin for a variety of reasons. Namely, bitcoin is a technology that:

1. allows everyday people to maintain their wealth in the face of corrupt or authoritarian governments and institutions,

2. permits displaced people to transport or safeguard their wealth despite forced migration movements,

3. offers solutions to sending remittances internationally while avoiding usurious middlemen and cumbersome settlement layers, and

4. helps people combat rampant inflation rates often caused by institutional monetary mismanagement and legacy neocolonial practices.

Bitcoin offers users two options, never before possible: the ability to opt out of oppressive regimes that are antithetical to US values and national security, while also letting them opt into the decentralized principles that undergird the United States Constitution. Bitcoin is a loud and unyielding advertisement for American values that wins the hearts and minds of people in troubled parts of the world without costing the US Government a thing.

Winning Hearts and Minds Without Boots on the Ground

Competition between nation-states is often viewed as a battle between competing ways of life, a competition between the ideals that underpin conflicting societies. Therefore, conquering nations often accompany physical power with softer inducements intended to convince others of the benefits of being conquered.

Classical Greeks and Romans often justified their perpetual states of warfare as the fight of democratic or republican virtues against the barbarism of autocratic Persians or unsophisticated Germanic tribes (the very word 'barbarian' stems from the Greek word for those that are not Greek or do not speak Greek).

Later, European colonial powers convinced themselves that their self-interested conquests across the world served as a "civilizing" force for good. Even the present century — following the 9/11 attacks on New York

City — saw nearly two decades of warfare by the United States and its allies that pitted the Western ideals of freedom and equality against the religious extremism of the Taliban, al-Qaeda, ISIS, and other groups.

And no matter what you may think of such stated ideals, whether they are of noble intent or mere justifications for baser goals, the actions taken are always aimed at swaying one society to eventually adhere to — and ally itself with — another's way of life. The perception being that such cultural adaptation serves to eliminate future conflict through the subjugation of one country or culture to another.

Alexander the Great, for example, insisted upon the intermarriage of himself and his officers into Persian royal society after his famous victory, which he hoped would promote the staying power of his conquest and win the hearts and minds of Persians (had he lived longer, he may have been more successful).[411]

Mohammad, for his part as a brilliant General, would not just conquer a particular territory but insist — under threat of death — its citizens adopt Islam to encourage social cohesion over time and expand what would become the caliphate.[412]

The modern era has seen a strong preference for softer power methodologies to persuade the hearts and minds of targeted populations, counterintuitively enacted during times of war. This often takes the form of asymmetric warfare coupled with humanitarian aid. Or proxy wars that buffer major powers from direct conflict but serve as a signaled advocacy for their way of life. Or military aid and advisement in exchange for political, economic, or cultural concessions to the wealthier nation.

But what if the United States Government could supplement its defense capabilities and promote its fundamental values — democracy, transparency, accountability, economic inclusion — without engaging in any of the power tactics discussed above? By encouraging the use of the bitcoin network, the US Government would be tapping into a decentralized network that promotes US values 24 hours a day, 7 days a week, 365 days a year. All for free, with no cost to the US taxpayer, and no risk to our US military service members.

Bitcoin does this by offering a constant and reliable alternative to autocratic regimes and their methods of financial control over their populations. Any citizen living in Putin's Russia, Xi's China, or even in stateless kleptocracies, can now opt out of centrally manipulated currencies and opt into preserving their wealth through the bitcoin network, which is beyond the control of any centralized entity and therefore insulated from political whim and corruption. This is especially true for places like Russia and China, where US dollars are highly controlled and monitored by the State and average people have limited access.

By encouraging the adoption of bitcoin where US Dollars are scarce or controlled, the United States can be seen as encouraging people to achieve financial freedom beyond the confines of their autocratic governments. And, as most autocratic governments are funded and supported by extracting wealth from their citizens through monetary debasement or outright theft, bitcoin offers a way for those citizens to defect financially from such oppressive regimes. Thus, a better way of thinking about this concept might be to consider bitcoin as a new kind of defection from autocracy that is available to all in society: Defection 2.0.

The best way to understand Defection 2.0 is to view it through the lens of Defection 1.0, most prominent and publicized during the 20th Century Cold War between the United States and Soviet Union.

Defection 1.0 vs. Defection 2.0

The legacy Cold War system of defection rewarded the elite few who chose to publicly opt out of authoritarian regimes in favor of Western democracies. The bitcoin network now allows all people, no matter their station or class, to privately opt out of tyranny by investing autocrat-controlled currencies into a decentralized global system of financial independence. But what is defection and how does defection 2.0 decentralize and de-risk the practice in favor of the United States?

A defector, in the traditional sense, is a person — usually someone in an elite position with access to important information — who abandons his or her country in favor of a new country that often has an opposing or differing ideology. A defector is offered physical protection and financial reward for the information they provide.

However, for US Intelligence during the Cold War, defectors represented a more troubling conundrum: how does one determine the veracity of a defector's information, especially if that defector is part of a sophisticated intelligence organization like the KGB? Are they genuinely defecting and revealing valuable intelligence? Or are they defecting as part of a larger intelligence operation meant to mislead the U.S.? Perhaps one false defector is simply defecting to discredit a legitimate defector — and the hall of mirrors circles round from there.

Perhaps the most controversial declassified defector case involved Anatoliy Golitsyn and Yuri Nosenko. Both Golitsyn and Nosenko were high-ranking KGB officers who were accepted as defectors to the United States, but each offered contradicting intelligence discrediting the other. Eventually, CIA Counter-Intelligence Chief James Jesus Angleton sided with Golitsyn,[413] locking Nosenko up in a dark site in Maryland where he was denied access to his possessions and occasionally dosed with LSD. Four years later Nosenko was determined to be a bona fide agent and released from solitary confinement. This is a clear case of how Defection 1.0 often resulted in cases where the confusion and ambiguity involved in soliciting traditional defectors wasn't worth the effort.

Due to the myriad doubts that defection raised regarding the legitimacy of the intelligence proffered (as illustrated in the extreme above), defectors generally became more valuable for their public propaganda than for their actual information. Many Soviet defectors to the United States were often paraded in front of the press to demonstrate the winning ideology of capitalism over communism.

The Soviet Union did the same with British defectors who had run their course as agents and were relocated to the Soviet Union. For example, notorious British Intelligence officer and arguably the greatest traitor of all time, Kim Philby, was toured around Moscow to demonstrate the failures of Western capitalism.[414] Thus defection during the Cold War eventually garnered more value as an ideological publicity statement than as a trusted source of human intelligence collection.

Another problem with Defection 1.0 is that the ability to defect from a perceived tyrannical or authoritarian regime has — until now — been limited to elites with access to sensitive information. There surely were many average citizens living under the draconian oppression of the Soviet Union who wished they could defect and opt out of the Soviet regime. Or, at the very least, safeguard their personal wealth from Stalin and his successors. But they had no access to anything of value to the opposing systems that might receive them, and therefore were left without options. They had to not only stay in the Soviet Union, but also to continue participating in and perpetuate its economic and cultural restrictions.

Bitcoin Fixes This with Defection 2.0

Bitcoin represents a monetary system that allows the average person, no matter where they live, to opt out of the economic chains of tyrannical and authoritarian regimes. Anybody with an internet connection can now cease all but the most necessary financial participation in the country in which they live by converting their state-controlled currency into a decentralized and incorruptible store of value. Value that can be stored privately or carried over borders by refugees without risk of confiscation. Value that is free of debasement by a corrupt or incompetent regime. Value that, while potentially volatile in the short term, has proven to be a hedge against inflationary policies in the long term.

Whereas those elite legacy defectors fleeing authoritarian regimes would be forced to leave their family and possessions behind, now anyone can opt out of the monetary shackles placed upon them by authoritarian regimes while still functioning in the society in which they live. By opting out of a tyrannical system and into a decentralized protocol like bitcoin, there is no longer the worry of your wealth being confiscated by prejudicial laws, as has happened so many times throughout history. In an age when so much of our identity and personal choices are tracked by governments and corporations, bitcoin offers the ultimate protection for the minority opinion in that it safeguards one's wealth from a corrupt regime's power players and political whims. Bitcoin is therefore the best safeguard for oppressed people living under regimes that are leveraging tools of digital authoritarianism such as Central Bank Digital Currencies (CBDC).

Since the United States has previously recognized that defection has more value as a public opportunity to champion Western ideals over those of tyranny, then we must now recognize that the bitcoin network is Defection 2.0. For it allows all people to opt into a free and decentralized monetary system that cannot be manipulated by tyrants for personal gain. The legacy cold war system rewarded a small group of elites by allowing them to defect from tyranny. In return, the receiving nation was able to publicly claim a small ideological victory.

But now, it is worth sacrificing the public nature of the defection of the few for the private monetary defection of the many across the world who do not wish to participate in the strictures of authoritarian regimes. It is for this reason that so many autocracies, like the Chinese Communist Party [415] and previously, the Supreme Leader of Iran,[416] have banned this technology. They do not want the public quietly opting out of their control.

The United States must embrace bitcoin as a symbol of the democratic and capitalist ideal, so that people can privately defect into a US-aligned monetary system that safeguards their personal wealth and independence from tyrannical systems that use CBDCs to enhance ubiquitous technical surveillance capabilities.

There is no better way of fighting corrupt autocratic regimes than supporting networks that enable the global public to opt out of all but the most necessary financial ties that bind them to such states. Of all these networks, bitcoin is by far the best choice due to its decentralized nature, instant settlement, transportability and unrivaled security.

The United States government must re-solidify its role as a beacon of democracy across the globe by offering its unwavering support for this technology. One that decentralizes and level-sets the opportunity for defection, toward liberty, all across the world.

QR Code to **Chapter 10** Endnote Links and Figures on the Bitcoin Today Coalition website:

404 Cryptocurrency Penetrates Key Markets in Sub-Saharan Africa as an Inflation Mitigation and Trading Vehicle – Chainalysis
405 Young People's Potential, the Key to Africa's Sustainable Development – Jason Mulikita, United Nations
406 How Africans Are Using Bitcoin Without Internet Access – Vladimir Fomene, Forbes Digital Assets
407 Remittances Grow 5% in 2022, Despite Global Headwinds – The World Bank
408 Top 10 African countries with the highest inflation rate, mid-way into 2023 – Chinedu Okafor, Business Insider Africa
409 Macron Isn't So Post-Colonial After All – M. Kelta and A. Gladstein, Foreign Policy
410 Neocolonialism and the IMF – Joyce Chen, Harvard Political Review
411 Anabasis of Alexander – Arrian of Nicomedia, Project Gutenberg
412 Muhammad: The Warrior Prophet – Richard Gabriel, Historynet
413 Wilderness of Mirrors – Jefferson Morley, The Intercept
414 A Spy Among Friends: Kim Philby and the Great Betrayal – Ben Macintyre
415 The People's Bank of China Bans Bitcoin, Again – McShane, Bitcoin Magazine
416 Iran Reportedly Bans Trading Of Bitcoin Mined Abroad – Namcios, Bitcoin Magazine

CONCLUSION

In just over a decade, bitcoin has grown from a niche software breakthrough into a potential solution for many of today's global challenges. What began as a peer-to-peer public ledger is now contributing to financial technology innovation, energy transformation, and — as illustrated in this book — strengthens a wide variety of international security interests. It only makes sense for the United States to be at the forefront in supporting this revolutionary technology.

China is on a mission to become the world's next dominant superpower, using global technology networks to exploit, surveil, and control other sovereign nations. Essays in this book have demonstrated how it has already spread its tentacles to the continent of Africa and beyond, and is decades ahead toward achieving its goals. However, its disdain for what it cannot control — in this case bitcoin — will prove to be a major strategic error, one that the United States can capitalize on to jump ahead.

In contrast, Africa is using bitcoin to achieve economic freedom away from outside forces. Its youthful population is using bitcoin mining technology to stand up local minigrids, bringing profitable electrification to areas that have none, and where it was previously economically unviable. Countries and villages alike are partnering with bitcoin mining companies to monetize their vast sustainable natural resources, breaking the grip of China-based infrastructure and technology debt.

The UAE is quickly adopting the benefits of bitcoin as well, promoting clear and simple regulations, and a business and innovation friendly culture, with tax incentives to attract growth in this emerging industry. Policymakers in the United States would do well to take a page from these new, global ingenuity hubs to gain valuable insights into how to excel at the forefront of digital and energy innovations.

Energy independence is crucial to the security of any nation, and nowhere is that more evident than in our energy resources here at home. Texas is taking the lead by utilizing its cheap and abundant renewable power, partnering with bitcoin miners to facilitate grid stability and demand response.

In the goal to reduce dependence on fossil fuels as reliable baseload power, clean and safe nuclear energy offers its synergies with bitcoin mining to fill that role. And as the world moves toward the electrification of everything, the United States must not dismiss any opportunity to incentivize advancements in national energy resiliency.

Far from facilitating illicit activity, bitcoin's ledger is transparent and open-source with very little room for criminals to hide.

Far from consuming too much energy, bitcoin largely consumes energy that no one else wants, that no one else can get to, or isn't otherwise economically feasible. Revenue from partnering with bitcoin miners is already facilitating the development of more renewable energy infrastructure, both at home and abroad, creating jobs, and empowering communities.

Financial empowerment is a guiding principle upon which bitcoin was created. Its decentralized, censorship-resistant, rules-based protocol prohibits any bias or exploitation. By leveraging bitcoin, all individuals now have the power to quietly defect from corrupt regimes, self-serving institutions, and short-sighted governments.

Failure to embrace bitcoin will not stop bitcoin. Like China's mining ban, it will merely send bitcoin, as well as the talent, innovation, and prosperity that comes with it, to other places. Investment in excellence in the United States must be prioritized over blind allegiance to outdated legacy systems, regardless of who those systems may enrich.

Like the printing press, the internet, or democracy itself, bitcoin is an innovation that decentralizes access from the few to the many. For the US to remain a beacon of equal opportunity, innovation, and prosperity, it must not resist a technology that holds so much promise. Instead, the United States must embrace its role as a global leader and advocate for this new paradigm, one that shares its core values with those upon which our country was established, values that remain true today.

STRATEGIC ADVISORY TEAM BIOGRAPHIES

Lyn Alden is the founder of Lyn Alden Investment Strategy, where she provides financial research to retail and institutional investors. With a background that blends engineering and finance, Lyn focuses on fundamental investing with a global macro overlay, and covers a broad array of asset classes including equities, currencies, commodities, and digital assets. She is an independent Board Director of Swan Bitcoin, a bitcoin-native financial services company, and is an advisor to Ego Death Capital, a venture firm that focuses on financing startups that are making use of the bitcoin network.

Alexandra DaCosta is a Board Member for the Bitcoin Today Coalition. Her work focuses on the intersection of finance, digital infrastructure, and the energy transition. She is a Managing Partner of United Integrity Advisors, a digital infrastructure advisory firm. Alex was a founding member and CEO of Aspen Creek Digital Corporation, catalyzing the decarbonization of power generation by standing up new renewable power paired with bitcoin mining and interruptible data centers. Prior to ACDC, Alex spent 18 years on Wall Street in Fixed Income Securitized Products and as head of ESG and Impact Investing. She is an Advisor to Synota, an Advisory Board member of Mass General for Children, and a Board Member of the University Cottage Club at Princeton University. Alex graduated cum laude from Princeton University with a Bachelor of Arts in Politics, and from LEAD at the Stanford Graduate School of Business.

Dr. Julia Nesheiwat is a distinguished fellow and Board Member with the Atlantic Council's Global Energy Center, as well as a recognized expert for energy, environment, climate change, and national security issues as a public servant, academic, former military officer, and US diplomat. In government, she most recently served in the White House as Homeland Security Advisor to the President and as Florida's first Chief Resilience Officer. Julia has served as the Corporate Advisor to TeraWulf, Inc. (NasdaqCM:WULF), as a Board Member for Bridger Solutions, and on the Advisory Council of Sustainable Bitcoin Protocol, PowerEdison, and others. She has also published numerous articles in the Stanford Review and Energy Source. In prior administrations, Julia served as Deputy Assistant Secretary of State for the Energy Resources Bureau at the US Department of State. Prior to holding those positions, she served as Chief of Staff to the US Special Envoy for Eurasian Energy as well as the Under Secretary for Energy, Environment, and Business. Her Ph.D. dissertation is from Tokyo Tech titled "Post-Disaster Reconstruction in Energy Policy & Resilience" and she's been a visiting professor at the Naval Post Graduate School on Energy Security. Julia served multiple combat tours in Afghanistan and Iraq and has been awarded the Bronze Star Medal.

CORE EDITORIAL TEAM BIOGRAPHIES

Alexander Brammer, PhD is a Director on the Board of the Bitcoin Today Coalition and has worked in the bitcoin mining industry since 2021 in both high-growth start-ups and large-scale energy infrastructure companies. Before starting his career in the digital infrastructure space, Alex served 15 years in the Army. While in uniform, Alex deployed four times to Iraq in both special operations and airborne infantry units, completed a Bachelor's in Economics from West Point, a Master's in Security Studies from King's College London, and a counterinsurgency focused Doctorate in Political Science from Queen's University Belfast as a 2014 Marshall Scholar. He medically retired from the Army in 2021 after leaving command as a Captain.

Jayson Browder, MPA is Vice President of Government Affairs for Marathon Digital Holdings and Third Way's Visiting Fellow for National Security, leading work around US-China cyber/digital power competition. Prior to Third Way, Jayson held several senior advisor roles, most recently at New York Abu Dhabi (NYUAD) as Assistant Dean/Chief of Staff to the Associate Vice Chancellor, Principal National Security Advisor to U.S. Congressman Beto O'Rourke, Presidential Management Fellow in the Obama Administration's White House Office of Management and Budget, and U.S. Fulbright Scholar. As a US Air Force and Iraq War Veteran, Jayson is passionately involved in Military and Veteran Affairs. In 2015, he founded Veterans in Global Leadership, an executive-level training and leadership development non-profit, advocating for veteran visibility within civilian government leadership. Jayson holds a Global Executive M.P.A. from New York University and the University College London and a B.A. in Sociology and Latin American and Latino Studies from Fordham University. He was awarded 40 Under 40 at the Middle East Policy Council and 40 Under 40 Latinos in Foreign Policy at New America, Diversity in National Security Network, and Huffington Post.

Victoria Corriere is the Operations Manager for the Bitcoin Today Coalition and Veterans for Energy and Technology Security as well as Project Manager for this book, National Security in the Digital Age: Bitcoin As A Tool For Modern Statecraft. With a background in business operations as well as writing, editing, design, and development for a variety of websites, she's the author of 21 Things To Know About Bitcoin. Victoria has also previously worked in software development as a Senior Business Analyst, as a Risk Management Specialist for a general and psychiatric hospital group, and as a Registered Representative for select multiple-CTA, limited partnership, commodity trading funds, holding Series 63, 22, and 7 securities licenses.

Ben Kincaid spent the first half of his career as a U.S. Diplomat, serving and leading teams in multiple countries in Africa, the Middle East, and South Asia. Ben worked across the U.S. interagency and with senior foreign officials to drive partnered approaches to pressing national security challenges in some of the world's most troubled places. Today, he's CEO of ReElement Technologies Africa, whose mission is to bring the critical mineral processing step to Africa, empowering nations to capture the value of their natural resources. Ben is also founding partner of Bridger Solutions, an Africa-focused bitcoin mining company. He serves as an advisor to Allegro Group, a Fargo-based talent and leadership transformation company. Ben lives in Santo Domingo, Dominican Republic where his wife is currently posted to the U.S. Embassy. He holds a BA in International Studies and Political Science from Virginia Military Institute and an MA in Latin American Studies from Georgetown University.

Robert Malka is a Board Member for the Bitcoin Today Coalition, where he has built relationships with dozens of offices on The Hill. He has also helped design the first required bitcoin certification program at a public high school in the world under Mi Primer Bitcoin, a nonprofit in El Salvador. He is co-founder and COO of a company that provides 24/7/365 interpreting services for the deaf in the United States, Canada, and the Middle East, and has also built socratic-centered alternatives to K-12 schooling. He has written on Deafness, the philosophy of Nietzsche, and bitcoin's relationship to culture. He has a Bachelor's in Philosophy and the History of Math and Science from St. John's College, Santa Fe.

Kyle Schneps is the co-founder of BTC VETS and an Advisor to the Bitcoin Today Coalition's Board of Directors. He has held a variety of Federal and State Government positions, most recently working as Special Advisor for State Operations in the New York State Executive Chamber. Prior to his role in NY State government, Kyle spent most of his career serving as a US Intelligence Officer, which was preceded by a diplomatic post as Advisor to the Special Envoy for Guantanamo Bay Closure at the US Department of State. He is a former White House Fellow, during which time he worked across different national security and federal budgeting roles. Kyle is now Vice President of Public Policy at Foundry, a Digital Currency Group Company. He holds two Masters degrees in International Affairs and Public Health from Columbia University.

Thank you to everyone who participated in this book's content, production, and distribution.

For press or other inquiries, please contact:

victoria@bitcointodaycoalition.org

© 2024 by: The Bitcoin Today Coalition

https:// bitcointodaycoalition.org

All rights reserved.

Made in the USA
Columbia, SC
19 July 2024

970f9a68-17d3-4af5-86ec-6ad114ab9464R01